Boston University

Boston homilies

Short sermons on the international Sunday-school lessons for 1892. Second Series

Boston University

Boston homilies
Short sermons on the international Sunday-school lessons for 1892. Second Series

ISBN/EAN: 9783337264680

Printed in Europe, USA, Canada, Australia, Japan

Cover: Foto ©Paul-Georg Meister /pixelio.de

More available books at **www.hansebooks.com**

BOSTON HOMILIES

SHORT SERMONS ON THE INTERNATIONAL
SUNDAY-SCHOOL LESSONS FOR 1892

*BY MEMBERS OF THE ALPHA CHAPTER OF THE
CONVOCATION OF BOSTON UNIVERSITY*

SECOND SERIES

*NEW YORK: HUNT & EATON
CINCINNATI: CRANSTON & STOWE*

1891

INTRODUCTION.

IN preparing this volume the aim has been to furnish Sunday-school teachers and older scholars with brief exegetical and illustrative studies of the Sunday-school lessons for the ensuing year. The contributors are members of the Alpha Chapter of Boston University, chosen from a wide range of territory, and from as many classes as possible. It is hoped that their work will not be entirely in vain.

FRED. H. KNIGHT,
EDWARD M. TAYLOR,
WILLIAM I. HAVEN,
Editors.

CONTENTS.

FIRST QUARTER.

LESSON		PAGE
I.	THE KINGDOM OF CHRIST. Isa. xi, 1–10. J. W. BASHFORD.	11
II.	A SONG OF SALVATION. Isa. xxvi, 1–10. GEORGE SHAW BUTTERS	20
III.	OVERCOME WITH WINE. Isa. xxviii, 1–13. W. H. MEREDITH	27
IV.	HEZEKIAH'S PRAYER AND DELIVERANCE. Isa. xxxvii, 14–21, 33–38. DAVIS W. CLARK	35
V.	THE SUFFERING SAVIOUR. Isa. liii, 1–12. W. I. HAVEN	41
VI.	THE GRACIOUS CALL. Isa. lv, 1–13. WILLIAM E. HUNTINGTON	49
VII.	THE NEW COVENANT. Jer. xxxi, 27–37. WILBUR S. SMITHERS	57
VIII.	JEHOIAKIM'S WICKEDNESS. Jer. xxxvi, 19–31. J. E. JACKLIN	66
IX.	JEREMIAH PERSECUTED. Jer. xxxvii, 11–21. JAMES HARRISON HUMPHREY	75
X.	THE DOWNFALL OF JUDAH. Jer. xxxix, 1–10. WALTER J. YATES	85
XI.	PROMISE OF A NEW HEART. Ezek. xxxvi, 25–38. ALEXANDER DIGHT	93
XIII.	THE BLESSINGS OF THE GOSPEL. Isa. xl, 1–10. STEPHEN L. BALDWIN	101

SECOND QUARTER.

I.	THE WAY OF THE RIGHTEOUS. Psa. i, 1–6. SAMUEL L. BEILER	113
II.	THE KING IN ZION. Psa. ii, 1–12. J. S. DAVIS	121

LESSON	PAGE
III. God's Works and Word. Psa. xix, 1-14. George A. Phinney	129
IV. The Lord My Shepherd. Psa. xxiii, 1-6. I. Simmons	138
V. The Prayer of the Penitent. Psa. li, 1-13. B. P. Raymond	146
VI. Delight in God's House. Psa. lxxxiv, 1-12. Fred. H. Knight	154
VII. A Song of Praise. Psa. ciii, 1-22. Katharine Lente Stevenson	163
VIII. Daniel and His Companions. Dan. i, 8-21. M. D. Hornbeck	171
IX. Nebuchadnezzar's Dream. Dan. ii, 36-49. Nicholas T. Whitaker	182
X. The Fiery Furnace. Dan. iii, 13-25. Henry A. Starks.	190
XI. The Den of Lions. Dan. vi, 16-28. John P. Otis	198
XIII. Messiah's Reign. Psa. lxxii, 1-19. W. G. Richardson	205

THIRD QUARTER.

I. The Ascension of Christ. Acts i, 1-12. J. W. Hamilton.	217
II. The Descent of the Spirit. Acts ii, 1-12. Marcus D. Buell	225
III. The First Christian Church. Acts ii, 37-47. William F. McDowell	234
IV. The Lame Man Healed. Acts iii, 1-16. Wilbur P. Thirkield	244
V. Peter and John Before the Council. Acts iv, 1-18. Joel M. Leonard	254
VI. The Apostles' Confidence in God. Acts iv, 19-31. John D. Pickles	262
VII. Ananias and Sapphira. Acts v, 1-11. Gilbert C. Osgood	269
VIII. The Apostles Persecuted. Acts v, 25-41. J. A. Story.	278
IX. The First Christian Martyr. Acts vii, 54-60; viii, 1-4. J. H. Allen	286

LESSON	PAGE
X. PHILIP PREACHING AT SAMARIA. Acts viii, 5–25. H. H. CLARK	294
XI. PHILIP AND THE ETHIOPIAN. Acts viii, 26–40. E. M. TAYLOR	303
XIII. THE LORD'S SUPPER. 1 Cor. xi, 23–32. R. C. GLASS	314

FOURTH QUARTER.

I. SAUL OF TARSUS CONVERTED. Acts ix, 1–20. A. W. TIRRELL	325
II. DORCAS RAISED TO LIFE. Acts ix, 32–43. J. M. DURRELL	331
III. PETER'S VISION. Acts x, 1–20. R. T. STEVENSON	339
IV. PETER AT CESAREA. Acts x, 30–48. GEORGE W. BROWN	348
V. THE GOSPEL PREACHED AT ANTIOCH. Acts xi, 19–30. H. H. FRENCH	355
VI. PETER DELIVERED FROM PRISON. Acts xii, 1–17. JOSEPH PULLMAN	364
VII. THE FIRST CHRISTIAN MISSIONARIES. Acts xiii, 1–13. M. F. COLBURN	373
VIII. PAUL'S FIRST MISSIONARY SERMON. Acts xiii, 26–43. JAMES MUDGE	381
IX. THE APOSTLES TURNING TO THE GENTILES. Acts xiii, 44–52; xiv, 1–7. J. D. SPRIGGS	389
X. WORK AMONG THE GENTILES. Acts xiv, 8–22. RAYMOND F. HOLWAY	397
XI. THE APOSTOLIC COUNCIL. Acts xv, 12–29. H. C. SHELDON	406
XIII. THE BIRTH OF CHRIST. Luke ii, 8–20. JOHN FAVILLE	415
XIII. A LESSON IN SELF-DENIAL. Rom. xiv, 12–23. J. WEARE DEARBORN	422

NOTE.—For the quarterly review lessons no homilies have been prepared. Homilies are given for the alternative lessons of the last Sunday in the year.

FIRST QUARTER.

BOSTON HOMILIES.

I.

THE KINGDOM OF CHRIST.

Isa. xi, 1-10.

GOLDEN TEXT.—He shall have dominion also from sea to sea, and from the river unto the ends of the earth. Psa. lxxii, 8.

OUR lesson should be considered under three heads:
1. The Prophet.
2. The Circumstances Attending the Prophecy.
3. The Prophecy.

1. *The Prophet* Isaiah prophesied between 758 and 690 B. C. His call is narrated in the sixth chapter. Probably that chapter is the story of Isaiah's conversion, as well as of his call to the ministry. It consists of four parts: (1) The vision of God in his holiness. (2) The deep conviction of the seer's sinfulness as the result of this vision. God sometimes smites us with conviction by showing us ideal purity, rather than by dwelling upon our sinfulness. Flash ideals before noble souls, flash consequences before the base, if you would produce conviction. Dr. Stalker, to whom I am indebted for these hints in regard to Isaiah's spiritual life, thinks the prophet may have been very sinful in his youth, like Bunyan or Augustine. I am inclined to think that the presenta-

tion of the heavenly vision to Isaiah and his immediate obedience to the call indicate that, like Paul, he was already struggling for an ideal life. (3) Water and fire are the two symbols of cleansing in the Bible, as they are the two agents for cleansing in nature. Fire is far more thorough and is used in purifying metals. So the touching of Isaiah's lips with the live coal was the symbol of his purification. (4) Unhesitating obedience, even eagerness to be God's messenger, follows the prophet's cleansing.

Isaiah is the St. John of the Old Testament. One might almost call him the St. John and the St. Paul of the old dispensation; for to the lofty insight and the spiritual nature of the former he unites the practical and statesmanlike traits of the latter. The richness of his style makes him the Shakespeare among the prophets. Ewald says in substance that he is not specially lyric, like Joel, or elegiac, like Hosea, or monitory, like Micah; but every style is at his command, and this constitutes his greatness. His fundamental peculiarity is his majestic repose of style proceeding from the full and sure command of the subject. It is not possible that Hezekiah's good reign was a coarse transcript of the glowing vision of this man of God.

2. *The Circumstances Attending the Prophecy.* Palestine lies between Assyria, Babylon, Media, and Persia on the one side, and Egypt, Greece, and Rome on the other. She was the highway for the commerce and the conquests of the world for a thousand years. In 739 B. C.

the northern kingdom became subject to Assyria, and in 727 it attempted to throw off the Assyrian yoke through an alliance with Egypt. Samaria was then invaded by Sargon and subjected in 722. Judah lay apparently at the mercy of Assyria when the prophecy was uttered, between 722 and 720.

The prophet advised the policy of strict neutrality between the two great kingdoms of Assyria and Egypt, with the righteous fulfillment of all obligations upon the part of Judah, both at home and abroad, and a firm reliance upon Jehovah as her providential defender. In case of invasion, which, indeed, the prophet anticipated by reason of national sin, Isaiah advised submission. Neutrality was the only wise course if Judah would escape desolation. If an alliance were made with either party Judah would be first exposed to the attack of the opposing kingdom. This policy of neutrality in modern times has saved Belgium, Holland, and Switzerland, lying between strong nations. The prophet, however, recognized that the real safety of Judah consisted not only in freedom from entangling alliances, but in the performance of the divine tasks committed to her. God would then guarantee her safety, because she would then be doing her providential work. What better defense of a weak nation can modern statesmen suggest than freedom from entangling alliances, a righteous discharge of all obligations, both at home and abroad, the fulfillment of her providential mission, and a reliance upon the Upholder of nations?

The older prophets had declared that Judah would be overthrown by reason of her sins, and only a remnant be saved. They had also declared that Jehovah's kingdom would triumph. Isaiah adds two additional elements to the prophecies of his predecessors, namely: the kingdom will be established by a personal Messiah; this Messiah will draw all nations unto him, so that the call to salvation will become universal and Judah's privileges will be extended to all. A personal Messiah and the spiritual equality of all nations is Isaiah's special contribution to the world.

3. *The Prophecy.* After foretelling that the Messiah will come from Jesse the prophet thus characterizes him: "The Spirit of the Lord shall rest upon him, the spirit of wisdom and understanding, the spirit of counsel and might, the spirit of knowledge and of the fear of the Lord." The first of the sevenfold blessings of the Spirit is a generic possession—the Spirit of the Lord. Under it are included three pairs of virtues. The first pair refers to the mind of the Messiah, the second to his executive and practical abilities, and the third to his character and his relation to Jehovah. The first pair refers to the powers by which a young man advances in the world. The second pair refers to the power by which one touches all the life around him. It indicates his growth in breadth as the first pair indicates his personal advancement. The third pair relates to the powers by which one grows upward into God. (See Phillips Brooks's sermon on "The Symmetry of Life," in the volume called *The Candle of the*

Lord.) The two Hebrew words for wisdom and understanding do not make a clear distinction in the mental qualities here set forth. Wisdom, however, seems to me to indicate the intuitions which Christ possessed in regard to mental, spiritual, and moral truth. By reason of sinlessness his vision was clearer and his intuitions were more numerous than ours. "Understanding" indicates the good judgment and common sense which he showed in regard to men and affairs. "The spirit of counsel and might" indicates the power by which one brings things to pass. "By the spirit of counsel" Christ formed wise plans for the spiritual conquest of the world, and by "the spirit of might" he is carrying these plans into successful execution. Many a man who has the spirit of wisdom and understanding lacks these practical faculties. Many a man who has the spirit of counsel, so that he can plan wisely in regard to action, lacks the executive faculty, the courage and patience, for carrying out his plans. But "he shall not fail nor be discouraged, till he have set judgment in the earth."

"The spirit of knowledge and the fear of the Lord." The knowledge here spoken of is the knowledge of God, and not simply an intellectual knowledge in regard to earthly objects. The next clause in the Revised Version reads: "And his delight shall be in the fear of the Lord." We know, therefore, that this fear is not a dread of Jehovah on the part of the Messiah. It is reverence melting into love of God and delight in him.

"He shall not judge after the sight of his eyes, neither

reprove after the hearing of his ears." This is not a condemnation of the use of the senses, but a limitation of them to their appointed functions. You cannot measure faith with a foot-rule, nor weigh character on the city scales. Modern science, and even the Church, is too prone to esteem men according to material tests.

" But with righteousness shall he judge the poor, and reprove with equity for the meek of the earth." Christ cited his preaching to the poor as one of the tests of his Messiahship. Yet some of us are glad to preach to rich congregations as a proof of our higher standing in the Christian ministry! " And he shall smite the earth with the rod of his mouth." The choice of truth and love as the means, and of preaching and service as the agencies, by which the Messiah would make the conquest of the world is one of the highest proofs of the inspired sagacity of Christ.

"With the breath of his lips shall he slay the wicked." How many men have been made dead to sin and brought to life in the spirit by the words of Christ. "And righteousness shall be the girdle of his loins, and faithfulness the girdle of his reins." Righteousness refers to rectitude of motive and faithfulness to fidelity in the practical details of life.

The prophet now passes to a description of the triumph of Christ in the physical universe. The question may arise as to why he did not dwell more fully upon his triumph in the Church and in political and social life. The passing over of these conquests in this place is probably due to the fact that Isaiah devotes special prophecies elsewhere to these phases of Christ's work.

The last four verses of our lesson form a prophecy yet unfulfilled in regard to the redemption of the earth and the regeneration of the animal kingdom. The language is doubtless figurative. But men of the common sense of Wesley, of the saintliness of Fletcher, of the philosophical breadth of Julius Müller and Richard Rothe, of the scholarship of Meyer, and of the spiritual insight of Godet hold that the earth has been affected by sin, and that it will be redeemed by Christ. God made no ideal world, but a world adapted to a sinful race. As soon, therefore, as sin disappears the earth will present an unsuitable environment for man. It will consequently be transformed to suit his new condition. Paul writes: "For the creation was subjected to vanity, not of its own will, but by reason of him who subjected it, in hope that the creation itself also shall be delivered from the bondage of corruption into the liberty of the glory of the children of God. For we know that the whole creation groaneth and travaileth in pain together [or with us] until now." The earth was once an Eden, and it shall become a Paradise again. The last triumph of chemistry, says Rothe, will be a spiritual body possessing immortality, and perfectly responsive to the will. John saw a new heaven *and a new earth* in his golden vision of the millennium.

The lesson, as a whole, brings hope to the despondent and furnishes the richest practical study of the finest character on earth. May we cultivate the sevenfold gifts of the Spirit. May men always be able to recognize in us the Spirit of the Lord. By obedience may we keep our moral vision so clear and strong that we shall have an intuitive perception of spiritual realities and a strong, clear judgment of men and measures. May we have the practical sagacity to wisely plan our work and the firmness and the executive ability to carry out our plan. Protestant Christianity has to a large extent been individual. Each soul has been pushing forward for itself. We are just now approaching a social phase of growth. We must reach out toward our brothers and sisters on each side of us. The danger of the Church of the next century is that we shall become so engrossed in social duties and in the service of our brethren as to lose sight of God and immortality. Above all, may we, therefore, grow upward into him, so that when we have found our brethren we shall be able to show them Christ incarnate in our lives. May we judge and be judged according to motives, and be especially interested in the poor and the meek of the earth. And so by love, by service, and by truth may we help to conquer the world and to bring in the millennium in which the earth shall become the garden of the Lord.

A final word as to the bearing of this prophecy upon higher criticism. As a rationalistic exegesis of the New Testament has been overthrown by the character and acts of Christ, so an antisupernatural theory of the Old Testament will break before the prophecies relating to

Christ. The Old Testament declared that the Messiah would come from the Jews. It described his character and suffering. It declared he would conquer the world by love and truth and service. A man appears later whose character was so original and so transcended, if it did not contradict, the spirit of his age, that it could not have been invented by ignorant and carnal fishermen. He assumed that he was the Messiah, and declared that he would conquer the world. His own nation joined the world in responding to this preposterous claim by crucifixion. We live nearly two thousand years after this being appeared. Strange to say, we find him now conquering the world by the very methods of humility and self-renunciation and death which the world despised. When we find prophecies uttered from four hundred to two thousand years before Christ came, and when we find his character exactly answering to the prophecies, and when, nearly two thousand years after his advent, we find his prophecies being fulfilled before our eyes, a candid criticism must confess that the Being who inspired these words is the Being who guides the unfolding history of the human race. Rationalistic exegesis will yet bow before the prophecies of Christ as it has already bowed before his cross.

J. W. BASHFORD.

II.
A SONG OF SALVATION.

Isa. xxvi, 1-10.

GOLDEN TEXT.—Trust ye in the Lord forever; for in the Lord Jehovah is everlasting strength. Isa. xxvi, 4.

THIS lesson has been fitly named. It follows closely the prophecies concerning the gospel times which are to bring great changes to the Lord's people. In the day of the fulfillment of divine promise this song is to be sung. The Church will then be a reality, and here it is represented as a city whose inhabitants are to give expression to their joy in this lesson we are to study. These verses are suggestive taken by themselves, but they become especially so when associated with the kingdom which Christ was to establish. We are not to limit the application of this prophecy, for it is broader than human conception. This city is Christ's Church. The song is descriptive of its glory and power in the world and at the same time the inward and heart experience of its members is beautifully expressed. It is the visible body of believers whose names are so many, and also the invisible company " that no man can number."

THE GLORIOUS CHURCH.
1. Its Security and Peace.
2. Its Victory and Power.
3. Its Trust and Devotion.

1. *Its Security and Peace.* It is a strong city, and so well fortified that no power can prevail against it. Its walls and bulwarks are indicative of what the city within must be, for the materials suggest strength and power, and also the value of the possessions to be guarded by their defense. The Church is not merely the building, but also the inhabitants who have some knowledge of salvation, the watchword and theme of all who enter within its gates. It is not strange that this seer said in another place: " Strengthen ye the weak hands, and confirm the feeble knees. Say to them that are of a fearful heart, Be strong, fear not: behold, your God will come with vengeance, even God with a recompense ; he will come and save you." Salvation is safety, and this lesson indicates that it may be present, complete, and eternal. The Saviour confirms this word of prophecy when he utters his " fear not " of encouragement. His angelic messengers repeat the same blessed word of security which is the gospel message to all who will listen to it.

In the second verse of this lesson there is a thought which looks forward to the time of the establishing of the Church on Christ's own foundation. In the prophet's view the city seems to be just completed and empty. It is to be filled, not with the chosen people alone, but the gates are to be thrown wide open that " every righteous nation which keepeth the truth may enter in." This is the forerunner of the Master's " whosoever." The " far off " were to be brought " nigh " by the provision which had been made. The old dividing wall was to fall of its own accord. The old lines of separation were to be snapped asunder and the veil of the temple rent in twain. Paul expresses this fulfillment in these words: " For through him we both [Jew and Gentile] have access by one Spirit unto the Father. Now therefore ye are no more strangers and foreigners, but fellow-citizens with the saints, and of the household of God; and are built upon the foundation of the apostles and prophets, Jesus Christ himself being the chief corner-stone ; in whom all the building fitly framed together groweth unto a holy temple in the Lord : in whom ye also are builded together for a habitation of God through the Spirit."

But there is something even stronger than mere security from enemies without in this city or church. Its inhabitants enjoy a peace which is the most perfect of any thing that can be described. It is " peace upon peace." It is the rest for the people of God in advance of the heavenly rest promised in the word. It is peace among themselves and also within themselves. Jesus thus speaks of it: " Peace I leave with you, my peace I give unto you: not as the world giveth, give I unto you." It is a blessing imparted and a condition in which the trusting soul can be constantly kept. It carries its reason in its condition and speaks in the happiness of its possessor. His mind is stayed on Him, and he sustains the staying soul. The everlasting strength comes from " ever trusting in the Lord Jehovah."

2. *Its Victory and Power.* Here is a pre-statement of "A little one shall become a thousand, and a small one a strong nation," and a re-statement of "One man of you shall chase a thousand: for the Lord your God, he it is that fighteth for you, as he hath promised you." There is nothing more helpful to the thoughtful Christian than to consider how the Church has moved forward in her successes. Her battles have been many and her victories have been more. Her losses have been only temporary —in appearance rather than in reality. The sneers and scoffs of unbelievers have found expression and have been forgotten. The proud conceit of him who claimed that he was undermining the cause of Christ has little to show for his work except the memory of his self-consciousness. Others have arisen after his disgrace to carry on his work, but the Church has moved on unmindful of them all. She seeks no battle, but never retreats when her foundations and walls are besieged. She has perfect confidence in the Captain of her salvation and has never misplaced her faith in him. "The weapons of our warfare are not carnal, but mighty through God to the pulling down of strongholds; casting down imaginations, and every high thing that exalteth itself against the knowledge of God, and bringing into captivity every thought to the obedience of Christ." We do not often enough let our thoughts dwell upon the power of the Church. Such meditation always strengthens faith. It was our Lord himself who said: "On this rock I will build my Church, and the gates of hell shall not prevail

against it." Daniel's picture is inspiring: "And the kingdom and dominion, and the greatness of the kingdom under the whole heaven, shall be given to the people of the saints of the Most High, whose kingdom is an everlasting kingdom, and all dominions shall serve and obey him." The strange part of this prophecy is to be found in that "the poor and the needy" are to be prominent factors in the establishing of this power in the world. In ministering to them we are helping to spread his kingdom and power.

> "Our Lord and Master,
> When he departed, left us in his will,
> As our best legacy on earth, the poor!
> These we have always with us; had we not
> Our hearts would grow as hard as are these stones."
> —*Longfellow.*

When John the Baptist seemed to be in doubt whether Jesus was really the Christ, the climax to the Saviour's answer was in these words: "And the poor have the gospel preached to them." If this was the Master's opinion of his ministry, how careful ought we to be that we "do not despise" one of the least in his kingdom.

3. *Its Trust and Devotion.* Here really is to be found the reason of the Church's security and peace, as well as its victory and power. This trust and devotion are expressed first as personal and then as an influence upon others. Not always as efficient as desirable, as the last verse of the lesson indicates, but the seventh states the case in general for those who are true, and the tenth is only the contrast on the part of those who will not see

and believe. It is so clear that all may understand it, and, best of all, we have the Lord's approval in, "The way of the just is uprightness: thou, most upright, dost weigh the path of the just." Matthew Henry translates this verse in this way: "The way of the just is evenness." He also says in explanation, "It is their endeavor and constant care to walk with God in an even, steady course of obedience and godly conversation." The beauty of this trust is in its constancy. It is not merely for great occasions, but for all times and for the greatest difficulties. When the devotion of the Church is thus even and constant she is at her greatest power. In the next two verses this trust is not so easy, because in the revealing of God's judgments there will come much to try the faith and to bring discouragement to the soul. But the trustful Christian clings to the thought of divine vindication, believing that

"God is his own interpreter,
And he will make it plain."

The little flock are told to "fear not," but when the time for fear seems to arise they are to hold on, faithful in their service. They are encouraged in their devotion by the devotion of their Lord to them. This is only a prophetic picture of what is simplest and grandest in the members of the true Church. This is the crowning part of her glory. She has wealth, and her resources have unlimited sway in the world. She builds her sanctuaries and colleges by the thousand. She enlarges her borders and is constantly seeking new and difficult fields of labor, but her glory and beauty and power reach their climax in the simple and constant trust and devotion of her adherents. Here, also, is the source of her greatness, and whenever weak the great secret of her weakness. This strong thought in this lesson can be suggested, but not fully described. Only he who lives it knows it, and he who lives it most knows it best. It is the simplest and most child-like; the highest and most human; the holiest and most divine. He who depends upon words for his knowledge of it must ever be ignorant, but the honest soul who trusts God learns more than volumes in a single act of saving faith. We must content ourselves with the oft-repeated assertion that "the half has never been told." In the midst of the blessings it brings to the believer it is constantly entreating favor for the man of unbelief, and how many times the devoted prayer has prevailed we may not know, but this constant testimony has not been in vain. These prophetic words are not mere prophecy given by the inspiration of our God. They have become the poetry of the trustful and devoted souls of the Church to-day. They are the "dew of the morning," the "light at eventide," and in darkest and most trying hours they are our "songs in the night." They have their part in the "new, new song" of experienced salvation, and also in the "old, old story" of redemption and love. They have been repeatedly sung in our "strong city," and in the "city that hath foundations" we shall recognize them in the "song of Moses and the Lamb."

GEORGE SHAW BUTTERS.

III.
OVERCOME WITH WINE.

Isa. xxviii, 1-13.

GOLDEN TEXT.—Wine is a mocker, strong drink is raging; and whosoever is deceived thereby is not wise. Prov. xx, 1.

THE last lesson was a song. This one is a malediction. Together they make two stanzas of the Bible song of "Mercy and of Judgment." Our lesson is the first of five woes pronounced against evil-doers. These woes make a distinct section (chaps. xxviii-xxxiii) of the prophecies of Isaiah, which, judging from his frequent quotations from it, must have been a favorite book with Jesus of Nazareth.

Four of these woes are directed to God's own people, the fifth to those whom he would use to punish them for their sins. The Israelites are not now one people, but for a long time past have been two kingdoms. Israel includes ten tribes and possesses the northern territory, with Samaria for its capital; Judah, with its two tribes, occupies the south, with Jerusalem for its center.

The evil fruitage of division is clearly seen in both kingdoms, and is especially manifest in connection with these woes from the lips of God's prophet.

1. The clouds gather, and woe is pealed forth over the

northern kingdom. "Woe to the crown of pride, to the drunkards of Ephraim" (ver. 1).

Ephraim, son of Joseph, declared fruitful, adopted into the tribes by dying Jacob, to which also Joshua belonged, becomes the leading tribe, and now it stands as the representative of the whole kingdom of Israel. "Woe to Ephraim" is woe to the whole northern kingdom. Why this malediction on Israel? Externally it would seem as though the divine benediction was repeatedly spoken to it. Occupying the middle portion of the land of Canaan, with possessions extending far to the north, it was beautiful for situation. Victory after victory had followed its northern invasions. Wealth it had in abundance. Samaria, its capital, sat in stately grandeur, enthroned upon one of its hills which sloped down into flat valleys fat with rich pastures. The sheep and kine grazed peacefully upon the sides of Mount Ephraim. The people of the land, being highly prosperous, were proud of their country and gloried in their imposing capital which crowned the nation. Even Jerusalem itself was not to be compared to Samaria in their estimation.

The body politic of Israel seems to be in the fullness of health and vigor; but looking closer, we find it is not the flush of health which glows on its cheeks, but the hectic blush of disease. The strength of its members is not the muscular strength of the strong man. Its movements are not the strides of a conqueror, but the faltering steps of the broken spirited and the conquered. For Ephraim, which should be an overcomer, is overcome—

broken, the margin says—broken with wine. Its political constitution is "broken" by the nation-destroying conqueror, Wine. Its intellectual power is "broken" so that judgment is lacking for the business to be transacted at the gates of its cities and in the high places of government. Its spiritual life is overcome and "broken" by the evil spirit of wine. The poison has entered subtly into the body politic of Israel, and is silently but surely working from within its utter destruction. Its vitality is being sapped by consuming wine. Moreover, the displeasure of Israel's God is aroused. His malediction is uttered against Samaria, "the crown of pride of the drunkards of Ephraim," "the fading flower of his glorious beauty, which is on the head of the fat valley." Because they are overcome with wine they shall be overcome by the mighty Assyrian, whom God will take into his hand and use to break them into pieces. He will hurl the Assyrians at them for their overthrow even "as a tempest of hail and a destroying storm, as a flood of mighty waters overflowing" (ver. 2). Samaria itself shall be pelted, beaten, and overwhelmed by their mighty foes, the Assyrians, who are now handled by God, whom they have dishonored, for their overthrow. The imposing city "shall be trodden under foot." The "fading flower of his glorious beauty" shall be consumed even as a fruit-hungry man quickly devours the choice first early ripe fig which comes into his hand. All of which ruin God wrought later by the hands of Shalmaneser and Sargon, who took the ten tribes into captivity. Thus ended the drunken kingdom of Israel.

But not Israel alone is the object of this uttered woe. It is directed to Judah also. Jerusalem also, as well as Samaria, shares the divine displeasure because of sin. Though not so wickedly drunken as Israel, Judah is not free from the curse of wine. A residue from Israel have escaped to Judah and thus break company with the topers of Israel. They have cut off their affiliations with the wine-dealers and wine-drinkers of Ephraim, and cast in their lot with Judah and Jerusalem. To this " residue " (ver. 6) " the Lord of hosts shall be for a crown of glory, and for a diadem of beauty." Their strength shall not be the strength of wine, but the strength of God. Their beauty not the consumptive beauty of disease, but the beauty of holiness. This shall radiate from them like the sparkling light from a diadem of beauty upon the brow of a royal conqueror. Having escaped the snare of the evil spirit of wine which perverts judgment, God will be to them " a spirit of judgment." Having conquered wine, they shall overcome all their foes and drive them back even to the gates whence they came.

But, alas! these strong and pure ones from Israel, and also they of like mind in Judah, form but a remnant. The conquering cup has been carried into Judah, even to Jerusalem (vers. 7-9). There also the people "reel" and "stagger" (margin) through strong drink. Walking the streets of its cities the eyes of the remnant were offended with the staggering gait of the drunkards, their fetid breath polluted the atmosphere, and their drunken speech grated upon their ears.

The hospitalities of the people had degenerated into debauchery. (See chap. v, 11, 12.) The gorgeously furnished homes of the entertainers, even the tables at which they ate, were poisoned with the filthiness of the drunkard's vomit (ver. 8). These things the temperance remnant met in the social life of Judah and Jerusalem.

On entering the realm of things religious similar scenes met their gaze. The priest at the altar, though by positive divine command prohibited from using wine before the service of the sanctuary (Lev. x, 9; Ezek. xliv, 21), yet is seen staggering to the altar to perform his heartless rites and ceremonies. The prophet, the chosen medium of the divine message to the people, has his vision beclouded and his judgment perverted by strong drink so that he cannot see the will of God nor declare his message to the people. (See Amos vi, 1-6; Mic. ii, 11.)

A dark picture certainly is this of both kingdoms, Israel and Judah. The strength of each nation is broken with wine. Even the ministers of religion are "drunk with wine wherein is excess," instead of being "filled with the Spirit." The common people, the best (?) families, the ministers of civil affairs, and the ministers of religion—all overcome with wine, a bare remnant only excepted! Physical resources, civil advantages, religious privileges—all prostituted to the service of the evil spirit of wine!

To such a people was Isaiah sent to utter the divine

maledictions of which our lesson is the first in this book of woes. How did they receive him? Verses 9 and 10 answer. They discuss Isaiah and his message over their cups. Listen to them in their drunken conceits as they ask, " Whom would he teach?" etc.! His moralizings and temperance talks may do for babies just weaned. Perhaps they also said, " Let him preach to women and children, not to us MEN." Certainly we hear in their words the stammerings of drunkards as they caricature the warning utterances of Isaiah, for the Hebrew monosyllables in verse 10 are repeated just as drunkards would utter them.

Isaiah takes the stammering words from their lips and hurls them back upon them by telling them that the Assyrian jargon shall soon fall upon their ears, and it shall be the shouts of their conquerors. The wine-smitten and broken shall be smitten and broken by their northern foes. Having rejected and incapacitated themselves for God's "rest" and "refreshing," the unrest of captivity shall be theirs. Being now overcome with wine, they shall be overcome by the Assyrians in the hand of God, whom they have dishonored. They shall recede from the high position they have taken as nations, shall stumble backward as do drunkards, shall be broken into fragments, snared as in a net, and be taken as prey by the spoilers, all because they disobeyed the God of David their father, and became a nation of drunkards. Overcome with wine, they shall be overcome by the Assyrians in the hand of God. The later history of Israel and Judah prove Isaiah to have been a true prophet of the Lord.

With equal force is this woe directed to the English, American, or any other nation which is under the foot of the god of wine. Physical resources, civil opportunities, educational facilities, religious advantages only heighten the condemnation and hasten the doom of a God-dishonoring and drunken nation in either hemisphere. Let the wandering, nationless Jew wherever seen be a temperance sermon in shoes, giving a loud warning to every man who meets him.

The remainder of this first woe is addressed to the rulers of the people (vers. 14-22). Let law-makers who make a covenant with death to furnish him victims from our own land at the rate of eighty thousand yearly, and who, by legalizing the rum-traffic, "with hell are at agreement" to rob heaven of its lawful subjects—let them know that already God's line and plummet are laid to their political structures, and the *waters* shall sweep away their refuges of lies. Then, as they made their bed so shall they lie on it, and find it too short for resting, and its covering too narrow to wrap themselves in (ver. 20). They must have new lodgings or die of unrest and cold neglect.

There was a saving remnant in Isaiah's day (i, 9; vi, 13) called a "residue" in our lesson (ver. 5). There is a temperance remnant in God's Israel to-day. It demands that the ministers of religion be free from the curse, that priests and people wholly abstain from all alcoholic bev-
2*

erages. While seeking the reformation of those already overcome, it especially seeks the formation of a sober rising generation by teachings in Sunday and day schools, and by securing such legislation as shall make the streets safe for the feet of both young and old.

All hail to the remnant of all denominations and parties who to-day are seeking to rescue those overcome with wine, and to save others from being smitten down by the rum fiend!

This first "woe to the drunkards" who have "erred," "stumbled," "are out of the way," "swallowed up," and are already "overcome," "broken, smitten down," and in "filthiness"—if this woe is not heeded the New Testament declaration, "No drunkard shall inherit the kingdom of God" (1 Cor. vi, 10), will surely be fulfilled. Let us, then, in the name of the Lord declare, "Woe to the drunkards of this and every place."

W. H. MEREDITH.

IV.

HEZEKIAH'S PRAYER AND DELIVERANCE.

Isa. xxxvii, 14-21, 33-38.

GOLDEN TEXT.—The righteous cry, and the Lord heareth, and delivereth them. Psa. xxxiv, 17.

"ALL history and all experience teach us that nature knows no difference between praying and cursing" is the affirmation of a Unitarian divine.* That word nature is a cover for much evasive nicety, it is true, but the context of the quotation, and especially the emphasis put upon "unvarying law," indicates that the speaker's practical intent was to show the inutility of prayer.

Does the ex-rector recognize the sacred Scriptures as authentic annals, then here is one history, at least, which teaches that there *is* a difference between praying and cursing, and that it is better to pray than to curse.

In the fascinating series of Bible pictures representing the ancient worthies in the act and attitude of prayer—Noah on the dripping rocks of Ararat, Jacob at Jabbok, Elijah on Carmel, Daniel in Babylon, Peter on the housetop at Joppa, and Paul in Street Straight in Damascus—all must yield the palm for scenic effect to the picture of the sack-clothed king kneeling in the awful presence of the Holy of Holies, with the blasphemous scroll of the world-

---
* Thomas Vickers, ex-Rector Cincinnati University.

conquering Assyrian spread out under the effulgence of the very Shekinah itself. Such a scene arrests attention, provokes thought.

Judah was a bagatelle for Sennacherib. The Nile was his real destination. It was the acme of his ambition to boast that he had dried up the irrigating canals of Eygpt, which would be equivalent to a complete desolation of the country. But to reach Egypt he must pass through the tiny realm of the Hebrews. Nothing, then, could prove more than a momentary impediment. The Ninevite was ignorantly omitting the invincible factor in his calculations, the God of the Hebrews.

The prophet describes the approach of the world-conqueror with nervous picturesqueness. Like an engulfing tide his army reaches the height of Lebanon, even the highest caravansary. The cedars feel his fire at their roots. Damascus is a heap. Hamath, Arphad, Sepharvaim, Hena, Ivah, Calno, Carchemish are mile-stones in the march of desolation. He pauses at Michmash, the " Rubicon of sacred territory." Ramah, Gibeah, Geba, Benjamite citadels, fall in a day. Two-score defended cities of Judah are taken. Jerusalem alone remains inviolate, and the ruthless invader even now stands at Nob and shakes his hand defiantly at the Daughter of Zion.

For the first time in his long and glorious reign Hezekiah falters in faith. He confers with flesh and blood. The indemnity, to pay which the house of God must needs be stripped, is as nothing compared with the loss to the nation of moral tone incurred by the defection from Jehovah and compounding with an idolatrous and blasphemous monarch. The loss of *morale* was quickly and sharply illustrated by the delirious excitement of the people as they watched the hostile cohorts passing by, their failure to heed their divine call to humiliation, their riotous gluttony, and want of appreciation of the sacrifice at which immunity had been purchased.

This historic incident is singularly apposite to some living issues. Any compromise, municipal, state, or national, with the enemy of Jehovah produces precisely the same results to-day as in Hezekiah's time. License saloons and prostitution, and you lower that inestimable quality of the community, its moral tone, and by that very means you indefinitely postpone and increase the difficulty of the final suppression of the evil. Yet there are not wanting those who would strip off the fine gold of our national temple and turn it over as an indemnity to the devil. Hezekiah's bitter experience is a warning. May it be heeded !

How short Judah's respite. In an incredibly brief time Sennacherib, who in his " gasconading inscriptions " at Korsabad describes himself as an " observer of sworn faith," is back under the walls of Jerusalem ; not in person, but represented by his chief captain, chief eunuch, and chief cup-bearer. The indemnity just paid is ignored, and surrender of the city is demanded. The embassy address themselves to the people crowding the wall, studiously slighting the king's representatives. With

Machiavelian skill they put the finishing touches to the *morale* of the garrison, already undermined by the king's concession.

This insulting embassy is quickly followed by a letter from Sennacherib—terrible in its language and terms—written "grievousness."

The extremity is reached. Jerusalem is an oasis in a desert of desolation. The destroying floods break in angry roar and foam around the rock of Zion. Hezekiah is as a bird shut in a cage. Sennacherib is about to thrust his hand into the Holy City, as he has into the nest of every nation, and irrevocably despoil it. The dilemma is fixed. Resistance and defeat on the one hand subject the captives to inhuman, ferocious barbarities, unsurpassed in history. For some, a ring in the nose, an iron bit through the lip, by means of which the captive shall be dragged whithersoever the merciless captor listeth; at length the eyes jabbed out with a spear. For others, that acme of human cruelty, flaying alive. Assyrian sculptors are even now cutting the *bass-reliefs* depicting the stubborn defenders of Lachish lying naked on the ground, each waiting the incision of the relentless knife.

The other horn of the dilemma is scarcely less appalling. It involves a moral humiliation and agony as insufferable as the physical: an ignoble surrender to the blasphemous idolater that involves denationalization and the deporting of the entire populace according to the fixed method of the Eastern conquerors; an exile imbittered, too, by the importation of an idolatrous colony (also part of the Eastern policy) into Judea; a motley, debased people who shall be encouraged to imitate the Hebrew ritual after the manner of the Samaritans—this, too, a part of that hated diplomacy which thought it wise thus to maintain the worship of local divinities by the colonists; a bastard race peopling even the holy hill of Zion, mimicking the Davidic psalmody and the Levitical sacrifices. Out on the very thought! Who can endure it?

Pity the ignoble, merciless fate of a people once exalted to heaven. On one or the other horn all that remains of the Hebrew nationality must be impaled. It is inevitable unless—Jehovah makes bare his arm!

In this emergency the ex-rector, Vickers, would have said, " Hezekiah, you might as well go to the wall and curse Sennacherib as to go to the temple and pray to God. All history and all experience teach us that there is no difference between praying and cursing. Every thing is subject to unvarying law."

A diviner wisdom possessed the soul of the glorious reformer, the Judean king. He believed the as yet unwritten Scripture, " The effectual fervent prayer of a righteous man availeth much." Chanting in his soul the psalm, " The Lord is our refuge and strength," and shoring up his faith with the "strophe-like" prophecies of Isaiah and the memory of the Red Sea and the wilderness, and justified by the awful emergency in what otherwise would have been a profanation, he enters even the holiest place and casts himself before the mercy-seat.

Hezekiah prays. Unvarying law varies. A *simoom* sweeps the *Judean valley at night*. Sleeping warriors drink in death through their uncovered mouths, and deliverance has come.

> O day-star [Sennacherib], son of the morning,
> How art thou cut down to the ground?

The crimson shields of Assyria cover the pillars of the temple so lately stripped to buy a worthless truce, trophies of the dead host " unsmote by the sword." The cedars of Lebanon shout for joy at the fall of their destroyer. A colossal page of history turns. On its under side Assyria disappears; on its upper, Babylonia comes to view.

In the turbid stream of the materialism and infidelity of our day this indubitable historic incident erects itself. Textual criticism and a something falsely called science and an evil unbelief all fret into a foam about it. It is unmoved, immovable! For three millenniums it has been a glorious, irrefutable memorial of answer to prayer. Hezekiah prayed. God delivered.

DAVIS W. CLARK.

V.

THE SUFFERING SAVIOUR.

Isa. liii, 1-12.

GOLDEN TEXT.—The Lord hath laid on him the iniquity of us all. Isa. liii, 6.

IN this chapter more than in any other portion of the Old Testament we breathe the atmosphere of the New. There may be some uncertainty as to its author; there is none as to its evangelical spirit. Whoever wrote it—Isaiah in his advancing years, meditating with an old man's yearning on the future of his nation and God's mystery of redemption as revealed to him by the Spirit, a pupil of the aged prophet chastened by the sufferings in Babylon so as to be translucent to the divine ray, or some unknown one sensitive to the heart of God—whoever was the author, he utters, hundreds of years before the ear of man is ready to receive it, the theme which is repeated over and over again with almost infinite variety in the writings of the New Testament. Here, under the discipline of a life constantly attentive to the whispers of God, a soul has received and given to the dull heart of his race the story of the coming incarnation, rejection, voluntary humiliation, sacrificial death, and exaltation of the servant of the Lord.

This mysterious Servant is one of the striking characters standing out in these later chapters of Isaiah. More and more distinctly he appears, until in this chapter he is seen with that full and sudden vividness that impresses him indelibly on the memory. No one who will take the pains to read slowly through these final chapters of Isaiah and trace the references to the Servant can finish this chapter without seeing One with marred visage, unattractively attired, gently ministering in uninteresting by-ways; stirring the conscience, making one uncomfortable in the neglect of duty, and yet so mildly reproachful, uttering not a word, simply turning and looking—such a look!—scorned, hated, forgotten, and yet not forgotten ; burdened with a heavy burden, a load you feel you ought yourself to carry ; pierced with an unseen thrust, quivering, still. Your eyes are riveted on him. There is a change ; the countenance is bathed in light; it itself becomes light; it is bright— brighter than the gleam of snows. The eyes rest on yours ; you feel yourself transformed ; shame changes to sorrow, and sorrow to joy. He, the marred One, is " clothed with a garment down to the foot, and girt about at the breasts with a golden girdle . . . And his eyes are as a flame of fire . . . and his voice as the voice of many waters."

Who is he, this wondrous personality ?

The prophet begins that description of him with which we are now concerned in the thirteenth verse of the fifty-second chapter. These last verses of the fifty-second chapter belong with the fifty-third chapter. They contain in outline what the fifty-third chapter gives in more detail. We will begin with the fuller description.

"*Who hath believed our report? and to whom hath the arm of the Lord been revealed?*" etc.

No one in the day when the Servant appears believes in him or sees in his acts any proof that the " Lord hath made bare his holy arm " through him, and is with him as he was with Moses and David. He comes with no pomp or show. He is but as a sucker springing from some root forgotten in the dry earth. " Is not this the carpenter's son?" There is nothing whatever interesting about him, nothing princely, nothing to show that he is servant of the great God. He is simply a servant, a menial. Therefore, the people despise him, and when he comes to give them his message they will have nothing to do with him. " They rose up, and cast him forth out of the city, and led him unto the brow of the hill whereon their city was built, that they might throw him down headlong."

His whole life is sad; he knows grief as one knows a familiar friend. Like Job, he is forsaken by his friends. They will not even look on him.

So far, then, we get this answer to our question. The Servant is the great rejected One, One who ought not to have been rejected, for he really has vital connection with the glorious past of the nation; he is of "the root," he belongs to the household, and ought to have been recognized.

A new paragraph gives us more light.

"*Surely he hath borne our griefs, and carried our sorrows: yet we did esteem him stricken, smitten of God, and afflicted,*" etc.

He is One whom the people of his time will think, and will some time confess that they thought, a special object of God's wrath, a leper, but really crushed beneath a load of griefs, sorrows, transgressions, and iniquities not his own, but theirs. He is a vicarious sufferer—that is, one who changes places with another (*vicis*, the Latin root of vicarious, means change), and takes his load upon his shoulders. "There are twelve distinct assertions of vicarious sufferings in this chapter."

These burdens, too, are not guiltless burdens, for the people are sinful, willful wanderers, all of them. Sometime they will confess

> "I was a wandering sheep,
> I did not love the fold,
> I did not love my Shepherd's voice,
> I would not be controlled."

The Servant, then, is a vicarious sufferer.

One thought is added here which is developed further on—the thought of the Golden Text.

Before this is emphasized a third paragraph tells us this Servant bore his load meekly.

"*He was oppressed, yet he humbled himself and opened not his mouth,*" etc.

He went voluntarily to his doom. "I lay down my life. . . . No one taketh it away from me, but I lay it down of myself." Still, the manner of the taking of his life is violent and unjust.

"*By oppression and judgment he was taken away.*"

And now a man of the far off time is represented as saying, for the whole chapter is dramatic and has many speakers: " Who of us that lived in his day considered that he was put to death because of our sins ? "

Then the awfulness of the violence is dwelt on, for this sinless, vicarious Victim has insult added to his injury; he is buried with the wicked, or what to the somewhat ascetic mind of the prophet amounts to the same thing, the rich. He is placed in an unhallowed grave.

The last paragraph opens with the thought noted before: This Servant is a victim.

"*It pleased the Lord to bruise him; he hath put him to grief.*"

We are accumulating evidence as to who this mysterious person is—this rejected One, a son of the household, a sorrowful One, the bearer of the grief of the sinful; a voluntary, uncomplaining victim, bruised of God, yet blameless.

One further fact is mentioned. This Servant is finally exalted. He is to have a following and carry forward prosperously the work of God. He is to be wholly satisfied in spite of his pain. He is to be wise in the purpose of God to make many righteous through his vicarious sufferings, and by his knowledge he is to further this end. He is to be given a royal rank and to share in the glory of the world.

Who is this Servant of the Lord?

Surely not the younger generation of the Jewish people, purified by the Babylonian captivity. Such an answer is absurd. Surely not Jeremiah, or any like hero. This is inadequate. Who is the mysterious One?

This was the question the Ethiopian eunuch asked himself as he was reading this chapter in his chariot on his way home from Jerusalem, when Philip met him by the appointment of the Spirit. What would we not give for the complete record of Philip's exposition of these verses? We have enough, however, to give us the answer to our question. "Philip opened his mouth, and beginning from this scripture preached unto him Jesus." Out of the Spirit-guided century of the apostles our question is answered.

Jesus is the Servant, "the man of sorrows and acquainted with grief," the rejected One, the vicarious Victim, the glorified One, "King of kings and Lord of lords."

This chapter is full of Jesus. It tells us of his incarnation, his agony, and his victory. It is the prophecy of the great confession when

> "Sinners, whose love can ne'er forget
> The wormwood and the gall,
> Shall spread their trophies at his feet,
> And crown him Lord of all."

A multitude of practical applications of the truths in these verses crowd in upon one. Only two that spring from the Golden Text can be mentioned:

1. What an awful thing is sin that makes it possible that such a burden of woe and pain can be laid upon a loving soul. Nothing brings out the exceeding sinfulness of sin more vividly than this picture of its blameless victim. This story of the cross repeated over and over will yet awaken the world and cause it to cry out: "We *all* . . . have gone astray." There is no meditation more helpful to the soul that desires to see its true state in sin and to be filled with a loathing for sin than a meditation on these words. It will profoundly stir one and be a curb on the unruly passions, a purifier of the intents of the heart. It will open the fountains of tears and lead to that contrite sorrow which satisfies the Lord for the travail of his soul.

2. Here is the great evangelical message: "The Lord hath laid on him the iniquity of us all." When the apostle Paul grasps this glad gospel he shouts: "There is therefore now no condemnation to them that are in Christ Jesus."

The awakened soul feels the need of a sacrifice. No one ever comes to himself after a wrong act or series of actions without instinctively thinking of what he can do, what he can offer to God whom he has wronged as an atonement for his sin. This instinct of the soul ought not to be weakened. It is right and true. Any form that it may take under a false system of religion is less hurtful than the absence of it altogether. Better the butter offerings of the priests of Thibet and the gifts of the guilt-conscious woman of India to her idol than the utterly empty hand of the cultivated sneerer against superstition. An offering is needed, and every awakened sinner should have this pressed upon his attention. His instinct should be assisted, and not hindered, in its exercise. But what shall we give? With what shall we fill our hands? Shall we bring lambs or turtle-doves and pigeons? No; our word tells us "the Lord hath laid on him the iniquity of us all." We are to take him as our sacrifice. Our lips may repeat for our hearts the words:

> "I lay my sins on Jesus,
>   The spotless Lamb of God;
> He bears them all, and frees us
>   From the accursèd load:
> I bring my guilt to Jesus,
>   To wash my crimson stains
> White in his blood most precious,
>   Till not a stain remains."

In this glad song our burdened hearts will find relief, and the endless joy of the blood-purchased life begin.

W. I. HAVEN.

VI.
THE GRACIOUS CALL.

Isa. lv, 1-13.

GOLDEN TEXT.—Seek ye the Lord while he may be found, call ye upon him while he is near. Isa. lv, 6.

THE evangelical prophet in this chapter rises to some of his most impressive utterances. The tenderness of the appeals, the strength and beauty of the language, the searching quality of the truth, make it a remarkable passage in prophetic Scripture. The majestic movement of Isaiah's mind is felt even in this brief chapter, just as the water of the bay opening out into the sea feels the pulsations that stir the entire Atlantic. Poetry with its imagery is here. Historic allusion—a secure basis for predictive statement—is here. Prophecy brightens the glowing strains with its story of the better time to come. There is in this passage that mystical quality which wide-reaching spiritual conceptions often have. There are also direct, pungent statements of practical truth fitted to stir the conscience and rouse the religious feeling. Every variety of appeal is here, from "the still small voice" of gracious entreaty to the trumpet-like announcement of final victory for the Church of God.

1. *The Invitation.* The Old Testament and the New alike say, Come. "The Spirit and the bride say, Come."

Prophets, apostles, and, above all, the Redeemer himself invite a weary, heavy-laden, thirsting, hungering world to come to the Fountain of life, to the Bread from heaven. Physical needs are put as figures for spiritual want. Hunger and thirst must be satisfied or the body perishes. The famishing soul must be supplied or spiritual death ensues. The prophet points to the herds and vineyards of Palestine in his allusion as types of the abundant, life-giving grace which God has to bestow upon fainting souls who will simply come to him. The transaction is taken far above the plane of the market-place. "Money" and "price" are not in this high reckoning by which immortal souls are redeemed. Salvation is above all commercial interests, language, and law. The impoverished sinner is bidden to partake of inexhaustible supplies freely and forever.

2. *The Rebuke.* The reproof, delicately but forcefully expressed in the second verse, is against the folly of men who lavish money upon things which do not nourish the real life, and which when bought leave the buyer restless and unsatisfied. This is the story of worldly desire. Feverish longing for gain, for glittering, material, perishable objects, is a desire which is never fully appeased. Indulgence only stimulates the covetous spirit, which grows more and more ravenous.

It is as foolish to spend and labor for that which does not feed and strengthen the essential life as it would be to buy stones for bread. Land and gold and wealth and honors are that which "satisfieth not" the real hunger of an immortal soul. Then the rebuke changes to exhortation. A better way is opened. Let desires wait upon God. Lift the powers of mind and heart toward his riches. Begin to feed on heavenly manna. Hunger and thirst after righteousness. Covet earnestly the best gifts. Lay hold, by all the loftier appetites of the soul, upon eternal things; then a great wholesome satisfaction takes the place of the old fitful fever. Life grows rich. Faith, love, holiness, heavenly-mindedness crowd out the former worldly desires. The shriveled worldling becomes the peaceful, happy saint.

3. *The Threefold Power of the Divine Guide.* The primary allusion in the third and fourth verses is evidently to David and the covenant which Jehovah had established between himself and the chosen nation which David had brought to its proud place as a victorious people. But it is a passage, like many others in prophetic writing, which is as evidently applicable to the Messianic Person for whom David and his kingdom were but foreshadowing types.

The great gift of God to the world is his Son. He proclaimed himself as a *Witness*. Truths which before he came had been only dreamed of or hoped for became, by Christ's testimony, the foundation of the world's faith. He came out from God; so that all he said about God and the divine purposes is the testimony of a true and faithful witness. He is also a *Leader*. He goes before his disciples in the path of obedience and self-sacrifice, and says, Come, follow me. He leads the nations in their progress. Christianity is foremost in all the best advances that civilization makes. He is a *Commander*. He spoke not as the scribes in his earthly ministry, not with hesitation, nor for the sake of sect or school, but with authority—an authority which his own majestic character enforced. The scene upon the tempestuous Sea of Galilee, when he commanded winds and waves to be still, or the scene in the Temple courts, when he put to flight a crowd of shameless, sacrilegious money-changers, give us glimpses of the commanding dignity and power which slumbered behind the humility of his earthly bearing.

4. *The Call to Paganism.* Through the somewhat obscure language of the fifth verse we have at least a hint of the great truth which Hebrew history embodies. Israel, with all its isolation and exclusiveness, was nevertheless the custodian of a revelation for all nations. Its sacred book, its completed and glorified law, its Prophet, Priest, and King, who consummated the best things of Jewish history in his person and work, all have a world-wide interest. The desire of all nations is for just the religion which the Jewish-Christian revelation discloses. No kindred, people, or race will be satisfied until it has "run unto" the Saviour and acknowledged him and his truth. The East, with its Oriental type of life—contemplative, reverent, yearning—is to come to Christ. The West, with its vigorous, aggressive forms of activity, must run toward, not away from, the Redeemer, if it would be safe in all its splendid movements of intelligence

and of power. The North and the South—opposite poles of human life—the white and the black, the Alaskan and the African, are all described under the prophetic vision as turning to this central figure of human history, running to meet the King of kings whom we love to call—the Christ.

5. *"Seek, and Ye Shall Find."* We are constantly reminded of gospel language in this stirring passage: Seek not money nor power, but seek the Lord, who holds all riches and might in the hollow of his hand. The searching heart need never lose courage in its search, for it is sure to find him who is near to just such souls. But he may not always be so readily found as *now*, in this accepted time. This is the warning implied. God is far away from the hardened, persistent wanderer who will not look for God; this is the apparent attitude of God, but even in these conditions it is the human disobedience that makes the separation. But to most men he is near. His Spirit broods over them, draws upon them by his tender ministries. He is near men by his providential watch-care, by the messages which come from earth and sky, from the still voice within, from revelation, and the impressive ordinances of the Church. These voices of divinity speak to the deep needs of the soul. The prophet appeals tenderly and warningly to men not to let this divine Friend who "besets us behind and before" pass beyond the reach of their prayers while they are indifferent, disobedient, and unloving. As the loadstone flies to the magnet, so ought the human soul,

with unresting eagerness, to press toward the life and love of God. If it has sinned, the fact of sin to be forgiven should only add wings to its returning flight as it comes penitently to Him who longs to forgive.

6. *Contrast Between God and Man.* It is very natural for us to project our human notions upon the divine mind, making our ways his ways, our thoughts his thoughts. The fact is that the Infinite is utterly beyond human power to conceive. We have a little knowledge of him, for he has condescended to our low estate. His self-limitation has graciously bridged the gulf which separates finite from infinite. It is not the Absolute whom we struggle to apprehend, but a self-revealing Father. Thus his majesty, his omnipotence, his omniscience are all the more adorable since we have knowledge of his love. With this conception as a basis of knowledge upon which we can rest—that God is love—the other fact which the prophet brings out is not dreary or discouraging ; we even rest with great confidence upon the truth that his infinite wisdom overreaches our fretful, anxious life ; his invincible power undergirds all our experiences. We beat about in our little circles ; he calmly rules from his everlasting throne. There is wonderful repose for the human heart as it settles with profound conviction upon the comforting doctrine of divine sovereignty.

7. *The Fruitfulness of God's Grace.* The law which rules for the grain of the field is an illustration of the law which controls in spiritual things. The sower is not

more confident of the effects of the early and latter rain than the child of God may be in the power of divine grace to quicken the germs of spiritual life in his heart. Earth and sky co-operate for the golden results of the harvests; two worlds unite their forces for the complete manifestations of Christian character. It cannot be evolved by merely human skill or will. Righteousness of the true type comes from above. It is the word of God that is the fructifying power. The truth which has gone forth through prophets and apostles and from the lips of Christ was spoken with divine wisdom for the salvation of the world. It will not fail to accomplish the glorious work of salvation. Men grow weary and disheartened; the word lives on, works on in its own resistless way. Human ignorance sometimes misinterprets the word, preachers fail to declare the whole counsel of God; yet its truth will finally shine out upon the world clear as the sun. There are periods of confusion and conflict when the region of dogma seems unsettled; but the word stands secure, for at least human thought is sure to rest confidently upon its everlasting truth. Substitutes for the word are often tried; but these, when the tests of human experience come upon them, are "like the chaff which the wind driveth away." The word of God abideth forever.

8. *The Joyful Victory.* The last two verses of the chapter have the cadence, the imagery, the antithetical force of a masterpiece in sacred poetry. We are not told when the glorious results foretokened here shall take

place. But the slow march of our race onward toward a better condition is certainly made significant, though weary and full of pain, when such illuminating pictures of the outcome are held up to the thought of the world. It will not always be battle and confusion, with many a defeat and backset for the cause of right. There will be a mighty triumph by and by. Joy and peace will reign instead of misery and war. Even the dumb hills will be vocal with the echoing gladness that will fill the air. The solemn mountains will vibrate to the world's great anthem of victory. The trees will be applauding witnesses. Nature will respond to the jubilant hearts of redeemed men. A transformed earth is the promised accompaniment of a regenerated race.

O blessed prophecy! We will wait and work and hope and pray that the time may be hastened when "thorns" and "briers" shall be plucked out of human hearts forever, and the earth, with all its fullness, shall be the Lord's.

WILLIAM E. HUNTINGTON.

VII.

THE NEW COVENANT.

Jer. xxxi, 27-37.

GOLDEN TEXT.—I will forgive their iniquity, and I will remember their sin no more. Jer. xxxi, 34.

THIS passage might fittingly be called the Gospel before Christ. It had not only an immediate application, but also a far-away reference, then not clearly understood, now plainly seen. Take out Christ, as represented in types, figures, and prophecy, from the old, or first, covenant, and it becomes worthless and lifeless. The basis of this new Messianic covenant is found in the declaration, "I will forgive their iniquity, and I will remember their sin no more." The new covenant accomplishes that nearness to God which the old but promises. How strikingly all the things foreshadowed are fulfilled in Christ.

Upon a dark background the prophet throws this marvelous picture. Like a gleam of sunshine through stormclouds these words light up the surrounding gloom. They form a bow of promise to troubled hearts.

Israel, through failure to keep the first covenant, had become subject to the King of Babylon. Many of her citizens were languishing as exiles in that far-away land. Those remaining regarded not the claims of Jehovah.

Zedekiah, a well-meaning but weak prince, sat upon the throne, a servant of Nebuchadnezzar. Attempting to throw off the foreign yoke, a large army soon encamped before Jerusalem to compel submission. The outcome was plainly declared by the prophet, who counseled immediate surrender. Zedekiah, however, feared his courtiers, while they hated Jeremiah, because he continued to proclaim to the people that longer resistance would be fruitless. His life was in constant jeopardy, while the people suffered great distress with the prospect of nothing better than death or exile before them. In the end the land was laid waste, her cities were torn down, her flocks and inhabitants carried away by the invader. The prophet, in a vision, sees a better day coming, when God shall again enter into covenant relations with his people. This prophecy forms the text of this lesson.

On examination we find:

1. *A Period of Preparation.* God is never in a hurry. When all things are ready he speaks, he acts, he sends the blessing the people are prepared to receive. Before the covenant is announced Israel is to be returned; the land is to be replenished; the waste places are to be builded. In those days her prosperity shall be greater than in former years. As Job was enriched in his old age beyond all that he had at the beginning, so Israel shall be more fruitful.

The return from Babylon but in part fulfills the prediction. It is an earnest of the full and final blessing which is future. When the days of chastisement were past the Jews returned in spite of all opposition. When God put it into the heart of Nehemiah to rebuild the walls of Jerusalem, no Sanballat or Tobiah was sufficient to cause the work to cease. The restoration of Jerusalem was a marvel to those who heard of it, and its final resurrection will be one of the grandest achievements of history. He who had faithfully carried out the conditions of the old covenant, resulting in their overthrow and dispersion, because of disobedience, will as faithfully watch over them to build up and renew as they obediently serve him.

In the light of accomplished facts the significance of unfulfilled prophecy may be realized. So these exiles came at last to find comfort in the promise that had accompanied the menaces now so clearly fulfilled. Two things had been predicted. The first is now accomplished. This they could not doubt. Does not this warrant faith that God will in his own time restore them again to the joys and blessings of their own land? What a pity that some eyes can be opened only by suffering! We should remember that God watches over men in their sin and wrong-doing as surely as in their uprightness.

Punishment is grounded in individual guilt. The Israelites bewailed the sins of their fathers on account of which they suffer, saying, "The fathers have eaten a sour grape, and the children's teeth are set on edge." Our fathers did wrong, we suffer for it. How easy to lay the blame on others and to excuse ourselves! Men complain of their ill-luck and bad chance, as they are pleased to call them, till they speak against God, saying his ways are unequal, partial, unfair.

It is true that God visits the sins of the fathers upon the children to the third and fourth generations; but of whom? Of them that hate him. If a nation or family become base or profligate they soon perish. How many nations, families, individuals have sunk out of sight, being worthless. But if nations turn from their sins—as Nineveh—if children hate the evil which caused the fathers to suffer, God is merciful. If punishment has worked out repentance and amendment, it ceases, for its work is done. While this proverb is most certainly true, and we are constantly witnesses of its truth in those with whom we associate, and possibly in our own experience, still it is not to be used to justify ourselves in our present condition. God's plan involves the best for every individual. To declare ourselves wrecked and ruined because of inherited fetters is to believe a lie and lose faith in God. Every man has the working out of life in his own hands. Every one shall die for his own iniquity. Now, if I perish I have no one to blame but myself.

2. *The New Covenant Declared.* The word covenant frequently refers to promises made to Abraham and his immediate descendants. Its most important use, however, relates to the two dispensations known as the old and the new; the one referring to the law, the other to the Gospel.

(1) *Who are embraced in its provisions?* A united Israel. If this covenant be understood to be made pri-

marily with a literal Israel and Judah, in a secondary sense, at least, it must refer to the spiritual Israel.

(2) *The old and new covenants contrasted.* The *old covenant* was given to God's chosen people through Moses, and had to do chiefly with such outward ceremonies and observances as the law enjoined. Because of man's disregard of its conditions it only "worked wrath." In its scope it was preparative, symbolic, and limited. Man found himself utterly unable to keep the obligations which it imposed. This prepared the way for a more willing acceptance of God's new provision in Christ.

The *new covenant* " was made through Christ, sealed by his own blood, and secures to every believer the blessings of salvation and eternal life." It consists in the gracious bestowal of good upon man.

1.) *It is essentially inward and spiritual.* It is no longer an outward law inscribed on stone, but an inner, spiritual truth written on the conscience, leading to quick obedience in outward details. Under the old covenant God took his people by the hand to instruct them. But they regarded not God, so God justly regarded them not. Under the new covenant he will put his laws into their minds. They shall now be influenced by principles of law and truth. They shall receive such an illumination as will enable them to comprehend their meaning. His laws will be stamped on men's hearts; not the heart of stone, but the new heart of flesh. There is a change in man as well as in God's covenant. No change can count so much for a man as that which changes him. "A new heart will I give you." Having changed the man, the world is changed. The affections are turned into new channels—to regard spiritual objects. The passions and appetites are purified. What once was hated is now loved; what once was loved is now loathed. A new motive—love, born of the forgiveness of sins—enables us to fulfill the law, and a new impulse is given by the Spirit's indwelling.

2.) *Its conditions.* I will be your God. Ye shall be my people. From him the people shall receive light, direction, defense, support, and happiness. God's presence means all this. They being his people, it is implied that as such they will serve him with all their hearts; that they will be obedient to all his commands; that they will have no other object of worship. If any of these conditions be disregarded the covenant becomes null and void.

3.) *Its results.* Under the old covenant knowledge must be sought from the priest. Under the new covenant every believer has God's revelation and receives light directly from the Holy Spirit. This does not exclude the teaching of one by another while the provisions of the new covenant are being made known. But when once the Holy Spirit shall have taught all the gracious truths of the Gospel there will be no further need of man teaching his fellow-man. Until that day shall dawn it is the duty of every believer to do what can be done, that all may know these wonderful facts.

"The teaching is not hard and forced, because grace renders all teachable; for it is not the ministry of the letter, but of the spirit. The believer's firmness does not depend on the authority of human teachers. God himself teaches."

The wide diffusion of the Bible among men is evidence that this prophecy is fast being fulfilled. If present indications are not misleading, the generation now living will see the day when all shall have the privilege of hearing the Gospel or of reading for themselves God's new covenant with man. This truth not only prophet and apostle often emphasized, but we find it in the rabbins as well. "When the days of the Messiah shall approach even the little children in this world shall find out the hidden things of wisdom; and in that time all things shall be revealed to all men." Again: "There shall be no time like this till the Messiah comes; and then the knowledge of God shall be found in every part of the world." Is not this the gracious day when many run to and fro and knowledge is increased; when every nation is open to the Gospel, and every man hears in his own tongue wherein he was born?

4.) *Its basis.* Forgiveness of sins will be the root of this new state of grace. This is made possible by the death of Jesus Christ, the covenant sacrifice. His blood has purchased redemption, and faith brings remission. So in Christ sin is no longer remembered.

3. *The Continuance and Stability of this Covenant Affirmed.* The old covenant was rendered null by the

disobedience of the people. May not this in like manner become void? No; its permanence is shown:

(1) *By a reference to what had already been done.* God's fingers fashioned the firmament, and the sea obeyed his voice. He placed in the heavens the sun, moon, and stars. By a breath of his mouth he caused the sea to roar. He is able to perform what he has promised. He is the God of hosts. All created things are obedient to his will. As surely as these ordinances shall remain God's covenant shall abide. This is an everlasting covenant which shall never be destroyed. God will regard his own word rather than the people's merit. The preservation of Israel as a distinct people, notwithstanding the repeated persecutions they have suffered, remains the standing miracle of the ages. And God will no more destroy Israel as a distinct people than he will blot out the lights of the material universe.

(2) *Its permanence is enforced* by a reference to the impossibility of man's measuring the heavens above or of searching the depths below. No more inconceivable is this than that God should cast off his people. They sinned grievously; yes, "but where sin abounded, grace did much more abound." The jeweler, in setting precious stones, often spreads beneath them a dark substance in order to throw out and heighten their brilliancy. So here God's wonderful love is more clearly seen when we remember the sins of the people.

What a gracious privilege to live in this day of fulfillment; in the day when Christ so sweetly talks with us that we may know that we have "redemption through his blood, the forgiveness of sins, according to the riches of his grace." We will gather all the riches of this world, both of mind and matter, and lay them down at his feet, for "'Worthy is the Lamb that was slain to receive might and majesty, riches and power, honor and glory;' his is the scepter, his is the right, his this universal world."

WILBUR S. SMITHERS.

VIII.

JEHOIAKIM'S WICKEDNESS.

Jer. xxxvi, 19-31.

GOLDEN TEXT.—To-day if ye will hear his voice, harden not your hearts. Heb. iii, 15.

JEHOIAKIM took a manuscript copy of inspired words —supposed to have been a portion of our present Bible—cut it in pieces defiantly, threw the fragments into a fire, and burned them. It was the only copy in existence. It was written to benefit himself and his countrymen. He scorned the instruction and warning, and intended to put the Scripture where it would never come to him again. After the destruction of the scroll he ordered the death of the men who had prepared it. This was Jehoiakim's wickedness. All the notoriety attaching to his name arose from this act. It is the one solitary thing for which he is remembered. Better be forgotten than live in history on account of iniquity! This is the earliest record of the burning of the Bible; and for bold and shameless impiety it has never been outdone. Jehoiakim succeeded in reducing the roll to ashes, but he failed to find the men who wrote it and who could duplicate it. They were safe and God was caring for them.

The man who committed this wickedness was a king.

The most favored people on earth were his subjects. At the age of twenty-five he had inherited the advantages, honors, and responsibilities of one of the highest positions in the world. He sat on the throne of David and Solomon. He could have done great good and won lasting fame. Responsibility is calculated to develop good character. He ought to have been a good man and refrained from impiety for the sake of his people as well as himself. But there is no position so high as to be above the reach of temptation. No external advantages are a sure defense against sin. Men may fall from the loftiest places into the depths of ruin. Jehoiakim had the further advantage of being the son of a noble sire. His father, Josiah, made his reign glorious both for piety and prosperity. He raised the kingdom of Judah to a better estate than he found it. He bequeathed a restored temple service, a revived religion, and an example of devotion to God. If any persons have unusual reasons for being righteous and God-fearing it is those who have been born and reared in good homes. The greater is their guilt if they commit wickedness. Jehoiakim had come to the throne about five years before the burning of the sacred manuscript. His crowning was a little irregular and suggestive. The people did not choose him king. Although he was the eldest son they preferred a younger brother. It is not creditable to a young person to be distrusted by those around him. And those who do not win confidence and favor in one position will not speedily be called to a higher. This man sided with a bad political party—the Egyptian. It was made up of those who favored alliance with Egypt. King Josiah opposed that party, and lost his life in resisting the passage of an Egyptian army through his country. Jeremiah and other prophets warned the people against Egypt. It was the King of Egypt that placed Jehoiakim on the throne of Judah, displacing and taking as prisoner the brother whom the people had crowned.

His use of the royal power during the nearly five years that preceded this burning prepared him for the deed. He had gone on from step to step in baseness. Josephus says of him that "he was neither pious toward God nor good-natured toward men." Jeremiah reveals that he was oppressive toward the poor, defrauding workmen of their wages. He occupied an elegant house, built in unrighteousness. He was hard-hearted, and paid no regard to the wrongs and sufferings of the lowly. A man who begins by oppressing his weaker fellow-man will end in flagrant sins toward God. He does sin against God every time he wrongs the poor. Covetousness was another evil the king indulged. The times were hard, the nation paid a heavy tribute, and the people groaned under their load of taxes, and yet Jehoiakim glutted his avarice. He had given play, also, to cruel passions, and had unjustly caused subjects to be put to death. Stopping his ears to the cries of suffering, treating his laboring people with injustice, and indulging in bloodshed, this young ruler had lived in ease and

JEHOIAKIM'S WICKEDNESS.

luxury. Such a course is fatal to conscience, reverence, and all the better impulses of the soul. By living after that fashion he became hardened for the daring wickedness he afterward committed.

Affairs in his kingdom had in the meanwhile rapidly grown worse and worse. The religious services declined. Idolatry crept in. The good work of Josiah was largely undone. Religious decay was attended by an increase of immorality. Hypocrisy, falsehood, bigotry, evil-speaking, injustice, violence, and licentiousness were the sins that the prophets found abounding. Some people profess great admiration for morality, but disparage religion. Thus far the world has failed to sustain a high type of morality apart from religion. The eras marked by religious prosperity have shown the best record for morality. On the other hand, in times of religious decline there has been a like decay in the morals of the people. So degenerate had this nation become that Jehovah proposed to suffer it to be overthrown and its people to be carried into captivity. The time was nearly at hand. A hundred and twenty years before the ten tribes had been carried away, never to return. For centuries God had been seeking to school this people in righteousness and holiness, and they had been slow to learn. Wisdom had been scorned and goodness had been abused. Gentle methods had often to give way to those more severe. The severest chastening of all is yet to come. The Holy City that had been the home of David and his royal descendants for four centuries would be pillaged. The Temple of Solomon, the shrine of Hebrew devotion, the glory of the race, would be thrown down, and its consecrated wealth fall into plundering hands. The hill-sides of Judea would be deserted, the homes would be left vacant, the villages in ruins, and the chosen people of God would be toiling captives in a foreign land.

That dark outlook was revealed to Jeremiah. He saw the time drawing near. What made it the more terrible was the fact that it could all be avoided. It lay with the nation itself. Safety, peace, and prosperity were within its own grasp. It made its own choice and determined its own destiny. Just so are the issues of every one's life within his own control. Each chooses his own fortune and makes his own destiny. Ruin never falls on any man who does not pull it down upon himself. Judah herself was preparing the oncoming calamity. The iniquity that prevailed in palace and peasants' homes, the sin that defiled the Temple precincts, the impiety that neglected the services of religion, the injustice that reigned in the places of trade, and the immorality that polluted society—these were the causes of the threatened downfall.

To escape was simple. It required the putting away of sin and the practice of righteousness. Let king and subjects humble themselves, repent and reform, and they can defy all the armies on earth to harm them. Jeremiah had been preaching righteousness for eighteen years, and his words had been disregarded. Under divine impulse he made one last supreme effort. Baruch, of noble family and fine culture, aided him. A parchment was secured, and Jeremiah rehearsed under divine illumination all the prophecies he had before uttered. Baruch wrote them. He read them afterward to the people on an appointed fast-day, and then by request repeated them to the chief men or princes of the nation. These statesmen counted the matter serious enough to receive attention from the king. Taking the precaution to have Baruch and Jeremiah hide themselves, they acquainted the king with the matter, and he ordered the roll to be brought and read to him. As he listened his anger burned, and seizing a knife he cut off the portion read and dropped the piece into a brazier filled with coals to warm his luxurious apartments. Whether he listened to the whole or not is uncertain, but he kept on cutting and burning until the sacred parchment was all consumed. Three of the mature men who were present besought the king to refrain. But they appealed in vain. His stout will prevailed, and repressed all opposition. No one showed any disposition to heed the prophet's voice. The ungovernable madness of the king destroyed the last hope of the nation.

The reason in Jehoiakim's mind for this act was his displeasure with the contents of the roll. It was not a question of truthfulness or falsity, but simply a matter of dislike. He hated the truths thrust upon him. Perhaps here is the explanation of very much of the hostility manifested against that book in later years. The thing that specially displeased Jehoiakim was the prophecy of the downfall of the nation, and its captivity. People do not like to contemplate the results of their wrong-doing. They are unwilling to hear them spoken about. It angers them to be warned about the consequences. Wicked men live in the present and refuse to look into the future. Future punishment is the part of the Bible most offensive to bad men.

Jehoiakim was wedded to his luxury and his vices. The preaching of Jeremiah was against these. The demand was their abandonment; the condition of escape was reformed living. The king was unwilling to change. The suggestion of it angered him. He was like bad men in all ages. They propose to cling to their sins, and will risk danger and ruin rather than forsake them. The writing condemned the monarch's life, and so the monarch hated the writing.

It was folly in him to vent his anger upon the unfeeling parchment. He could not hurt it, nor by burning it injure any person but himself. Did he suppose for a moment that in the destruction of the words of prophecy the reality would be avoided? Laws are not repealed by burning statute-books. History is not unmade by consigning its records to the flames. The consequences of the sins of Jehoiakim and Judah were not to be turned aside by destroying the roll of Jeremiah and Baruch. Nebuchadnezzar's army moved up with unslackened pace. Its strength and prowess were undiminished. Jerusalem fell, and Jehoiakim was slain and Judea's men were overpowered and borne into captivity just as inevitably. Burning the Bible does not annihilate perdition nor ward off from evil-doers the consequences of their sins. Truth and law, like God, are indestructible. They existed before man learned the art of writing, and remain unchanged when written declarations are destroyed.

As if to show the king how futile was his attempt, God prompted the hidden prophet to reproduce another roll with the same awful words of prophecy. Wicked men will fight in vain against the testimony that will stand against them. God cannot be outwitted. He who sets himself against the Lord contends with infinite odds. Man may assume the airs of insolent defiance, but he will prove puny before the divine majesty. Jeremiah was directed to add a little to the first writing, and to announce the addition to the king. First, he should not have successors to sit upon his throne. With his own downfall should be the extinction of the family. Alas! how the sins of the fathers do come upon the children! Secondly, his own dead body, instead of receiving royal sepulture, as did the honored body of Josiah, should be cast out like the body of a dead dog, exposed to the heat of day and the frost of night. The new roll was made, and is probably a portion of the Book of Jeremiah.

The word of God has always survived the assaults of men, and "abideth forever." The wickedness of Jehoiakim was as great as his folly. If man welcomes any thing it should be the light that shines upon the darkened pathway of life, showing him how to live, what to seek, and what to shun. God's word is such a light. He sent that warning message to enlighten the erring Jehoiakim. He sent it as an act of kindness. Love prompted him. It would have proved a great blessing to the king. It was the last appeal to him. It was his last chance. His treatment of it settled once and forever his doom. He repelled the approaches of God, met good with evil, smote the hand that was stretched out in love to rescue him, and precipitated ruin upon himself and his people.

J. E. JACKLIN.

IX.

JEREMIAH PERSECUTED.

Jer. xxxvii, 11-21.

GOLDEN TEXT.—I am with thee, saith the Lord, to deliver thee. Jer. i, 19.

THIS lesson gives us a view of Jeremiah under stress of persecution. He is called to stand alone and make known the divine will in the face of great opposition, and falters not.

The situation is briefly as follows: The kingdom of Israel has been destroyed and the people carried off. The kingdom of Judah no longer exists as an independent power. Its king, Zedekiah, is a satrap or governor under Nebuchadnezzar, King of Babylon, to whom he has sworn allegiance and to whom he is indebted, indeed, for his kingly honors. He is surrounded by counselors who lead the nation into frightful corruptions and into a suicidal policy of rebellion against Babylon.

Against this tide of corruption and folly Jeremiah was called to stand. For a period of more than twenty years he witnessed for God in the face of the bitterest opposition and at the expense of great personal peril and suffering. Arrayed against him were the kings, princes, priests, the false prophets, and the people; on his side was—God. Intensely loyal to the theocracy, he was compelled to counsel submission to Babylon, while the mole-blind politicians and ecclesiastics—apostates all—enjoyed the transient glory of being the champions of loyalty. In this position he stood like a wall of brass, witnessing to the divine will. Neither the stocks, the bastinado, nor the dungeon could daunt his intrepid spirit, nor induce him to prophesy smooth things. "Obey God, repent of your idolatries, submit to Babylon, and live," this was the burden of his prophecy. Over and over again he declared, as from God, that their only hope of saving the city and the beloved Temple was in remaining loyal to Babylon. But in this position he stood alone. Led by the false prophets and princes, Zedekiah repudiated his oath of allegiance and exposed himself to the wrath of Nebuchadnezzar.

The city is besieged. Zedekiah and his counselors madly resist. Jeremiah reiterates, " Submit, submit to Babylon, and live!"

At the point where our lesson opens, Nebuchadnezzar has raised the siege to do battle to an Egyptian army that gives vain promise of relief to Jerusalem. Jeremiah is again consulted by the king, whose deepest conviction, no doubt, is that Jeremiah's word is God's word.

" Now, Jeremiah, the tide is turned. If you are loyal you will join in the general sentiment and prophesy the destruction of Nebuchadnezzar's army and deliverance to God's people. This will greatly strengthen the hands of the men of war in the city. It will make you personally popular and be better all round." This, we may imagine, was the advice of the tempter, if not of Jehucal and Zephaniah, priests whom the king sent to Jeremiah to ask an interest in his prayers. What answer will he send back? Listen. " Behold, Pharaoh's army . . . shall return . . . into their own land. And the Chaldeans shall come again, and fight against this city, and take it, and burn it with fire. . . . Deceive not yourselves, . . . the Chaldeans shall . . . not depart. For though ye had smitten the whole army of the Chaldeans, . . . and there remain but wounded men among them, yet should they rise up every man in his tent, and burn this city with fire."

That is plain enough. Jehucal cannot fail to understand that, and will have no difficulty in making it plain to Zedekiah and the rest. What is to be done? Here is a man who counsels submission to a retreating enemy simply on the ground that God has commanded him to do so.

The princes could interpret Jeremiah's motives only on a level with their own. Such counsel from the lips of their ilk would be a sure sign of sympathy with Babylon and disloyalty to Jerusalem, therefore Jeremiah is a traitor to be watched and put out of the way. He is arrested while going quietly about his business, on the assumed charge of desertion, beaten, imprisoned, neglected.

But the man who has a mission from God cannot be neglected for long. The king has silenced Jeremiah, but he cannot silence himself. A man may put away the word of God as spoken by the prophets, but he cannot put away the voice of God in his own soul.

The king has his misgivings. He has counselors

enough, but he is without counsel. Jeremiah is recalled. What will he now say? He has had "many days" of fasting and solitary confinement in which to try the spirits. Perhaps his prophetic ardor has cooled, and he will now prophesy smooth things. Listen, as this man of God, standing before the king, undaunted, replies: "Word from the Lord do you ask?" Word enough if you will hear it. The same old word, short, clear, crisp: "Thou shalt be delivered into the hand of the king of Babylon."

Jeremiah is sent back to prison, and why? If he is enough a true prophet to be consulted by the king, is he not altogether too much a true prophet to be held in durance vile? If he had prophesied to the king's liking, think you he would have been sent back to prison? He would probably have been promoted to some high office as a man of sound *practical* sense.

Events move on apace. God's flail of judgment, Nebuchadnezzar, returns to Jerusalem and prepares to strike. Jeremiah abates not his testimony: "The sword and the famine are here and are to come yet more. Remain in the city and die, or go out to the Chaldeans and live, for thus saith the Lord, This city shall surely be given into the hand of the king of Babylon's army, which shall take it."

The princes are exasperated beyond measure. This counsel is the truth of God, or it is treason. It must be followed or Jeremiah must be destroyed. But they have already determined to resist to the bitter end; therefore, "Let this man be put to death."

JEREMIAH PERSECUTED. 79

The king is a weak man, therefore cruel and unjust. He pleads his weakness, and turns Jeremiah, whom in his heart of hearts he believes to be a man of God, over to the tender mercies of the princes. " Behold, he is in your hand : for the king is not he that can do any thing against you." In a dungeon now, sinking in the mire, left to perish, what are the prophet's meditations ? Does he lose confidence in God, and cry out, "O Lord, thou hast deceived me and I was deceived?" Does he curse the day of his birth and the man who brought tidings of it to his father, saying, "Wherefore came I forth out of the womb to see labor and sorrow, that my days should be consumed with shame?" Or does he plead the divine promise contained in his call to the prophetic office, " For, behold, I have made thee this day a defensed city, and an iron pillar, and brazen walls against the whole land, against the kings of Judah, against the princes thereof, against the priests thereof, and against the people of the land. And they shall fight against thee; but they shall not prevail against thee; for I am with thee . . . to deliver thee." And does this bring him to his normal attitude of victorious trust ? " But the Lord is with me as a mighty terrible one: therefore my persecutors shall stumble, and they shall not prevail: they shall be greatly ashamed; for they shall not prosper: their everlasting confusion shall never be forgotten."

There was never yet dungeon with doors double barred deep enough to keep down the man whom God has commissioned to speak his truth. If God cannot find an Israelite to rescue his prophet, an Ethiopian he can find, and Ebed-melech comes to the rescue.

Again the king seeks from Jeremiah the word of the Lord. Once more Jeremiah, hollow-eyed from suffering, earnest-visaged from conviction of the truth of his message, stands before the king. Again he counsels the king to surrender and save the city and the nation's sacred, passionately cherished shrine, the Temple. Again the pusillanimous king draws back from the line of duty. He knows the will of God and does it not, and is beaten with many stripes. The vials of divine wrath are full. The crisis comes.

What a mournful tragedy greets our eyes! Jerusalem and the sacred Temple a heap of smoldering ruins; a captive nation toiling in mournful procession over the burning sands of the desert. Among them is their one-time king reaping the reward of his timidity and self-seeking—doomed to see his children murdered before his eyes, to have his own eyes put out, and to spend the remnant of his days in low drudgery and disgrace. "He that saveth his life shall lose it." Jeremiah, on the contrary, enjoys the sweet light of day, the blessings of liberty, the good opinion of his fellow-men, continues for many years to exercise his prophetic gifts and enjoy the divine protection. "He that loseth his life for my sake and the gospel's shall find it."

This lesson suggests a few practical questions.

1. *Why was Jeremiah persecuted?* He was naturally of a mild and gentle disposition, he did not love strife,

he shrank from publicity, he was extremely sensitive to the opinion of others, and yet he was constantly coming into conflict with the people around him. How will you explain it? If he could not prophesy smooth things, why couldn't he keep still? He couldn't keep still— tried to, couldn't. When he resolved not to speak any more in His name then there was, as it were, a burning fire shut up in his bones, and he was weary with forbearing, and said, "I cannot keep still!" He must utter his message. His message brought him into conflict with every element of power in the land. The priests and prophets persecuted him because he, a priest and a prophet, ventured to attack his own order and announce truths which had not received their sanction.

The princes strove to put him out of the way because he denounced the corruptions and the idolatries of the court and the folly of their nation's policy. From his more elevated standing-place he took a broader and more extended view than others of public affairs. He looked the evils of his times squarely in the face. He was called to fulfill the most melancholy mission that ever fell to the lot of prophet or reformer. Isaiah, in the general apostasy of the northern kingdom, took a more hopeful view of the southern. Not so Jeremiah; he saw no hope for the theocracy save in a general breaking up of the national life.

His persecution is an inevitable accompaniment of his career as a faithful and true witness to divinely given truth. The man who bears witness to truths that bring the lives of his contemporaries under condemnation will suffer persecution. If he is called to denounce political institutions, long established, honored, or social customs inwrought into family, church, and national life—as, for example, caste, slavery, the drink evil—he will be denounced as a visionary, a fanatic, a crank, a disturber of the peace, an incendiary, or a traitor, according to the force and directness of the attack and the sensitiveness of the body politic or the body ecclesiastical at the point attacked.

It is, however, our duty and privilege to bear witness to the truth as God gives us to see it. Some who are of the truth will hear our voice, will attach themselves to the truth, and to the Lord of it, and hasten the final triumph of the kingdom of truth among men.

And that brings us to ask:

2. *In what sense was God with Jeremiah to deliver him?* How is it that God permits those whom he calls to bear witness to the truth to be persecuted, and sometimes to suffer martyrdom for it? In what sense is God with such to deliver them? Precisely in this, the triumph of the truth through the testimony of those who are persecuted for it. Was God with Jeremiah to deliver him while in the stocks, the mire? If the promise pertained to temporal deliverance merely, methinks Ebed-melech would have been a little more prompt. What constitutes divine deliverance? Exemption from suffering? No. A life of ease and self-indulgence? No. That life is divinely delivered which God utilizes

for his glory. That man reaches life's chief end in spite of rack and dungeon whom God uses to root out the evil and plant the good; to hunt down the honored error and bring to place of power the despised truth. Devout men took Stephen to his burial, and no doubt lamented his *untimely* taking off. Did not God deliver him in the broadcast sowing of his martyr-blood? Any life spent for God is a fulfillment of God's promise to be with and deliver, even though that life be spent in a series of apparent defeats, or though it be cut off in the beginning of what promised to be a brilliant career.

3. *How may we know what is the will of God?* If it is important that we stand firm, it is not less important that we stand for the right thing.

For a man to embrace an error thinking it to be very truth, and to imagine that God has called him to propagate this supposed truth and suffer for it, is a sad but not uncommon folly from which, we should pray, "Good Lord, deliver us!"

Several safeguards are to be suggested, one to be emphasized.

(1) Consult the word of God prayerfully, with all available helps; not as an arsenal of projectiles to be hurled at the other party; not as a book of rules and precepts, but as a book of principles, and as bringing us under the influence of that divine life which is the source of all spiritual life, discernment, and power.

(2) Seek guidance in direct communion with God. The source of truth is the mind of God; the organ for

apprehending truth is the human understanding. The earnest, consecrated soul in communion with God will not fail to receive light on the path of duty.

But are these sufficient? Not always. There are fanatics who conscientiously follow the Bible as they understand it. Freeman, of Pocasset, thought he was following the guidance of the Spirit and the teachings of the word when he interpreted the narrative of the offering of Isaac as a command to himself to take the life of his daughter. What follies are sometimes wrought by those who vainly imagine that they are led by the Spirit of God—who mistake willfulness for the will of God, party spirit for holy zeal!

(3) Have regard to the consensus of thought, or the prevailing sentiment in the Church of Christ.

The combined judgment of the body of believers is more likely to be in accordance with the mind of the Spirit than the judgment of the individual. If some one says, "How about Luther?" I must remark that this last safeguard is important in inverse ratio to the probability that the Church is corrupt and that you are called to be a reformer.

(4) The safeguard to be emphasized is this: Seek prayerfully and in a spirit of absolute personal surrender to the will of God when known. So seeking we shall not walk in darkness, but shall have the light of life, and experience the fulfillment of the promise, "I am with thee to deliver thee."

JAMES HARRISON HUMPHREY.

X.
THE DOWNFALL OF JUDAH.

Jer. xxxix, 1-10.

GOLDEN TEXT.—Behold, your house is left unto you desolate.
Matt. xxiii, 38.

THE storm-clouds have long been gathering. Deep gloom has settled over the whole prospect. Ominous rumblings and fierce flashes give warning of the near tempest. All unheeded by the people are the plainest signs of coming danger till the cloud-burst of divine indignation sweeps with resistless fury upon them. From the highest hill-tops to the deepest glen every water-course of woe becomes a torrent. Barriers break as straws. The work of centuries is lost in a moment in the mad swirls of the rushing flood. The whole fabric of the national life totters and falls in one vast, hopeless ruin. Destruction is every-where. No path of flight to safety remains open. Desolation, anguish, despair, like blackest night, close over the scene of Judah's downfall. Will morning ever come! And if it come, can it bring help, or only show more hideously the utter wreck?

No more dramatic scenes are shown in history than those connected with the sieges and destruction of Jerusalem by Nebuchadnezzar. The horrors of the time are unparalleled save by those witnessed during the siege of the same place by Titus, nearly seven centuries later. Through all the conflict and confusion one figure stands calm and majestic, towering above all others. Priests, prophets, princes, soldiers, common people, in one mad, struggling mass surge around him. He alone is confident of the issue. Above the clash of arms, the shouts of brutal soldiery, the shrieks of wounded, crazed, and famished wretches, his voice rings out with trumpet clearness. The central figure is not the king, Zedekiah, contemptible and despised; not the high-priest, whose very name has perished; not the general-in-chief of the Chaldean forces; not even the great monarch of Babylon himself. The son of Hilkiah the priest, Jeremiah of Anathoth, gentle and shrinking by nature from scenes of violence, retiring in disposition—he is the one upon whom all eyes turn. Possessed by the spirit of inspiration from Jehovah, God of Israel, he was transformed into the fearless, outspoken prophet, denouncing the sins of the nation and threatening its complete destruction, but promising peace and prosperity on condition of repentance of heart and reformation of life.

Zedekiah, now thirty years of age, was in the ninth year of his reign. He had come to the throne in troublous times, when the strongest arm and wisest head were needed in the direction of the affairs of state to keep the vessel from the rocks. He possessed neither political sagacity nor moral integrity, and by his baseness hastened the disaster already threatening. His father was the godly Josiah, who had attempted to reform the nation by law. Aided by such men as Hilkiah the high-priest, Shaphan the chief secretary, and the young prophet Jeremiah, he had done what was possible to reestablish the worship of Jehovah according to the law given by Moses. Six years before the birth of Zedekiah, the book of the law, long neglected and lost to sight, had been discovered in the Temple, and its directions had been diligently followed by the king. But the evils of idolatry had become too deeply rooted in the thoughts and habits of the people to be easily eradicated. Alliances with heathen nations had been prohibited by the statutes of Moses and denounced by all the prophets of Jehovah. All the surrounding nations were deeply idolatrous, and in consequence morally corrupt. The great kingdom of Egypt on the south-west had for ages stood unrivaled in power, laying under tribute the whole of western Asia. In spite of all prohibitions there had from the first been a strong party always favorable to close political and commercial relations with the Egyptians. Solomon's marriage with the daughter of Pharaoh was intended as a shrewd stroke of state policy. It proved to be consummate folly. By it the abominations of animal-worship were introduced and fastened upon the people by royal sanction and example. The worthlessness of the political alliance was proved when Jeroboam was harbored by Pharaoh, and when Rehoboam ransomed his kingdom from being plundered by Shishak by delivering up the immense treasures of the Temple of Solomon.

All the wealth accumulated with such labor through years was lost at one stroke, never to be recovered. Bravely did the national party struggle during the reigns of Asa, Jehoshaphat, Joash, Hezekiah, and Josiah to establish a policy based on righteousness and allegiance to Jehovah. Persuasion and denunciation, precept and example, were exhausted in displaying the corruptions of idolatry and the ruinous consequences to individuals and the realm sure to follow any compromise with the evil. The rising power of Assyria and Babylonia was watched with eager interest by the court at Jerusalem. The chances of victory in the struggle for world supremacy between the ancient power on the Nile and the new civilization by the Tigris and Euphrates were balanced, and opinions divided sharply on the line of policy to be pursued by Judah in the conflict all saw as inevitable. In vain did the prophets strive to arouse the spirit of the nation to a true loyalty to their God. After every spasm of reform the nobles sank into deeper evil, and the mass of the people, never thoroughly imbued with devotion to purity, turned quickly to the unspeakably vile practices of their heathen neighbors. Avarice, cruelty, licentiousness, deceit, and murder in large measure ruled the times.

Every crime was tolerated, and even committed, by those responsible for the enforcement of the laws against crime. Priests became leaders in iniquity; prophets, claiming to be inspired of God, promised peace and prosperity, and encouraged the people in their wickedness.

Those who still stood for obedience to the laws of Moses and commands of Jehovah did so at the peril of their lives. It was amid scenes and under circumstances like these that Jeremiah and Zedekiah grew to manhood, each developing for the decisive hour of destiny; but developing how differently!

At nine years of age the young Prince Zedekiah saw his father Josiah set forth at the head of his army for that ill-advised campaign against Pharaoh-Necho which resulted in the defeat of the army of Judah at Megiddo and the mortal wounding of the king. The burial of Josiah; the national mourning led by the touching lament of Jeremiah; the crowning of Johanan, Jehoahaz, or Shallum, as he is variously called; his overthrow by Necho and exile to Egypt; the elevation of his brother Eliakim (Jehoiakim, Jakim) to the throne, all passed in swift succession, and could not fail to impress the boy prince.

Egyptian influence must have prevailed at the court of Jerusalem during the succeeding years. Even when the young Nebuchadnezzar of Babylon overran and subdued the whole country from the Euphrates to the confines of Egypt, and laid Jehoiakim under tribute and exacted from him an oath of allegiance, the spirit of the nation was adverse to submission to the distant empire on the Euphrates. Bitterly was it remembered that many of the sacred vessels of the Temple, with immense sums from its treasury, and the flower of the young princes and nobles, had been sent to Babylon as an offering by Nebuchadnezzar to his god for the service of a foreign temple. Revolt from the hated power was followed by the re-appearance of the Chaldean army, the close investment of the city, its capture, and the ignominious death of the treacherous Jehoiakim. His body was thrown without the city walls unburied. The whole strength of the army and all the artisans from the cities followed the earlier captives into the lands of the conqueror. Jehoiachin (Jeconiah, Coniah) and many of the nobles, after a few months of power, take up their long march to the East to end their days in Babylon. Zedekiah, at twenty-one years of age, is placed upon the throne of his fathers. Has he learned through these long years of calamity and bloodshed that safety for himself and nation lies only in the path of righteousness? Jeremiah, who has so faithfully warned the father, the brothers, and nephew, is equally faithful to the new king, destined to be the last of his line to sit on the throne of David. But all is to no purpose. The priests, the prophets, and the princes are in deadly opposition to all truth and virtue. Jeremiah owes his life to the influence of Ahikam, the son of Shaphan, the friend of his early years, and to a kind-hearted eunuch of the palace.

Zedekiah vacillates between his knowledge of duty and inclination to evil. Revolt is determined upon in reliance upon the promise of help from Egypt. Swift comes the retribution and terrible. The hosts of Babylonia swarm over the land. The forces from Pharaoh

THE DOWNFALL OF JUDAH. 91

are driven back. Two years of siege bring famine and unutterable misery upon Jerusalem. The walls go down before determined assault. By night the guilty Zedekiah, with wives and children, and the miserable, starved remnant of his army, steal out of the city at an unguarded point at the south, but by morning light their flight is discovered. Pursuit is made, and they are captured near Jericho. Brought before Nebuchadnezzar at Riblah, near the northern end of Lebanon, he is punished for his treason. His children and nobles are slain before his face, and then, his own eyes put out, he is shackled with fetters of brass to be led to Babylon. The climax of his calamity comes in the news that the walls of the holy city Zion are razed to their foundations, the gates and palace and Temple burned, the inhabitants removed, and the land left in utter desolation. The end has come. The doom of disobedience, long threatened, has fallen.

From the view-point of secular history the overthrow of the nation was an inevitable consequence of its treachery and disregard of treaty obligations. From the higher plane of spiritual insight it was the natural consequence of sinfulness and rebellion against the Lord of hosts. The pure, spiritual worship of Jehovah was rejected, with all that was divine and helpful to men. All that was vile in human and Satanic nature was cherished in the worship of Baal and Ashtoreth, of Molech and Chemosh.

The lesson was not alone for the men of that age. It

is an object-lesson to all ages and for all men, teaching that sin always and every-where brings suffering. Disobedience to God ends ever in disaster. Though penalty is deferred the punishment cannot be evaded. The offers of mercy are long continued, but if persistently rejected the sentence is pronounced upon nations, upon individuals, " Behold, your house is left unto you desolate."

WALTER J. YATES.

XI.

PROMISE OF A NEW HEART.

Ezek. xxxvi, 25-38.

GOLDEN TEXT.—A new heart also will I give you, and a new spirit will I put within you. Ezek. xxxvi, 26.

EZEKIEL is the prophet of visions. Great truths appear to him, not in logical formulas, but in vivid pictures. The literal condition of Israel in captivity is to him a picture of the spiritual condition of every soul in sin. The literal restoration which God promises to Israel is a picture of the spiritual restoration promised to all who forsake their sins.

The great facts of the lesson are:

1. Israel is in Captivity.
2. God Promises Deliverance.
3. A New Heart Shall be Given to Her.

The old dispositions and tendencies and desires which made God's law a burden shall all pass away, and new dispositions and desires and purposes, which shall make his law a delight, shall take their place.

4. The Land also Shall be Greatly Changed.

When they went out it was a land of famine, a land that ate up the inhabitants thereof; but when they return it shall be a land where the corn is increased and the fruit of the tree and the fruit of the field are multiplied.

5. With the New Heart will Come New Ability to Honor God.

6. Prayer and Blessings are Inseparable.

All this, though uttered 587 B. C., and literal as to Israel, is a gospel picture of sin and its results, salvation and its blessings, vivid as any that can be found in the New Testament.

1. *The Sinful Soul, like Israel, is Captive in a Foreign Land.* God is the home of the soul. In him it lives and moves and has its being. Out of God it can no more have a spiritual life than the fish out of water, or the bird out of the air. The seed has power wrapped up in it which, when brought into proper connection with sunlight and soil and rain, will unfold into a beautiful flower. You may bring it into contact with every thing else in the world, but keep it from these and it can never unfold. So the soul has powers which, brought into proper relations with God, will unfold into a beautiful spiritual life; but without him they must forever lie dormant. God is the atmosphere, the only atmosphere, in which the spiritual life can bloom.

The instrument that is out of tune cannot produce harmony. The soul that is away from God cannot be at ease. The soul that is in Christ has its longing, but it is longing for more of the same that it has. The soul that is out of Christ has its longing—longing for something different from what it already has. Here is the secret of the unrest of the sinner. He is out of his atmosphere, away from his native land, held captive there, and his spiritual powers long to be free and return home.

2. *God's Promise of Restoration* (ver. 24). This promise of restoration does not depend upon any good feelings we may have or good deeds we may do. There would be great cause for discouragement if it did. Upon something within God himself it rests. " Not for your sakes," but for my holy name's sake I do this, saith the Lord God (ver. 32). A really good man is anxious that his name shall be untarnished. God is very jealous of his name—his holiness. A besotted son reflects upon his father's honor, and for his name's sake he cannot rest without making efforts to restore that one. So one of God's children left in sin with no effort to restore him would reflect upon God's love for holiness. The very same reason—a display of his holiness—that prompted God to create man prompts him to seek his restoration to righteousness. This promise, moreover, is to all, and God is abundantly able to fulfill it. No souls have wandered so far away that he has lost sight of them; none have been so long away that he has forgotten them; none have so far wasted their substance in riotous living that he cannot renew them. Christ is greater than Adam. Grace is mightier than sin. The robe and the ring on the returned prodigal were richer than the garments he wore when he left the father's house.

3. *The New Heart.* In God's store-house are many rich gifts, but among them all none is more valuable than the new heart. It is a *heart* God is to give us.

The Christian life is a life of duty; but what is wanted is something that will make *duty* a *delight*. Clear *intellectual perception* will not do this. We may have a clear knowledge of right and a perfect hatred of doing it. Indeed, to the unregenerated soul clear perception of duty brings any thing but delight—it brings remorse.

Neither is the new heart a *controlling purpose*. A deep purpose will overcome every thing but impossibilities; but a deep purpose cannot make duty a delight. A general who is dominated by a deep sense of duty to his country, and has a purpose of loyalty which nothing can overcome, may, nevertheless, find his fingers itching for the gold an act of treachery would bring him. But he who *loves* his country more than all things else is moved only to burning indignation if a bribe should be offered him.

The controlling purpose may accomplish the same as the controlling love ; but in the one case there has been a great struggle to remain loyal, in the other to remain loyal has been easy and delightful. The new heart will undoubtedly give clearness of vision, it will strengthen the will; but these are rather the results of it than the new heart itself.

A *controlling love* is the essence of the new heart. Love makes all things easy. However clear our vision or strong our purpose of will may be, without love to God his yoke is not easy, his burden is not light; but with a supreme love to him his yoke is just such a burden as wings are to a bird. What God purposes to give his children is a new heart—a controlling love, a power at the center of their being which makes them feel that duty is a delight.

This new heart comes only by our coming into harmonious relations with the Holy Spirit (ver. 27). About all life there is something mysterious; but about the "new birth," or Christian life, there is nothing more mysterious than there is about the birth of an oak.

There is your acorn. Within it is a something which, when brought into proper relations with sunlight and soil and moisture, will spring into an oak. Deny it relation with these elements, lay it away in the dark and dry, and it never can produce an oak.

There is your soul. Within it is a something which, when brought into proper relations with the Holy Spirit, springs up into a Christian life. Deny it proper relations with that Spirit, and there never can be Christian life. As this life starts in union with the Spirit, so its continuance is dependent at every moment on that union. Remove the oak from soil and sunlight and moisture, and it dies. Cut off the soul from connection with the Spirit, and Christian life expires.

This Christian life must be carefully distinguished from much that only resembles it. Our *surroundings* may be so changed that we literally come into a *new* life, but not a *Christian* life. A child taken from a home of filth and squalor, where the only salutations have been blows and curses, and placed in a home of luxury, where it is caressed and fondled, will have new experiences of joys and hopes—will literally have entered into a new life. But this is not being "born from above;" it is only being born from around; and when the surroundings which brought the new experience shall depart the experience shall go with them. The birth from above rests upon connection with the Holy Spirit; it can be destroyed only by destroying that connection; change of surroundings cannot affect it.

4. *The Promise of Changed Conditions* (vers. 33-35). The bitterest draughts in every man's cup are those which his own hand mixes. But these are by no means all the bitter potions in the cup of life. The relations in which we are placed with others oftentimes bring most bitter sorrow.

The sinfulness of sin is that its evil effects fall upon the innocent. The innocent wife and child must suffer because of the drunken husband.

When God gives the new heart he promises there shall come with it new and better surroundings. It is the very nature of the new heart to create new surroundings.

As soon as the drunkard is converted he seeks new associates. He begins to be cleanly about his person and about his home; he becomes industrious and saving; he has noble aspirations after the good of this world as well as the next, and very soon that which was a waste becomes a garden.

If all would at once accept this new heart earth would at once become an Eden. If you, reader, will accept it the bitterest potion will be taken from your cup, and your surroundings will be vastly better than if you remain away from the loving Father.

5. *With the New Heart will Come New Ability to Honor God.* The prophet declared that the blessings and prosperity which should come upon restored Israel would cause the heathen round about to know that the Lord builds the ruined places and plants that which was desolate. So every renewed life is a testimony to the goodness and greatness of God. A shepherd is known by his flock. A poor, sick, weakly flock proclaims a worthless shepherd. A strong, healthy, vigorous flock proclaims a noble shepherd. So nothing honors God like noble, vigorous, joyous Christian lives. The miracles Christ wrought nineteen hundred years ago are a great recommendation to him ; but the miracle of a life transformed and made daily to walk in unspotted purity amid the sin of this world is a much greater recommendation. That, reader, is the way God promises you may honor him.

6. *Prayer and Blessings are Inseparable.* " I will yet for this be inquired of by the house of Israel, to do it for them."

When God promised Israel he would bring her back again to her native land he declared, " Not for your sakes do I this, but for my name's sake." So God for his name's sake is to-day bestowing many blessings alike upon those who pray and those who do not pray. " He sends the rain upon the just and the unjust." Yet he wants us to ask him for the blessings which we need. (1) Because if we are not desiring them enough to come and ask for them we cannot receive the full benefit of them. The rain came upon the good and the stony ground alike, but to the one it was only a temporary, to the other a permanent, blessing. He who has no desire for gold would not be benefited by a goldmine if it were at his disposal. (2) Because there are many blessings God would like to bestow upon us, but cannot because we are in no condition to receive them. God is never doing for us the absolutely best, but only the best he can under the circumstances. The heart that is longing for something is in a condition to receive it when otherwise it would not be. God's blessings are limited only by our capacity to receive them, and lack of desire destroys capacity. Prayer and blessings form the ladder that reaches from earth to heaven. The first round is blessing; that used brings prayer, and prayer again brings blessing. And so we ascend round over round till we shall stand in his presence.

ALEXANDER DIGHT.

XIII.*

THE BLESSINGS OF THE GOSPEL.

Isa. xl, 1-10.

GOLDEN TEXT.—The glory of the Lord shall be revealed, and all flesh shall see it together. Isa. xl, 5.

THE thought which stands out at the beginning of this lesson is that God's word is a word of comfort. Not only is the injunction, "Comfort ye," repeated, but to this repetition is added, "Speak ye comfortably to Jerusalem." At the time the prophecy was uttered the true people of God were in a state of great apprehension because of the prevailing corruption and the intense sinfulness which characterized the times. While they were depressed and in sadness and fear on this account, the prophet was sent with a message of comfort to them. Surely, here is a lesson for all gospel ministers. They should be sons of consolation. Having in their own hearts the experience of divine comfort, they should be able to minister it to others. A minister who has no taste for the work of comforting the sorrowing children of God is out of place. No eloquence of diction in the pulpit, no proficiency in theological lore, no accumulation of scientific knowledge, no splendid literary attainments, can compensate in any degree for the lack of deep and

---

* No homily is given for Lesson XII, which is a review.

earnest sympathy with the people in their trials and the power born of a divine experience to bring God's comfort to them in their hours of need.

Another point to be especially noticed is that God's comfort is for his people ; "Comfort ye my people " is the word of God to the prophet. It is impossible to bring real and substantial comfort to those who refuse to be the people of God; but for those who are loving him and trusting him there is abundant comfort always.

Notice, again, that this comfort is to be derived from the word of God. The passage at the close of the fifth verse, " For the mouth of the Lord hath spoken it," is the key to the whole situation. However dark may have been the surroundings, however destitute of comfort they may have seemed to mere human observation, because of what the mouth of the Lord had spoken there was to every trusting child of his a permanent source of richest comfort ; and we should enforce upon those who are under our instruction the fact that this is just as true to-day as when the prophet uttered it; that there is no need of any soul for which there is not an adequate supply; no sorrow for which there is not abundant comfort; no hours of bereavement and affliction in which God's word is not able to bring richest consolation.

The comfort brought to Jerusalem at this time was based upon three facts.

First, " Her warfare is accomplished." That is to say, her time of struggle was pretty nearly over. The conflict of tribulations and anxieties through which she had passed was near its end, and this in itself was a source of great comfort.

Secondly, " Her iniquity is pardoned." Sin was at the bottom of all her troubles. It was the fruitful cause of every disaster that had happened to her. The severest trials through which she had passed were simply a necessary outgrowth of the sin into which she had fallen, and for the removal of which she was utterly helpless. The announcement that God, who alone had the power, had pardoned her iniquity was a source of richest comfort and encouragement.

Thirdly, the punishment designed had been executed. " She hath received of the Lord's hand double for all her sins." This must be regarded as simply a strong rhetorical expression to indicate that her punishment had been severe and sufficient. It cannot be intended to imply that the penalty had been twice as great as was appropriate, for that could not be true in the just administration of God. It is simply an intense expression to signify that the penalty had been fully imposed. This being the case, of course no further treatment of the kind was needed. It is a divine proclamation that her punishment is at an end, that that darkest of all hours which is just before day had arrived, and the sunrise of hope and encouragement was just at hand.

The phrase, " The voice of him that crieth in the wilderness," no doubt has reference to the custom of Oriental monarchs to send heralds in advance of their coming and give notice of their approach. It doubtless has primary reference to the prophets, who spoke by divine authority in those troublous times, but unquestionably had special regard to John the Baptist, as our Saviour clearly indicates that this passage was fulfilled in his ministry. The object of this divine cry was to notify the people to prepare the way of the Lord. It was the custom of Eastern monarchs to send men in advance, when they would journey in any direction, to fill up the valleys and dig down the hills, so that an easy and nearly level highway might be prepared for their advance. At this day when the Emperor of China is about to make a visit to the tombs of his ancestors, a host of men are sent out in advance to prepare the roads and put every thing in perfect order for the monarch's approach. So the prophets were called upon to admonish the people to prepare the way of the Lord. This was to be done then, and is to be done now, by repentance, by sincere sorrow for the sins that have brought trouble upon ourselves and others, by humbling ourselves before God in the dust, acknowledging with sorrow the sins which have separated between him and us, and by reverently seeking to know his will, holding ourselves in a receptive attitude before him, so that his slightest whispers may be heard by our awakened and alert souls. It is under these circumstances that hindrances get out of the way, valleys are exalted, mountains and hills are made low, crooked places easily become straight, and rough places plain. The way of the Lord is so prepared that his messages of love and mercy at once penetrate and infuse the soul.

God has always sought such preparation on the part of his people. He longed for it among the Jews in their time of captivity, and when it was in his heart to bring them out of their bondage and return them in joy to their native land. He longs now for this preparation in the hearts of his people. He desires to open the heavens to pour out his richest blessings in seasons of great and sweeping revivals, turning the hearts of multitudes unto himself, and quickening his people in their holy faith; and that he may do this he seeks that they may be prepared. He commands the messengers of his truth to proclaim, as they did in Isaiah's time, " Prepare ye the way of the Lord." When this is done " the glory of the Lord shall be revealed."

The ministry of repentance and reformation, such as John's was in the wilderness, must always precede the coming of the Messiah and the revelation of God's glory. It is not in the divine order, it is a spiritual impossibility, that the revelation of God's glory should come to an unrepentant and unreformed people. The ministry of John the Baptist comes in its natural order before the ministry of Christ, the loving and all powerful Saviour; but when this ministry has done its work, and souls are filled with repentance and bringing forth works meet for repentance, the voice of God will soon be heard, saying, "This is my beloved Son, hear ye him;" and in due time will come the glories of the transfiguration scene,
5*

when God's chosen and prepared ones will be filled with the transporting delight of the Saviour's glorious presence.

As soon as the prophet reaches this theme of the revelation of the glory of God he bursts from the narrowness of Judaism, and exclaims that "All flesh shall see it together." And this glorious truth, which "the mouth of the Lord hath spoken," is repeatedly revealed in the clearest possible terms by this same prophet in many other passages. So that the Golden Text of this lesson is a missionary text, and gives all teachers an excellent opportunity to bring before their classes the missionary character of this prophecy.

This declaration of Isaiah differs not at all from the Saviour's own proclamation, "I, if I be lifted up from the earth, will draw all men unto me." Isaiah's declaration is a gospel of hope, a message of good cheer for the whole world. The angel over the plains of Bethlehem re-echoed this word of Isaiah when he said, "Behold, I bring you good tidings of great joy which shall be to all people." And Luke makes very clear what the meaning of this "glory of the Lord" is when he renders this passage, "All flesh shall see the salvation of God."

Let this glad evangel of Isaiah sound out over the whole world. Let the Church awake to its duty of making known this glorious truth wherever men are in darkness and in need.

Next, the perishable character of earthly things is alluded to in order to emphasize the enduring nature of

THE BLESSINGS OF THE GOSPEL. 107

God's word. "All flesh is grass, and all the goodliness thereof is as the flower of the field : the grass withereth, the flower fadeth; because the spirit of the Lord bloweth upon it : surely the people is grass. The grass withereth, the flower fadeth : but the word of our God shall stand forever."

These familiar statements in regard to the transitory character of earthly and material things seem to be introduced for the purpose of emphasizing by contrast the enduring nature of God's word. We are virtually admonished to loosen our hold on material things that we may take a stronger grasp on that which is immortal, as the apostle says: "While we look not at the things which are seen, but at the things which are not seen: for the things which are seen are temporal; but the things which are not seen are eternal" (2 Cor. iv, 18). The apostle Peter quotes this very passage, and adds that this word "is the word which by the gospel is preached unto you." This enduring word of our God is the Gospel of Christ which brings peace and comfort wherever its joyful sound is heard.

The verse which follows this, and which seems to be an address to Zion and Jerusalem, should rather read : "O thou that tellest good tidings to Zion, get thee up into the high mountain ; O thou that tellest good tidings to Jerusalem, lift up thy voice with strength ; lift it up, be not afraid." This is an exhortation to make known with clearness, and with as wide a range as possible, the glad tidings of salvation. Let it ring out over all the land!

Speak it so that all can hear! These words of help and comfort are not to be kept for the select few, but are to be made known with energy and to come with power of help and comfort wherever their messages of love and mercy are needed.

The message to all the cities of Judah was, "Behold your God." Not as an object of fear, not as one coming with a message of destruction to exercise his omnipotent power in blotting out his rebellious subjects from existence, but he was to come " with strong hand," and his arm should rule for him ; that is, his own strength, his omnipotent power should secure for him that which he designed to accomplish.

" His reward is with him." This is an intimation that he will recompense punishment to those who are flagrantly in rebellion and will not repent, and rewards of mercy and blessing to those who are faithful. The phrase, " His work before him," is differently interpreted. It may signify that he has his divine plan and purposes, which he knows how to accomplish, and that he will certainly do it.

The eleventh verse is not connected with this lesson, but seems to belong here ; and its simple language is a most touching expression of the tenderness of God in his care for his people: " He shall feed his flock like a shepherd: he shall gather the lambs with his arms, and carry them in his bosom, and shall gently lead those that are with young." The whole passage is one full of the tender and encouraging spirit of the Gospel. It might be called the Gospel by Isaiah, so full is it of the very spirit of the Master himself. It ought to be made the occasion of unfolding the love of God to every listening pupil, and under its faithful teaching many young hearts ought to be won for the Master.

STEPHEN L. BALDWIN.

SECOND QUARTER.

I.
THE WAY OF THE RIGHTEOUS.

Psa. i, 1-6.

GOLDEN TEXT.—Blessed is the man that walketh not in the counsel of the ungodly, nor standeth in the way of sinners, nor sitteth in the seat of the scornful. Psa. i, 1.

THE Bible has a grand purpose. It is revelation in order to salvation. Each book of the Bible may be said to have a subordinate purpose. It has a special truth to emphasize, makes an appeal to some special part of human nature, or deals with a special phase of human life or history. Our lesson is an introduction to the Book of Psalms. This Psalter is the heart's book. Here the heart opens itself that we may see in it the workings and results of wickedness, the victories and blessings of righteousness. In history we see the streams of life; here we see the fountains. The book is a mirror of my heart, your heart, all hearts. Here may be studied the heart, in itself, under the varied conditions of life; in its manifold fellowships with men, its different movements toward God. The importance of this is seen in these Bible expressions, "The heart is deep," "Who can know it?" "Out of it are the issues of life."

But these revelations of the heart are not blunt and so plain-spoken as to shock us. They come in the form of Oriental poetry, like living forms unclothed, yet veiled, chaste, and sacred.

This first Psalm is without any inscription. We are not told who wrote it. Its thought, imagery, and words suggest Solomon as a possible author. It may be one of his one thousand and five songs. Like his proverbs, it is full of sententious wisdom, and never rises to the height of passion. Still, we are not sure of the human author. But while we cannot repress the wish to know who penned this Psalm—his circumstances, feelings, and purposes when he wrote—may it not be well sometimes for the human to vanish that the feeling may grow more definite that God is now speaking to my heart about my life? There is here the "certain sound," the very spirit of authority that fills the words with assurance that the hand of the Master is on the harp. There are no queries, doubts, or proofs, but truth that wakes in me the consciousness that it is truth—truth that has the ring and tone of divinity.

How shall we study it? There are two great methods of interpretation. One is that of Luther, called the subjective, which ever looks for the principle, the truth, the food for the soul that is in the word just as it stands. The other is that of Calvin, called the objective, which looks for the sure ground of historical interpretation, and illuminates the text from all the side-lights of history till the word lives again for us just as it lived for him who penned it. Not knowing the author, time, or circumstances of this Psalm, we are shut up to the former method, the subjective.

In fact, we are inclined to think this is a subjective

hymn. It is not likely that the singer had before him two men, one righteous, who found his delight in the law and meditated in it constantly, and therefore his outer business life was always prosperous, and his relations with the natural forces of the world and with society always full of blessedness; and the other unrighteous and joined with the wicked, and therefore his projects all failed, and he was blown away by the winds of disaster to utterly perish in misery in this life. Such objective poetry, thus picturing the outer relations of life as the result of inner character, would not be true to history. Job was perfect and upright, a man who eschewed evil, and yet he was stricken, smitten, and afflicted, but in the depths of his trials insisted upon his integrity. The wicked often flourish as the green bay tree, are fat and prosperous in life, and have no pains in their death; but is their inner life full of blessedness?

The real blessedness of man is not in his outer circumstances, but in his inner heart life. Riches may fly away or be a source of trouble, friends may fail or even wound us, society is often not in accord with righteousness, and Dame Nature seems to be a cruel mother. But if a man have a fountain of peace, gladness, and joy in his own heart, if he have God and heaven in his own soul, he is greater than Diogenes in his tub and richer than Solomon on his throne.

It is this inner blessedness of the inner life of which the Psalmist sings. By a series of contrasted pictures he would show us the fountain on which the heart feeds, the way along which it moves, the end which it reaches. We see more plainly by contrasts than by looking at a single object with nothing by which to measure it. How striking the contrasts here! This Psalm is both dark and bright—like the pillar of fire and of cloud—it is darkness on the way of the wicked; it is light on the way of the righteous. "The way of the wicked is as darkness," "The path of the just is as the shining light, that shineth more and more unto the perfect day."

1. *The Negative Pictures of Progress and Results.* Let us note briefly the way the righteous man does not take. It is set forth in six pictures; three are the steps of progress and three are the results.

The first negative picture is "walketh not in the counsel of the ungodly." The ungodly are the restless, dissatisfied, unrighteous (Job iii, 17; Isa. lvii, 20). "The counsel of the ungodly" means hidden designs, secret thoughts, evil imaginations. These are the fountains of evil-doing. They precede open sin. They are the seed of wicked harvests. As a man thinks so is he. Reading accounts of crime and descriptions of vice in the daily press or in vicious literature, or seeing them represented in immoral theaters, and then meditating on them and living them over again in our imagination, is walking in the counsel of the ungodly. The righteous man does not even stroll through such thought-realms of impurity.

The second picture is doubtless a little more than a poetical repetition. "Nor standeth in the way of sinners." Sinners are active habitual doers of iniquity.

THE WAY OF THE RIGHTEOUS. 117

The dishonest, peculators, Sabbath-breakers, gamblers, profane are some of those meant here. To "stand" in their "way" is to agree with them in heart and mind. To be in any sense a party to wrong-doing in business, social, or political relations is to stand in the way of sinners. It includes the licensing of evil. The righteous man will not be entangled in or compromise with the world's sin. He hears the divine voice, "Come out from among them and be ye separate."

The third picture is still stronger. "Nor sitteth in the seat of the scornful." The scorners are those who make an open scoff at religion, and blaspheme and ridicule it. These, in varying degree, are as many now as in the Psalmist's day. They still have their "seat" or assembly and form a deliberate confederacy in wickedness. To "sit" in their "seat" does not necessitate being an open-mouthed blasphemer, but may only imply a silent member of such a company, who in his own heart at home harbors such feelings. Beware of mocking, ridiculing, scoffing, scorning sacred things. Such a spirit indicates a heart empty of good and of God, near to destruction.

The three pictures showing the results of such a heart-life are given in the fourth and fifth verses. The ungodly, with heart empty of good, of worth, and of life, will be as the chaff blown away by the wind when thrown in the air on the elevated threshing-floor. In the great day of judgment the hearts that are like empty shells will be found wanting, and the wicked spoiled by evil-doing will be condemned. When the congregation of the righteous are gathered in heaven, the "sinners" with hearts full of bitterness and scorn will not be there. "The way of the ungodly shall perish."

2. *The Positive Pictures of Progress and Results.* The way of the righteous begins well. See the righteous man *delighting* in the *law* of Jehovah! What a contrast to the counsel of the wicked! Delighting in the *law!* What law? The same law that to Paul was so bitter, so sin-reviving, so death-dealing. Doubtless the same law, the book of the law which was then about the only Scripture. The criminal finds no sweetness in the law. It has no delight for him. To him it means death. It was from that point of view Paul wrote. But the loyal citizen finds pleasure in the just and beneficial laws of his beloved country. So the righteous man in God's law. "Delight" is a strong word. It describes the whole inner man as in a state of exhilaration as he reads the law. "The precepts of Jehovah are right, rejoicing the heart." (See Psa. xix, 7–11.) In the revelations of God's holiness and his holy purposes concerning man, his own high destiny and great blessedness here revealed and made possible through God's grace, man finds such enlightenment for his eyes, such food for his heart, such inspiration for his soul, that he seeks no other delight.

"In his law doth he meditate day and night." A man will continue in that in which he delights; the real painter at his painting, the musician at his music, the scientist at his science, the debauchee at his pleasure.

The Gadarene possessed of devils found his delight in the tombs full of death, and dwelt there. Why should not the righteous man delight in a holy law and be wont to meditate therein day and night? The man after God's own heart will find his delight in the revelations of God's heart and want to make it his dwelling-place. To such a one the law will not be a mere rule by which he must frame his life, but it will be food and aliment to his spirit. To the righteous the law is like manna, tasting to every man like that he likes best, and "he who hath once tasted its excellence will desire to taste it again, and he who tastes it oftenest will relish it best." In the law, put under the mercy-seat in the Holy of Holies, and so put under grace in Christ, the human heart may find its purest delight in meditation, its richest food in earth's pilgrimage, and its highest inspiration in life's endeavors.

Such a one "shall be like a tree planted by the rivers of water." A striking picture to the Eastern mind! At certain seasons all verdure wilts and withers under the burning heat of the time of drought, save along the banks of the little mountain streams, where all is fresh and vigorous, full of leaves and of fruit in its season. And just so is the inner life of one who is constantly nourished by God's law, by the Bible as we have it to-day. All other sources may fail, but this is sure. It will keep the heart young, tender, growing, fruitful. Thought and faith and hope and love will ever bloom and fruit. There will be continual prosperity in such a heart. December will be as pleasant as May. Each season from youth to old age will have its fruit. Such a heart will not die. "His leaf also shall not wither." There will be no sign of lack of nourishment to the heart that is constantly nourished on God's word.

"Whatsoever he doeth shall prosper." All he does is in harmony with the law, and that insures prosperity. It is so in all departments of life. But here the righteous feel that they have not only law, but God in the law, helping them, "for the Lord knoweth [participle, "knowing," is knowing, watching over, caring for] the way of the righteous." While Jehovah lives the righteous need not fear. His way shall not perish, but shall end in fruition, even the fruition of God.

SAMUEL L. BEILER.

II.

THE KING IN ZION.

Psa. ii, 1-12.

GOLDEN TEXT—Blessed are all they that put their trust in him.
Psa. ii, 12.

THAT this Psalm was written by King David is expressly stated in Acts iv, 25. He had been victorious over his enemies. He was firmly established in his kingdom. His best friend and counselor, Nathan, had assured him that God would greatly bless and prosper him and his heirs. When full of courage and hope there seems to have come to him the vision recorded in this Psalm of the Messiah, born in his own royal line, yet in very truth the Son of God, whose dominion would be over all men and whose kingdom would be forever.

We believe that David here wrote of the Messiah who was called Jesus, both because his words are so interpreted in Acts iv, and because the Psalm wonderfully applies to the opposition of wicked men to Jesus Christ, and describes his victory over them.

The Psalm is divided into four stanzas of three verses each, and in form it is dramatic, four different speakers taking part.

Stanza I. In the first stanza the heathen nations are shown as united in their rebellion against Christ. In their impotent rage they repeat the words of the third verse.

With amazement the Psalmist asks why men are arrayed against the Lord. The question is apt to-day. Why are people opposed to the pure teaching of God's book? Because the laws of God, of righteousness, are considered mere cords and bands that unnecessarily restrain the natural tendencies and hold in check the heart's impulses. Men are opposed to God because they are self-willed. Many people regard religion as bit and bridle to keep one who wears them in the dusty road, even as a pack-horse is kept submissive to a master's will, and burdened with a heavy load. But that which is here called bands and cords is rather the touch of God's hand to guide the children of his care into safety and permanent happiness.

Those who think they can cast off the authority of God imagine a vain thing, since the laws of growth and decay are not more certain than the laws that obtain in the moral and religious domain. One can no more escape the law that an evil act brings an evil consequence to him who does it than he can the law of gravitation. Any man who believes he can find permanent good in any but God's way imagines a vain thing. All those who seek the gratification of passions and appetites in unlawful ways finally discover that such imagined pleasure ends in sorrow and trouble.

Ever since Christ came people have been trying to overthrow his kingdom, and some of them have vainly imagined that they have succeeded. In the third century Diocletian believed he had utterly destroyed Christianity. A medal was struck in his honor bearing the words, " The name of Christian being extinguished," and a monument was erected to him for " having every-where abolished the superstition of Christ." Voltaire said: " In less than a hundred years Christianity will have been swept from existence, and will have passed into history." But the house where Voltaire lived has become a depot for a Bible society and is packed full of Bibles, while his old printing-press has been used to print the Word of God. It was said in the French Revolution that the superstitions of eighteen centuries had been overthrown; but to satisfy the religious instinct that was not overthrown a mock religion was instituted which lived but for a day, and now Christ's kingdom prospers among the children of the Revolution.

Stanza II. In the second stanza the scene is entirely changed, and we have a picture of God secure on his throne in heaven. We have seen kings and rulers in confusion and rage, seeking to throw off divine authority. Here we see the Almighty in peace and tranquillity on the throne of his power. While God is everywhere present, the center of his kingdom is in heaven. He is far above, and unmoved by, the passions and vain conceits of foolish men. In wisdom and power he looks upon the weakness and folly of wicked men, and in his perfect comprehension of their puny, mad efforts he is said to laugh and to hold them in derision. Every man violating the law of God, as that law is revealed to him in the Bible, or in his own conscience, should be startled and confounded by the thought that his course brings him into derision of One who is absolutely wise and holy.

But God not only has knowledge of men; he also has an active bearing toward men. Because of their wickedness he feels toward them wrath, and in his dealing with them he will manifest his sore displeasure. Divine wrath is not simply against sin, but it is against those who commit sin. There is no abstract sin apart from the heart and will where it is born, and the hands or the tongues which commit it. Sin is made to appear less awful by the frequent declaration that the heavenly Father is angry at sin, but holds no wrath against the sinner. In God's wrath there may always be pity, and toward the sinner who forsakes his evil-doing there is tender mercy; but God's indignation against sin is hatred of an abstraction, but anger against a person. Just as a shepherd traces the slaughter of his lambs back to the wolf, so God traces all wrong-doing back to him who committed it; and as the shepherd's anger is directed against the wolf, so God's sore displeasure is directed against the sinner.

But notwithstanding man's sin and God's wrath he has established his King upon the holy hill of Zion. God's King is to reign for him, and the earthly kingdom is to have as its ideal the heavenly kingdom. While the worldly kingdom was entitled to cover the whole earth, it began upon the holy hill of Zion, the fortified stronghold where was King David's palace, where David's greater Son, Christ, taught and was crucified. The purpose of God in establishing his King is a purely merciful one. If we are astonished at human rebellion against God we have no less cause of astonishment at God's loving-kindness and long-suffering toward humanity.

Stanza III. Again the scene changes, and we have a prophetic picture of the anointed Son announcing the Father's purpose to give him final dominion over all the earth. The Sonship of Christ was declared by the voice from heaven, both at his baptism and his transfiguration, in the words, " This is my beloved Son in whom I am well pleased."

To Christ are promised the heathen nations and the farthest parts of the earth. He inherits by right as God's Son, and possesses by virtue of his power as a moral and religious conqueror. At the end of his few weary years on earth Jesus sent out his embassadors to every nation and people to teach them the laws of his life and his kingdom. He had said, " Heaven and earth shall pass away, but my words shall not pass away." And with that assurance those embassadors went out to bring all the world into subjection to him. The prophecy that Christ is to prevail over all the nations is not simply recorded in the Bible, but is scarcely less plainly written in every Christian heart; for every one who has faith in the living God must believe that truth and justice and right, the very principles of Christ's kingdom, will eventually completely triumph.

It has been well said, "It is written in the reddest of American blood that no question is settled till it is settled right." Just as the question of slavery would not down till it was settled right, so the terrible problem of intemperance will rest only when sobriety every-where prevails; and, indeed, every political, social, moral, and religious problem will sometime be solved according to the law of Christ.

The dominion of Christ has spread farther and farther during all the Christian era, but never has there been so rapid progress as at the present time. It seems probable that in twenty-five years every creature will have heard the Gospel. In a single year over one million heathen people were converted and joined Christian churches. More than one-tenth of the American Indians are now Christians in faith and character. Nearly one-fourth of the people of this nation are to-day church members, while at the beginning of this century only one-fifteenth were members of the Church. There is a net gain of nearly thirteen new churches for every working day of the year, and the gain in the number of Christian ministers is eleven for each day, including Sunday.

In reading the prophecy that Christ will break the heathen with a rod of iron, and dash them to pieces like a potter's vessel, we must never forget Christ's own words: "The Son of man is not come to destroy men's lives, but to save them." Christ destroys his enemies when he makes them his friends. He dashes them in pieces when national governments, bound to idolatry and iniquity, both by civil laws and social customs, are overthrown, and new governments are inaugurated that will be more favorable to the admission of the true faith and life. But it is also to be remembered that those who will not yield to truth and righteousness will finally be destroyed. The man who throws himself in unyielding rebellion against God cannot but dash himself to pieces, even as the sea-wave rushes against the mighty rocks.

Stanza IV. We have in the fourth stanza the conclusion and admonition of the poet-preacher. He exhorts men to receive the Son with affectionate obedience as Master and Lord. It is the part of wisdom to welcome instruction. Only the foolish are satisfied and conceited in their own notions. Wisdom transmutes knowledge into character and power. Wisdom leads men in safety into the kingdom of the Messiah. When Christ came it was the wise men who came to him with their glad recognition of his Kingship, and the wise in all the ages have found him the Son of God. It has been said Christianity is not for the learned, but for the lowly in knowledge; but learning keeps no man from finding God. Gladstone declares: "During the many years I was in the cabinet I was brought into association with sixty master minds, and all of them but five were Christians."

To serve the Lord with fear is the true wisdom. To sin against him is the supreme folly. Obedience to the divine word is obedience to the law of our being. What

God commands in the Bible he demonstrates in human experience. The man who discovers the will of the Lord may well rejoice, for in doing that will there is the highest good and the truest happiness. But not only obedience is demanded by Christ, but also affectionate homage; since the will cannot fully yield if the heart is not given to him. They who merely serve the Lord may find only galling slavery, but they who also kiss the Son enter into the most perfect liberty.

"In man's brief space on earth it is possible to perish from the way," to lose the road to happiness and heaven.

The practical teaching of the Psalm is summed up in its last sentence, the Golden Text, the blessed are those who are happy because of their rightness. They are first of all true, and therefore they are happy. People can be right just as they trust in, intrust themselves with, the Son of God, who thus becomes their loved Master and their complete Saviour.

J. S. DAVIS.

III.

GOD'S WORKS AND WORD.

Psa. xix, 1-14.

GOLDEN TEXT.—The law of the Lord is perfect, converting the soul. Psa. xix, 7.

THIS Psalm reflects the memories of David when alone with God among the hills of Bethlehem. "The fresh mountain air of Bethlehem blows through it, and the dew of life's quiet morning is on it." This whole Psalm is a unit. It is the song of one continuous inspiration. The three central thoughts which these fourteen verses contain are Nature, Scripture, and Humanity.

1. *Nature.* These first few verses remind us of the young shepherd boy busy with his pastoral work among his father's sheep. There yonder in the pastures or in the olive-yards of the ancient hamlet is seen a boy of a dozen summers. His eyes are lovely. They are large and liquid, as becomes a poet's eye. His face, so fair, has a touch of youthful color on it. In striking difference from his swarthy and burly brothers passing through the pastures, his hair is golden, like an autumn sunset. But a boy! There he stands leaning on his shepherd's staff, looking up to God in self-forgetful contemplation. It is now night. O, the beauty of this Syrian sky! As the stars stood out in numberless array before the wander-

ing eye of Abraham, they seemed to fill with peculiar brightness some of those calm nights in his shepherd life. The heavens speak to him. The glory of God is revealed. The air sweet with the fragrance of some neighboring vineyard, the dews now gathering, the brooks now running, some bird alone with the night in song, the west wind bringing an unexpected shower, all talk to him of God. Now it is daybreak. The sun is rising over the mountains of Moab. Suddenly, so unlike the long twilight in northern lands, the morning breaks in the beauty of a bridegroom coming from his bridal chamber and going forth like a runner anxious to begin his task. And through the whole day he follows him as he swiftly runs his course, until the valley of the Jordan feels the heat of that Eastern noon and the treeless hills on the south burn under his scorching eye.

The work shows the character of the workman. God's goodness, wisdom, patience, and power are seen in the things he hath wrought.

One of our great American prose-poets describes the glories of the morning. What is the difference between them? It is the difference in the inspiration. David's harp is touched by the fingers of heaven. The one is a message of God in man to men; David's is a message of God to man for men.

2. *Scripture.* From the seventh to the eleventh verses the Psalmist speaks of the revelation of God in his written word. The sudden transition in thought and rhythm is in harmony with the progress made in the

Psalm from nature to the written book. The law which is referred to, according to the marginal reading, is the teaching of our Lord, and, therefore, includes the Testaments. The Bible is the holy, inspired Scriptures. We do not assume that all parts of Scripture are of equal value or have the same degree of inspiration; but we can say with Martin Luther as we turn its sacred pages, " God's word here, God's word there."

In general terms we do not claim for the Bible that it is a great book, a good book, a peculiar book only. We do not say merely that it contains the deepest philosophy, the grandest ethics, the finest rhetoric. It is not enough to declare that its Christ is an unimpeachable character; that as an agency among men it is most beneficent; that its writers were filled with holy enthusiasm; that for our rapidly growing civilization it is the necessity of the age. *The Bible* is the *one, final, eternal* revelation of God to men. There has been no other written record sent us. In the richness of its contents, in the comprehensiveness of its truth, in the sublimity of its purpose, this book speaks as a finality to the world. The divine will is unchangeable. What God said yesterday is the law of the to-morrow of eternity. There are no more Only Begotten Sons for sacrifice. Three things the soul must know about—Deity, humanity, and immortality. As one has said, " Sometime, somehow, somewhere God must send messages." The question of our day is whether Biblical Christianity or ritual religion shall be supreme. It shall be, it is, the Bible. For it is what the king requires to guide him in the administration of the kingdom. Victoria leans gracefully on her Bible. It is what the man of affairs must have to help him in many business cares. It is what the widow needs for her days of mourning. It is what the children look to in the times of their sorrow. We all fly to it as to a rock for safest shelter. It is the book that goes to the hamlet as quickly as to the palace. It knows no sunset. Its history is sunrise. It is God's carrier of love, and has gone out from him on its great errand and rested in the heart of humanity.

David says, regarding the Scriptures, that they are his "law," "testimonies," "statutes," "fear of the Lord," and his "judgments." As "law," it is the teaching of his will. As "testimonies," it reveals his nature and man's need. As "statutes," it indicates established ordinances. As "judgments," it is his declaration of his mind concerning human conduct.

David gives in these verses several distinct characteristics of the Scriptures. The Word of God is *divine*. Seven times he says in this Psalm that the "law" is the covenant of Jehovah. The Scriptures speak out what God has spoken into them. Sometimes it contains the verbal utterance of God, sometimes the expression of illumined consciousness, sometimes the mere narration under divine guidance of familiar historic facts. Paul gave us the best classification of literature when he said, "All *Scripture* is given by inspiration of God." This reveals its origin. Its mission is defined as one of doctrine, reproof, correction, and instruction in righteousness. It is the *perfect* word, and hence it is *sufficient*. Its sufficiency is seen in its opportuneness. It gets us hence to our Cheriths or tells us to arise and go to our Zarephaths just when we ought to do it. It is adapted to all human circumstances, so that when we are in the rocky stronghold like David in Adullam it has the tender word, " In the secret of his tabernacle will he hide me." It tells humanity of the privileges it affords the soul, for " Whoso looketh into the perfect law of liberty, and continueth therein, . . . this man shall be blessed in his deed."

The law of the Lord is *mighty*, " converting the soul." The word of God is quick and powerful. It tells men what they are, what they should do, and where they are going. Two persons are necessary in the study of the Scriptures, a seeking soul and a saving God. The work of the Holy Spirit is to teach men wisdom out of the Word, and lead them to careful consideration for this life and the life that is to come.

David taught the disputed doctrine of *infallibility*. The Christian's intuitive judgment and certain external evidences, such as the honesty, earnestness, and intelligence of the apostles and the prophets, the sinlessness of our Saviour taught by them, their own testimony to the inspiration of the Holy Spirit, the divine attestation of God by miracles, fulfillment of prophecy, atonement through Christ, make it the authoritative voice for us to follow. Though it does not teach philosophy, history, or science, it is philosophical, historical, and scientific. We accept it.

It is *exhilarating;* for, as David says here, it " rejoiceth the heart." God's word convicts of sin, and so in a troubled conscience produces sorrow. Otherwise, as Jeremiah says, " Thy words were found, and I did eat them; and thy word was unto me the joy and rejoicing of mine heart." It is *illuminating;* for it enlightens the eyes.

> " Lord, everlasting thanks be thine
> For such a bright display,
> As makes the world of darkness shine
> With beams of heavenly day."

Its *purity* is displayed in the counsels which it gives us, for it says, " Whatsoever things are true, honest, just, pure, lovely, of good report," are to be the subjects of our meditation; and it works purity in our lives, for it makes us pure in heart, so that we shall see God. It is *everlasting*, or, as one has more literally translated it, it is the word which is " standing up to perpetuity." The everlasting Father speaks only the everlasting word. It is *equitable*, for it teaches universal salvation as conditioned on personal faith, and is alive with living interest in our times to the great need of human fraternity. Communism and anarchism are answered by its equity with a " Masters, give unto your servants that which is just and equal," and " Servants, be obedient to them that are your masters according to the flesh."

David shared his son's estimate of the *invaluableness*

of the truth, for Solomon said, " Wisdom is better than rubies." The spirit of the times and the spirit of eternity are in a conflict as to the relative supremacy of gold over Scripture. Mammon and God are face to face. How beautiful the words of David, " Sweeter than honey and the honey-comb." The word of God is *palatable* to them that are spiritual—that is, they who " hunger and thirst after righteousness." It is full also of *admonitions*. There is a warning in it issuing in the midst of the stillness of Eden. It breaks forth from the flaming top of Sinai. How Ebal thunders with her curses, and Gerizim sings her numerous blessings!

" Woe unto thee, Chorazin!" " Woe unto thee, Bethsaida!" " Woe unto thee, scribes and Pharisees!" " Woe unto him by whom the Son of man is betrayed!" Undeviating loyalty to God is rewarded. God's word *rewards* us in two ways: by perfecting character—" Whoso keepeth his word, in him verily is the love of God perfected "—and by bringing us to final triumph; for Christ's promise to John was, " Because thou hast kept the word of my patience I also will keep thee from the hour of temptation."

3. *Humanity.* This Psalm, so beautiful in its diction, spoken as Wordsworth says all true poetry must be spoken, from the heart to the heart, a lyric of the highest order, so grand in its conception, closes with a revelation of the human heart. It is a searching confession of the sinfulness of humanity. With what keen analysis David describes our errors, faults, and presumptions! By

errors he means weaknesses. Our greatest weakness is the misfortune of heredity, our selfishness. Our faults are those which appear to others as they look at us, but are unknown to ourselves. Burns was repeating David when he wished we had power to see ourselves as others see us. What we really are is not what we appear to be to ourselves, but the picture we cast on the lives of others. The truest estimate of a man is in his neighbor. Presumptuous sins are serious crimes of a nature that has fallen little by little from God. But David believed in deliverance. Here is the twofold view: fallen humanity ruled by sin; restored humanity regulated by love. This deliverance from sin is found in humility and trust. The Psalmist calls himself a servant. That man will reach perfect deliverance who first has reached perfect humility. David believed that to be a servant of the devil was not wise, but to be, like Paul, a "slave of God," was to get lordship through Christ over himself.

And now this Psalm that opened with this reference to an ideal picture of nature, in which the "heavens declare the glory of God, and the firmament showeth his handiwork," closes with another, an ideal for the soul, in which the glory is that of Christ's tranquillity within us, and his handiwork in the operation of grace upon us. There are three characteristics of a perfect life which the Psalmist emphasizes in the closing verses. Practice, for "he that committeth sin is the servant of sin." Speech, both of free conversation and silent reflection. A holy man not only does not say impure things, but he does not think them. And, finally, the realization of personal union with God, so that we can say, "O Lord, my strength, and my redeemer."

The Psalmist reminds one of a young golden eagle who is soaring under the bright sky and is looking for his eyrie in a distant and lofty cliff; and as David comes nearer God he hears his voice in Scripture, and still nearer he comes until his own redeemed soul alights on the bosom of God, saying, "My Rock, and my Redeemer."

GEORGE A. PHINNEY.

IV.

THE LORD MY SHEPHERD.

Psa. xxiii, 1-6.

GOLDEN TEXT.—The Lord is my shepherd; I shall not want.
Psa. xxiii, 1.

THIS is a purely devotional Psalm. The royal writer remembered his early craft. He led his flock with an affectionate solicitude. He delivered them from the lion and the bear. He sought for them the most fertile pastures. He restored the straying to the safe paths again. With his crook and staff he scaled the rough places to return them to the shelter of the fold.

The early training often fashions the thoughts of later years. The holy soldier prays and talks in military language, the sailor embellishes his religious utterances with nautical phrases. Thus David associates his Lord with the scenes of a pastoral life. Of the two hundred and fifty-four names ascribed to Christ in the Scriptures, no one more tenderly touches the human instincts than "Shepherd." He says of himself, "I am the good shepherd. My sheep hear my voice, and I know them, and they follow me : and they shall never perish, neither shall any pluck them out of my hand."

The Psalm presents five fundamental truths.

1. *Divine Sustenance.* "I shall not want." The bane

of human life is worry. Though well supplied for to-day, we are painfully apprehensive of future famine. The present bliss is drowned in the restless struggle to make to-morrow sure. What a contrast with this feverish rush after possessions as a prop for coming needs is the opening strain, " I shall not want. He maketh me to lie down in green pastures."

Contentment is a pillar of strength to the soul. Not to want nor fear want is a perennial supply. To lie down in pastures of tender grass is a figure of refreshing rest amid luxuriant growth and fruitfulness. " Why art thou cast down, O my soul?" Here is a present luxury. Not in the "sweet fields beyond the swelling flood," but here among anxious multitudes struggling for bread we may contentedly nestle in the fertile meadows of his grace and have abiding rest.

2. *Divine Guidance.* " He leadeth me beside the waters of stillness." The quiet lamb reposing on the grassy bank represents the calmness of the soul whom the Good Shepherd leads. His gentleness and meekness, unmoved by the surrounding agitations, are models of the characters who learn to implicitly follow where he guides. It is to such he says, " My peace I give unto you." If weak human nature breaks from the path at any point, " He restoreth my soul ; " and by his gentleness makes it great, and leads it " in the paths of righteousness for his name's sake."

3. *He not only Guides, but he Protects.* There are dreaded evils in this daily path, and before the final fold

is reached comes one greater than all. It appears in the distance like a deep valley between huge and rugged heights. Through the dense darkness no sun ever shone but the Sun of righteousness. No torch ever illumined it but that of faith. No gleam of philosophy, no smile of a fellow-pilgrim, ever cheers the lonely passer that way. But the Good Shepherd has pioneered that path. His rod and staff are familiar to the hideous journey. Leaning upon these the valley is transmuted into summits and the darkness into light. Bishop Gilbert Haven declared as he stepped into it : " There is no valley, no river," and walked on mountain peaks blazing with ineffable glory into the city of light.

4. *Royal Abundance.* " Thou preparest a table before me," etc. Enemies throng the way of a good man. They do not always resemble wolves, but may be mistaken for one of the flock. They are clothed in raiment of light, and assume forms of angelic beauty. They present plausible questions on practical life, and bewilder the judgment on the daily tests of necessity and supply. What shall I eat, and wherewithal shall I be clothed? Who can set a table when there is no food in the larder? The Good Shepherd hushes these insinuations of doubt by preparing us a king's feast. It is not a sufficiency only, but a superabundance. Like the grass that springs up every-where, and the millions of blossoms blown from over-laden boughs, the royal banquet is a miracle of supply. His pardon is an abundant pardon. His gifts are "how much more" than an earthly father's good

bestowments. Twelve gates open into his treasury announcing that " He is able to do exceeding abundantly above all that we ask or think."

And all this in the presence of the enemies who plot our ruin. They shall see our royal bounty. They shall witness our running-over cup of blessing. When the Egyptians sought to destroy Israel by slaying the male children at birth, and by cruel bondage, " the more they afflicted them the more they multiplied and grew. "And they were grieved because of the children of Israel." The enemies of the righteous are maddened at their prosperity.

5. *Divine Faithfulness.* "Surely goodness and mercy shall follow me," etc. The flock follows the shepherd, and is itself followed by the vigilant dogs who guard the rear against hostile attacks. The Psalmist's life was one of danger and sometimes defection from the path of righteousness, and he remembered that goodness and mercy had followed him in those perilous times. Goodness is the permanent quality in love that pervades all the works of our Father. It makes the sun to rise on the evil and on the good, and sends rain upon the just and unjust. It patiently nurses and nourishes the refractory and rebellious. It supplies with loving continuance and long-suffering those who requite divine favors with hate and disobedience. But to those who follow him fully his goodness is wonderful. There are special providences, divine interferences, and interceptions that sweetly work the will without coercing it; and

there are systems of reward for virtuous deeds that make even the gift of a cup of cold water worthy of remembrance when given for goodness' sake.

Mercy is goodness operating in behalf of the suffering. "The Lord is very pitiful, and of tender mercy" toward all. Not a throb of pain that does not find a response in his sympathetic nature. But mercy can be resisted and refused. There is, therefore, a method in mercy. It is mercy to the righteous that penalties follow sin. It is mercy to the evil that they suffer while in the paths of disobedience. Mercy follows the righteous as a distinctive form of divine compassion. "For as the heaven is high above the earth, so great is his mercy *toward them that fear him*." "Like as a father pitieth his children, so the Lord pitieth them that fear him." There is a significant emphasis upon the classification, "Them that fear him." It is the sheep who hear his voice, and follow him, who are followed by these watchful guardians, Goodness and Mercy. With such faithful guiding and following all the days of an earthly life, one is surely made meet to "dwell in the house of the Lord forever."

This beautiful Psalm, illustrating by its simple pastoral references the solicitude, protection, and promise of our Lord Jesus Christ, "that great Shepherd of the sheep," is rich in its phases of religious experience.

1. *The Individuality of Religious Experience.* Seventeen times in these brief sentences is the first personal pronoun used. It is the one sheep that is conscious that all the power and love of the Shepherd are pledged to

its safety and sustenance. A wide distribution of faith is commendable; the parish for our prayers and charities is the world, but soul-strength comes of personal appropriations of the divine nature and promises.

The brute creation is the object of God's care. Not a sparrow falls to the ground without his notice. Not an insect flits in the sunlight in which is not the miracle of life sustained by his hand. But these are not his children. They cannot say of him, "Our Father." Of the birds he says, "*Your* heavenly Father feedeth them."

The personal consciousness that God is mine gives the key to this Psalm. It is this that gives the writings of St. Paul their power to stir the soul with the highest aspirations. "I know whom I have believed;" "I can do all things through Christ which strengtheneth me;" "I live, yet not I, but Christ liveth in me;" these, like the opening strain of the song, "The Lord is my shepherd; I shall not want," are enough to fill any station in life with sweetest contentment.

2. *The Victory of Religious Experience.* "This is the victory that overcometh the world, even our faith." This Psalm is rapturously triumphant. It proclaims deliverance from the three great fears that beset human life: the fear of want, the fear of death, and the fear of being overcome by the mighty antagonisms created by sin. The victory over such well-grounded fears must arise from a faith begotten of the Holy Spirit.

(1) That the Lord is *my* Shepherd.

(2) That my experience of his grace in the past

warrants this shout over things yet to come. He who can exult that "I have been young, and now a mold; yet have I not seen the righteous forsaken, nor his seed begging bread" can surely rejoice that "I shall not want."

(3) This victory also arises from the present attitude of the soul before God. No one can positively know that he will not be terrified when in the agonies of death, nor that he will never turn from the path of righteousness through unknown possible evils, except the soul who is at present conqueror over existing evils. God will do for us what he is doing. Paul says: "Shall tribulation, distress, persecution, famine, nakedness, peril, or sword be able to separate us from the love of Christ? Nay, in all these things we *are* more than conquerors." We shall, because we can shout, We are.

3. *The Exuberance of Religious Experience.* There is a sweet sense of fullness and overflow in the soul that does not limit the Holy One of Israel. The cup running over is a fitting simile of the exceeding joy, perfect peace, and restful quiet from the ghostly forebodings that shadow the future. And it is the overflow that gives the impressions to others of the truth and power of our holy religion.

Emotion is dangerous when it takes the lead, especially if the deep principles of piety, regulated by a godly judgment, are wanting. In a climax the Psalmist rises from a firm faith that the Lord is his Shepherd, leads him into luxurious supplies, guides him into paths of righteousness, robs death of its terrors and foes of their power; then his exultant spirit bursts out with great joy, "My cup runneth over." Sterling principle based on steady faith will save emotion from fanatical excesses. The outbursts of joy that called for their accompaniments of praise from every thing that had breath, with mountains and hills and trees, were but the cup running over. A gladsome salvation, too full of spiritual vitality for merely ceremonial service, singing songs in adversity till prisons rock and fears fly, is the running-over cup to be coveted by every child of God.

4. *The Fellowship of Religious Experience.* The fellowship of kindred minds is beautifully set forth in the figure of a flock of sheep. The shepherd knows and superintends each, but the flock is one. Each one is happier for its fellowship with all. The heavenly Shepherd deals with each soul separately. He walks with him alone in the fertile lands of "corn and wine and oil;" he goes alone with him into the valley of the shadow of death; but he leads the flock as one. His fellowship with the one is the bond that binds the whole together, therefore the Church. Life is richer for its associations with the people of God, and its highest hope is to dwell in such associations and fellowship forever.

I. SIMMONS.

V.

THE PRAYER OF THE PENITENT.

Psa. li, 1-13.

GOLDEN TEXT.—Create in me a clean heart, O God; and renew a right spirit within me. Psa. li, 10.

EVERY interpretation of a text of Scripture in isolation is a misinterpretation. This text discloses at once the deep sense of need which the Psalmist felt, and also his knowledge of the fact that the help he needed, the cleansing and the renewal, must come from God. We must seek to understand this text by the help of the broad context, not only of the Psalm, but of the individual life and times out of which it came.

The vigor and variety of words used reveal the fact that the consciousness of need was painfully real.

The soul of the penitent was in agony. If we follow the order of the Psalm we find the penitent speaking of "my transgressions," "mine iniquity," "my sin," and my "blood-guiltiness." His confession is, "I acknowledge my transgressions: and my sin is ever before me. Against thee, thee only, have I sinned." He acknowledges the justice of God's judgments against him, and vivifies and intensifies his consciousness of his own guilt and the offensive deformity of his life before God by a recognition of the bad heritage that came to him as his very birthright. For it can hardly be supposed that this language is used for the purpose of extenuating his sin or throwing back the responsibility for his wickedness upon his mother. No suggestion of such a sentiment can be made consistent with the current of thought running through the Psalm.

He prays, " Have mercy upon me," and, " blot out my transgressions." They stand out before him indelibly written in God's great book. " Wash me thoroughly . . . and cleanse me." " Purge me with hyssop." The dreadful dye is too deep for any ordinary washing. " Make me to hear joy and gladness." O, the misery of the guilty soul! Crushed bones cannot express the agony. " Hide thy face from my sins." He cannot bear the thought that they are ever before God. " Blot out all mine iniquities." And then, as though he realized that God might at any moment cast him off, he cries out, " Cast me not away from thy presence." Dreadful as is the thought of his sins as ever before God, the thought of being cast away from his presence is more dreadful.

His language points to conscious guilt, and to suffering that is a torture ; both of which are intensified by every ray of light that shines upon his quivering, sensitive soul. And under the fire of conscience enkindled by Nathan's parable the burning rays shine in upon him from every quarter of the moral universe—from the confusion and peril of his soul, the disintegration of his confidence in God, and of his consciousness of God's gracious presence; from the disgrace in relation to his people; and from the forebodings he has of evil and calamities that will follow him and his house. Sin is so central that it runs into and perverts the sinner's relations with all moral beings in the universe.

This is not a general confession of sin. It is personal. As one reads the Psalm through he seems almost to be listening to the great criminal and sinner, as he alone in his secret chamber pours out his soul to the God of all grace; we almost feel that it is an intrusion to listen, so intensely personal is the prayer. The suppliant turns not aside from the thought that the whole case is between him and God. He has in mind the case of Uriah the Hittite in his "blood-guiltiness," and his sin is pre-eminently the planning of his murder and the taking of Bath-sheba for his wife. It is amazing that the great, generous-hearted David, capable of such friendship as that with Jonathan, and of such generosity as that shown to Saul, could bring himself to plot the murder of one of his own brave captains, or, worse than this, that he could rob him of his beautiful wife, Bath-sheba. We will not pause to say one word of what other Oriental monarchs were accustomed to do, as every writer on this subject has felt called upon to do. David was a Hebrew monarch. His motive, his several deeds in connection with this case, his device for protecting himself, and his final plot: "Set ye Uriah in the forefront of the hottest battle, and retire ye from him, that he may be smitten, and die;" his comforting word to Joab when the news of

Uriah's death is brought to him: " Let not this thing displease thee, for the sword devoureth one as well as another "—these are all dastardly from beginning to end, worthy only of the unclean, the false, and the murderous devil to whom he had sold himself. Had David pleaded extenuating circumstances, his Psalm would have been ethically false and spiritually worthless. We may be sure that not the least among the causes of bitter repentance was the fate that was to follow the kingdom of which he was the head, and which was dearer to him than life, for he knew that Nathan's words, " the sword shall never depart from thine house," were as true as the parable which aroused his conscience. " The crime itself had sprung from the lawless and licentious life, fostered by the polygamy which David had been the first to introduce; and out of this polygamy sprang the terrible retribution." To extenuate our sin is to hug the asp to the heart.

With some quickened sense of David's need we may well pause to gather up the lessons that may be learned by the way. We have here a clear case of genuine repentance. There is certainly very deep moral emotion. It is not sorrow that his sin has found him out. No word of this Psalm or of the thirty-second, which belongs with it, suggests such a thought. It is not a superficial emotion. It seems to be as deep as the sin and as true as the truth itself. It is a repentance toward God, and not toward men to be seen of them. All sin is against God; and, more than all else, repentance is an abandonment of sin. He turns his back upon it, he loathes it. He prays to be delivered from its power and to be upheld in the righteous attitude toward God. This is genuine New Testament repentance. This is the work of the Holy Ghost. In a sermon on "The Sin of Sins" Dr. McClintock says: "The Holy Spirit is not sent to convince man of the sinfulness of the transgression of God's law in the obvious and outward way. . . . The thief knows it is wrong to steal without any operation of the Holy Ghost; the adulterer practices his devilish arts of seduction in the face of a reproving law and in spite of an accusing conscience; he does not need the Holy Ghost to inform him of the evil of his course. . . . The Holy Spirit has a higher mission." It is "to point out the deep hidden root from which all sin springs." He is to "reprove the world of sin because they believe not in me." The sin of sins is a wrong attitude toward God of intellect, heart, and will. This is the unbelief that goes out into all sin. David under the work of the Spirit recognizes this clearly. "Against thee, thee only, have I sinned," is his way of expressing it.

It is of little consequence what our emotions may be; of little account how deeply we feel, or how violently we express our feelings; unless we turn away from sin and turn unto God, all our emotions and tears are vain and our cries will prove to be but as sounding brass. God will hear none of them. It will mean literally nothing in the way of reformation or character; literally nothing to God.

THE PRAYER OF THE PENITENT.   151

We must neither palliate nor excuse our sins. All sins are essentially alike. They are different in external act or form of expression, but inwardly they are one in their false attitude of intellect, rebellious attitude of will and heart toward God. It is this essential oneness of sin that led James, under the inspiration of the Spirit, to write, " For whosoever shall keep the whole law, and yet stumble in one point, he is become guilty of all." And it is this essential oneness that has made David's prayer the prayer of millions of penitents through all the ages. It would probably be claiming too much to say that every prayer in our social meetings and in the more formal public service is directly influenced by this Psalm; but every one may observe how dependent he is upon its words, its figures of speech, and its direct petitions and suggestions of promise and mercy, and may at the same time learn how much of the sacred literature, which in its origin is temporal and local, is in its spirit applicable to all the ages.

We must not suppose that the method which thought follows in getting an idea of sin is the actual method in experience. Thought is likely to set sin up by itself, and, when conviction has been wrought, bring God in as the helper and deliverer. We have studied that phase of the Psalm which sets forth David's great need by isolating it. But in the actual history the course of sin becomes clear and intense as the divine presence becomes evident and the divine nature revealed to the soul. The only response David makes to the charge of

Nathan is, "I have sinned against the Lord." His child sickens, and he beseeches the Lord for his life. The Lord is before his eyes constantly because his sins are now ever before him. What other help shall he seek? Why not offer sacrifices? or repeat his creed—a very long creed, perchance? or call in the priest or the prophet? O, no! None of these nostrums answer now. The soul is sick with a mortal malady. His cry is well voiced by the words of another soul smitten with the same dread malady: "Who shall deliver me from the body of this death?" He can only fall back upon God, God the Creator, who alone can re-create. "Create in me a clean heart, O God."

This is the constant teaching of the New Testament. Paul teaches that "Paul may sow and Apollos may water, but God alone can give the increase." All regenerative power is from him. In these days of growing dependence upon machinery in the material world, where its worth is so evident, we need to beware lest we come to feel that more machinery and better organization are all that we need. First of all we need to keep and intensify this sense of dependence upon the Holy Spirit.

There is another lesson for us in the way in which David magnifies the mercies of God. This is his only hope. The manifestation of God's favor toward him in the past, calling him from the duties of the shepherd boy to the duties of the throne of Israel, warrants his hope in God in this spiritual emergency. Let us often recall and continually magnify the mercies of God toward us if we would strengthen our faith for larger manifestations of his grace. And, finally, let us note that the condition of successful work with sinners is, first of all, that we ourselves have the *joy* of this salvation; and if the sustaining power of God's Spirit be ours, then may we successfully teach transgressors his ways and sinners will be converted unto him.

B. P. RAYMOND.

VI.

DELIGHT IN GOD'S HOUSE.

Psa. lxxxiv, 1-12.

GOLDEN TEXT.—Blessed are they that dwell in thy house.
Psa. lxxxiv, 4.

THE proper setting of the Psalm is not surely known. It may have been the song of a pious Jew denied the privilege of joining the happy throng of pilgrims in their journey to the Holy City. Or, after weary years of absence, a stranger finds himself again upon the threshold of the great Temple. This more probable view would make this pearl of Psalms the expression of emotions which fill the soul of one whose long pilgrimage is at last completed.

To such a one the sight of familiar scenes usually suggests a multitude of memories. In this Psalm, however, we miss what we expect to find and do find elsewhere. Memory appears to be inactive. There is no mention of Jerusalem, nor of anything in it save the tabernacles of God. The thoughts of home and friends, the companions of other days, the familiar haunts of childhood, are all absent from the pilgrim's mind. His face, his thought, his heart are toward the Temple. And even here we are surprised that no mention is made of priest or chant or sacrifice. Our pilgrim is a worshiper. The one great thought filling and consuming his soul is unhindered and unmingled communion with God.

In striking contrast with this scene is a more modern one. In a certain city church crowds gather every Sunday morning in such numbers as to fill not only the pews, but frequently the standing-room also. They come from far and near to listen to the performance of a famous public singer, and go out largely when the performance is ended, leaving the minister to preach to a half-emptied house. Many people, few worshipers! We need in these days a revival of that love of pure worship which breathes through this pilgrim's song. More than any thing else just now we need to learn to worship God in the great congregation. How few are they, even among those who are called worshipers, who could find a just expression of their deepest emotions in words like these:

> " How lovely is thy habitation,
> Jehovah Sabaoth !
> My soul longs, yea, even pines for the courts of Jehovah ;
> My heart and my flesh ring out their joy unto the living God."

The remainder of the Psalm divides itself into two chief parts, the division being marked by the word " Selah " at the close of the eighth verse.

After the outburst of fervent desire for the pure worship of God, the singer in a beautiful figure sings a strain of peace :

> " Even as the sparrow finds a house, and the swallow a nest,
> Where she lays her callow brood,
> [So have I found, even I,
> A home] by thine altars,
> O my King and my God."

The author of this version imagines the pilgrim as already sharing the blessing of which he speaks. Others picture a soul pursued by enemies, longing for the rest and security afforded by the sacred precincts of the Temple. Whatever view we take, the deep truth remains that the true worshiper finds peace and safety in the place of public worship. The thoughts which belong to other days and places may be excluded from this place if one can only truly worship. The sermon critic, the one who insists upon perfect music, he who brings into God's house the dusty garb of week-day toil, may be sorely tempted even while performing the acts of worship; but the true worshiper finds peace and is safe.

But listen again:

"Happy are they that dwell in thy house! they can be alway praising thee."

We are reminded of Peter's words on the Mount of Transfiguration. To do literally what is suggested would not be well for the individual and would be a calamity to the world. The desire to dwell always in God's house is, however, far better than the tendency to worship God with his people as infrequently and briefly as possible. Too much of one's time may be spent in the assembly of saints and too little in one's home.

With the multitudes there is danger that too little time shall be spent in both church and home. But, to return to the text, we in our day have a better interpretation of this passage than even David—if he is the writer— could have had. The time has come when not in Samaria's mountain, nor in Jerusalem, nor yet alone in places set apart for that purpose, must men worship the Father. God's dwelling-place is the trusting and obedient heart. Those who trust and obey may also commune constantly and shall find the secret of always praising God.

Another strain is heard:

" Happy the man who has thee for a stronghold, in whose heart are thy ways."

The singer's thought has turned to the days of pilgrimage. The journey is not irksome; there is something within which exultantly responds to the call of duty and which shortens and makes smooth the way. Life is frequently in Scripture called a path or way. " The path of the just is as the shining light, that shineth more and more," is the figure of Proverbs. The path of the just is through the " valley of balsams," but the sandy, dry, and barren valley " becomes the source of fountains, and the early rain mantles it with blessing." This is the figure of the Psalmist. We find here an illustration of the fullness and honesty of Scripture. So far from attempting to conceal the darker phases of a righteous life, infinite pains are taken to inform him who would become a pilgrim of a certain valley through which, sooner or later, he must pass, and which, from the reports of travelers, has gained the name " valley of weeping." " In this world ye shall have tribulation," said Christ. It was an old truth. But Christ added, as in some form the Scriptures always add, " Be of good cheer." The philosopher's stone of ancient lore, which was reputed to have power to transform the meanest material into gold, was a myth. The myth, however, was prophetic of a power that should make "all things work together for good to them that love God." This is no myth.

We are not surprised, therefore, that the pilgrim, in whose heart are God's ways, comes out of the valley stronger than when he went down into it. Whatever life's experiences, such as he go from strength to strength. Knowing the value of even the hard things of life, they do not desire to be coddled. They despise softness. What they endure produces lasting effects upon character. Their souls develop nerve and spiritual fiber. Therefore, when weaker ones fall they stand; they are brave and manfully resist when others tremble and draw back. They are the giants of their generation. Sometimes God honors them with partnership in the sufferings of his Son. But out of great tribulation they at length emerge, and without spot, and blameless, stand before the throne. Every one of them "shall appear before God in Zion." Then comes the petition:

"Jehovah Sabaoth, hear thou my prayer·
Give ear, O God of Jacob."

Thus closes the first division of our Psalm. As we study the remaining verses it becomes evident that diverse thoughts are crowding in upon the Psalmist's mind and clamoring for expression. As is common in such

cases, the expression is obscure. Who is meant by
"thine anointed?" It is highly improbable that the
slightest reference is here made to our Saviour. The
king, the high-priest, the whole chosen people, were all
his "anointed." As to which of these is in the writer's
mind authorities cannot agree. If David the king is
also the pilgrim, one possible meaning is evident. In his
admirable work on the Psalms Professor Cheyne gives
an interpretation which to us seems highly probable:

"Several thoughts are in the writer's mind, and he
embodies them in successive quatrains. One is religious
loyalty to the king or high-priest. Another, suggested
by the original lyric" (the first seven verses, according
to his idea) " is the incomparable delights of God's
house. A third is the completeness of the believer in
his God. The first of these thoughts to arise in the
Psalmist's mind is that of loyalty to Israel's earthly
head, and he clothes this thought in the language of
prayer."

We have in these days no earthly head corresponding
to Israel's king or high-priest. The thought of religious
loyalty has nevertheless a meaning for us. Paul's words
to Timothy have not lost all their force: "I exhort
therefore, that, first of all, supplications, prayers, intercessions, and giving of thanks, be made for all men; for
kings, and for all that are in authority; that we may
lead a quiet and peaceable life in all godliness and honesty." Our bishops, presiding elders, and pastors, our
church editors and publishers, those who control the

secular press, and all others in positions of influence, certainly need divine help. Religious loyalty would lead us to clothe our thought in the language of prayer for them.

Next comes to the singer's mind the thought of "the incomparable delights of God's house:"

" For better is a day in thy courts than a thousand [spent abroad]; I would rather be at the threshold in the house of my God, than dwell in the tents of ungodliness."

Let us not put the word *church* with its usual meaning in place of *the house of my God*. The church can never be to an intelligent Christian what the Temple was to a pious Jew. For us the meaning of the thought is this: Let the position of a true worshiper be the humblest, the joys which are his are incomparably beyond those of the man who forgets God and lives in sin, even though he be highly exalted among men. The narrower view, according to which God's house and our meeting-houses are synonymous, would make it needful to say something about making church services attractive. Especially is this true if church attendance is to be treated as obligatory. Incomparable delights do not usually result from enforced obedience, nor do they of necessity attend upon much that passes for sermonizing and music. Better nothing at all than that which is sometimes called music; better the simple reading of God's word than some kinds of talks called sermons.

A single thought in the Psalm remains to be noticed.

It is that of the believer's completeness in God. The language of the Psalmist can hardly be improved:

> "For Jehovah Elohim is a sun and shield,
> Jehovah gives grace and glory:
> No good thing will he withhold from them that walk blamelessly."

God is a sun and shield—as some one has said, a sun for dark days and a shield for dangerous ones. Our increased knowledge of the solar system enables us to put much more into the first of these terms than the Psalmist could; yet to him both figures must have been most suggestive. The sun revealed the beauties of the land through which his pilgrimage lay, but the dangers which beset his path were also made apparent. The shield was his protection, sufficient, however great or numerous the dangers might be. The sun enabled the traveler to find the springs of water where, under the palm-trees, as at Elim, he might drink and be satisfied. The shield rendered the time of refreshing peaceful and secure. In these two figures are wrapped up "all manner of excellency, provision, and prosperity," and " all manner of protection whatsoever."

"Jehovah gives grace and glory." We must keep ever in mind the thought of pilgrimage. Grace to the traveler is help over rough places, the healing of bruised feet, protection from heat and hunger and thirst. Have his adversaries cruel designs against him? Grace thwarts them. Does strength wane and courage fail? Grace revives his courage and renews his strength.

Has the traveler lost his way? Grace causes a voice behind him to whisper, "This is the way." Glory, to a pilgrim, is "grace matured." It is to know the end of the long, hard journey, to be at length at the very threshold of the Temple, to appear before God in Zion, to inherit the kingdom, and to enter in. "Happy is the man who trusts in thee." Many desired things, but no good thing, will God withhold from him. Abounding grace shall be his along the way, infinite glory when the pilgrimage shall end.

FRED. H. KNIGHT.

VII.

A SONG OF PRAISE.

Psa. ciii, 1-22.

GOLDEN TEXT.—Bless the Lord, O my soul, and forget not all his benefits. Psa. ciii, 2.

THIS Psalm belongs to the last period of Hebrew poetry. It is thought by Ewald to have been written about the middle of the fifth century B. C. Its author is unknown, but it is evident that the one hundred and fourth Psalm is the work of the same master hand; while both breathe a broader spirit than the mere intense Jewish devoutness which characterizes the first "Songs of Restored Jerusalem."

Some perception of a God too great to be the God of the Jews only seems to have glimmered in this man's soul; his inspiration rises to the sublimity of a thankoffering for the universe.

The two Psalms are so manifestly one—the first considering Jehovah in the greatness of his character and his dealings with the individual man; the second rising to the impassioned heights of a veritable Psalm of creation—that it is difficult to separate them in our thought and study.

The one is the complement of the other, and they together paint a soul-picture which, if viewed in the true spirit of devotion, will indeed cause our "meditation of him" to be "sweet."

But it is of the one hundred and third Psalm that our lesson treats. It is well called "A Song of Praise." From the first word to the last it is a pouring forth of the heart's treasure of praise and thanksgiving; a breaking of an alabaster-box of very precious ointment, the perfume of which has filled the ages.

Notice: 1. The personal element in the Psalmist's praise. "Bless the Lord, O *my* soul: and all that is within *me*, bless his holy name." This personal element must ever be the key-note of genuine praise, as it is the key-note of all vital piety. We cannot "praise the Lord in the great congregation" until we have first praised him in the sanctuary of our own hearts. We may cry out with all earnestness of word and tone, "O that *men* would praise the Lord for his goodness!" but the words upon our lips will be but as sounding brass unless we have first taken upon ourselves the vow of his servant: "*I* will bless the Lord at all times; his praise shall continually be in my mouth."

That symphony of praise which some day shall fill the universe, when we shall hear "the sound of a great multitude, as the voice of many waters," can come only from the harmonious blending of the myriad individual voices.

If our notes are sweet and true, God will take care of the harmony.

2. Note that the Psalmist excepts no part of his nat-

ure from the obligation of praise: "*All* that is within me, bless his holy name."

Manifestly there must be heart and soul cleansing before this can be possible. Sin cannot praise God. The thought is blasphemy; but when once the clean heart is created within and the right spirit renewed, then there may be a glad dedication of our every power to the service of praise.

Our power of heart and mind, our love, our hope, our faith, our imagination, our reasoning faculties, our judgment, our memory, our wit and humor, are all to be dedicated to the high and holy office of a life-long praise of God. God wants our all; greater thought even than this, God can use our all.

In that perfect temple of his creation, where there is room for the sparrow and swallow—" the most useless and most restless of birds"—to nest, there is room for each faculty of our being to expand—to find its normal unfoldment " in him " in whom, indeed, " we live, and move, and have our being."

3. Note how the Psalmist quickens his praise through the faculty of memory: " Forget not all his benefits."

In verses 3-5 he enumerates what some of those benefits have been. Forgiveness, healing, redemption, lovingkindness, tender mercies, *satisfiedness*, renewal of youth.

" Surely," you say, " it is small wonder *he* should praise the Lord."

Ah! but notice those little words, " Forget not." There must have been danger of forgetfulness, else this exhortation would not have been given. There were hours in this life, as in our own, when the sunshine was dimmed by the shadow, when the present sorrow threatened to drive away all thought of past or present blessing. Perhaps in the depths of just such an hour, like perfume from a crushed rose, this Psalm was wrung from an aching, bleeding heart. "It is dark now, but it has been light; it will be light; there is sunshine behind the cloud. Forget not all his benefits."

Do we, in our dark hours, ever pause to take an inventory of our blessings? We shall find the list a long one; and if we practice the divine rule of forgetting sorrow and remembering joy, our lives will expand in perpetual praise.

Ewald's translation of verse 5 is more forcible than the Authorized or Revised Versions. "Who satisfies thy spirit with good, that like the eagles thy youth becomes new." The man does not live whom *things*, however good, can satisfy; and if a "mouth" satisfied with "good things" were the *summum bonum*, then were the Epicureans the true philosophers. But a "spirit satisfied with good"—such a one has found indeed the secret of perpetually renewing youth.

4. Note how the perception of personal blessings broadens the Psalmist's mind to take in the blessings of others. Hitherto he has thought only of God's dealings with himself; now his soul's eye takes a larger range.

God is good to me; yes, but that is not all; that is not sufficient reason for praise. "The Lord executeth righteousness and judgment for *all* that are oppressed." Not good to me only, not picking me out, with a capricious fancy, as an object of special benefaction, but embracing me in that universal love whose tides flow eternally, whose waves kiss in blessing the parched shores of each human life.

George McDonald makes Robert Falconer cry out in boyish indignation at his grandmother's teaching of the doctrine of election: "I don't want God to love me if he don't love every body." What true soul could! Who would not feel that he had lost his God and found instead the power of evil, if he could for one moment bring himself to believe that there was a being in the universe whom God did not love? Forever and forever must the soul of man respond in glad harmony to that eternal chord, "God so loved *the world*."

It is one of the highest proofs of our sonship to the Eternal that we, too, in our weak humanity, are "not willing that *any* should perish."

5. Note that it is the *quality* of God's love which causes the Psalmist to rejoice. All love should be a thing for which to give thanks. Most love is. And yet there are human loves which are banes, not blessings; which drag down rather than lift up both the lover and the loved. It is not enough that our friends love us; how do they love? Wisely or foolishly? selfishly or unselfishly? helpfully or hurtfully? It is not enough—we say it reverently—that God should love humanity. How does he love it?

The heathen have had conceptions of divine powers capable of love ; but the objects upon which their love was lavished were mere pampered favorites, spoiled children, made weaker, not stronger, by the love.

How does Jehovah love ? He himself answered the question centuries later: " God so loved the world, that he gave his only begotten Son, that whosoever believeth in him should not perish, but have everlasting life." The Psalmist answers it in the same spirit here: " The Lord executeth righteousness and judgment for all that are oppressed." A God whose love is manifested in an infinite helpfulness—whose helpfulness is the essence of righteousness and justice—this is the God we adore.

From this point to verse 19 the whole thought of the Psalmist is filled with God's attributes. He has gotten beyond blessings into the Blesser. The character of God —not his gifts—is filling his soul with the rapture of praise.

The force of comparison is well-nigh exhausted in showing forth the goodness, the long-suffering, the tender compassion of God. Whose heart has not been thrilled by the thought of that thirteenth verse : " Like as a father pitieth his children, so the Lord pitieth them that fear him." We know of but one other comparison which equals it in tenderness, and that is Isa. lxvi, 13 : " As one whom his mother comforteth, so will I comfort you."

We have pushed away from the shore, and are beginning to know something of the surgings of the infinite ocean of divine love, when the thought of what God *is* is more to us than any thought of what he does; when the thought of his righteousness is dearer to us than any personal blessing; when we stay our tired souls, not on any manifestation of his favor, but on the eternal verity that God is good. What though "man's days are as grass." "The mercy of the Lord is from everlasting to everlasting." "They shall perish; but thou remainest."

O, there must come hours in each true life when the fact that God is, that he is a God of righteousness and holiness, is enough to satisfy, though every gift and every blessing and every outward manifestation of his love were swept from the individual experience forever.

6. Note the Psalmist's conception of what it is to praise God. We find it expressed in the three last verses of this Psalm.

"Bless the Lord, ye his angels, . . . *that do his commandments, hearkening unto the voice of his word.* Bless ye the Lord, all ye his hosts; *ye ministers of his, that do his pleasure.*"

Surely this conception of praise is a something other and deeper than a mere verbal outpouring of thanksgiving. How are we to praise God? Even as the angels do. Our Master taught us to pray, "Thy will be done, in earth as it is in heaven." This Psalm teaches us that God's will is done in heaven through the angelic host "Keeping his commandments, hearkening unto the voice of his word."

A praise which is obedience, an obedience which seeks continually to know that wherein it may further obey, this is the divine ideal of praise. It is well to speak God's praises; it is better to live them. The speaking may help the living; it may hinder. There is danger that the soul's vital force, which should be expended in deeds, may explode in hallelujahs. If the hallelujahs help the deeds, let them come; if they constitute, in any sense, an end, and not the means toward that end, let them be suppressed. "Why call ye me Lord, Lord, and do not the things which I say?"

Surely, if "he prayeth best who loveth best," he praiseth best who best obeys. And what are his commandments? The Master epitomizes them all. "A new commandment I give unto you, that ye love one another, as I have loved you." Did you ever think that the very highest teaching Christ has for us concerns our relations to our fellow-men? The incarnation means just that; it was an object-lesson through which man might learn how to live with his brother-man. John caught its root-meaning when he cried, " Hereby perceive we the love of God, because he laid down his life for us: and we ought to lay down our lives for the brethren." " As the Father hath sent me into the world, even so have I also sent them into the world."

"For all behind the starry sky,
　Behind the world so broad,
Behind men's hearts and souls doth lie
　The Infinite of God.

"If true to men, though troubled sore,
　I cannot choose but be,
Thou, who art peace for evermore,
　Art very true to me."

KATHARINE LENTE STEVENSON.

VIII.

DANIEL AND HIS COMPANIONS.

Dan. i, 8-21.

GOLDEN TEXT.—Daniel purposed in his heart that he would not defile himself with the portion of the king's meat, nor with the wine which he drank. Dan. i, 8.

FOR breadth of character, Moses; for loftiness, Daniel. Men are broad for what they do; lofty, for what they are. Moses planned and carried out great things. Daniel's character stands like a great mountain in a vast plain. How shall we encompass it, how scale its height? We can do neither. We can only look at him and feel the power of his grandeur. Let us view him in the light of his temptation, his resistance, and his reward.

1. TEMPTATION. Can it be that these young men, well-named, well-trained, and of lofty character, were tempted? tempted just like other young men—young men of our day, surrounded with palace saloons, halls of enchantment, temptations of a fast age, social, mercantile, political? O tempter, thy name is legion. In the guise of kings and courts dost thou come. The young are thy choice victims; the comely, the courtly, the witty, thy booty. The innocent fall by thy craft, and the pure dost thou defile. "Death loves a shining mark;" much more dost thou pant for the blood of the

priceless fair. Thy hot breath is upon every land to wither and blast; thy presence in every home to rend.

Young princes of chosen and illustrious ancestry, " children in whom was no blemish, but well-favored, and skillful in all wisdom, and cunning in knowledge, and understanding science, and such as had ability in them to stand in the king's palace, and whom they might teach the learning and the tongue of the Chaldeans "—what could more whet the appetite of the all-devouring tempter? What wonder that far-reaching strategy, the finest of tactics, and a diversity of forces were employed to make sure the seizure.

Did you ever know temptation to come openly and direct? Ah, what skulking, what hiding under "reasonable claims." Now in the cloak of authority, now in the guise of friendship, now drawing into ambush by some fancied personal good. Even in that subtle charm of " holy charity " does he too frequently glove his hideous hand.

Human nature is somewhat combative, and usually resists open attack. When one expects an assault upon his integrity, his sense of self-defense at once thwarts the enemy. Satan has no pleasure in religious watch-towers. He wastes not his strength on strongholds. He contends not with resisting spirits. He fills the mind with the glamour of royalty, the phantasy of good-fellowship, the spirit of chivalry. He leads his victim on; he does not drive. If Daniel was to be overthrown, it must be by subtle methods, and what were some of these?

(1) *Royal Authority.* "And the king appointed them a daily provision." Now, one of the things that Daniel had early learned, and learned well, was reverence for and obedience to constituted authority. Himself a prince, he knew and appreciated the majesty of the law. He respected the kingly office, recognizing the divine right of kings. See with what appreciation he addressed the King of Babylon: "Thou, O king, art a king of kings: for the God of heaven hath given thee a kingdom, power, and strength, and glory" (chap. ii, 37.)

Daniel was a captive under subjection. He had not the rights of the lowest subject of the realm. It were enough for which to be devoutly thankful should he by readiest obedience save his head. But Daniel with all his appreciation of authority, and with full recognition of his critical condition, "purposed in his heart that he would not defile himself."

When viewing the character of Daniel we are not to forget the virtues of the three faithful companions. They shared in the temptations with which our lesson deals, united with Daniel in prayer to the "God of heaven," and were saved by miracle, as was he—they from the fiery furnace, he from the lions' den.

(2) *By Appeal to the Natural Appetite.* "And the king appointed them a daily provision of the king's meat, and of the wine which he drank." *Meat* and *wine*— very common temptations. Although wine had caused Noah's disgrace, and was at the root of Canaan's curse, and had caused the loss of Ben-hadad's army, since he

"was drinking himself drunk in the pavilions, he and the kings, the thirty and two kings that helped him" (1 Kings xx, 16), and its use was strongly denounced by Solomon and the prophets, it had not at that time become the cause of so much sin, crime, and sorrow as it is charged with at the present time. But "Daniel purposed in his heart that he would not defile himself with the portion of the king's meat, nor with the wine which he drank."

By subsisting upon the king's viands, Daniel would have 1.) compromised his faith in the true God. "To have partaken of such a feast would have been to sanction idolatry."—*Jamieson, Faussett, and Brown.* Much of it was no doubt the flesh of animals offered in idol-worship. "They sacrificed unto devils, not to God; to gods whom they knew not. . . . Their wine is the poison of dragons, and the cruel venom of asps" (Deut. xxxii, 17, 33).

2.) There was danger that the use of the king's meat and wine would lead to voluptuousness. The free use of such viands does not foster the instincts of manliness and scholarship. "When thou sittest to eat with a ruler, consider diligently what is before thee: and put a knife to thy throat, if thou be a man given to appetite. Be not desirous of his dainties: for they are deceitful meat" (Prov. xxiii, 1-3). "Let me not eat of their dainties" (Psa. cxli, 4).

3.) Daniel may have felt called to the exercise of the priestly office. "Not all priests were descendants of Aaron."—*Schaff-Herzog.* The priests were prohibited from using wine while on duty. The best way to keep free from the use of strong drink when on duty is to abstain from its use when off duty. It is evident that Daniel desired all the advantages favorable to successful study which the habits of the priests could give; for if any knew the arts of scholarly attainments it was the priesthood. It is accepted now by the best authorities that total abstinence is best for all men in all pursuits.

(3) *Appeal to Pride.* Dazzling prospects! "To stand in the king's palace;" to study "the learning and tongue of the Chaldeans;" to live in "great Babylon!" What opportunities! It is said that every man will break down if touched at his passion-point. Now, these youths had a passion for learning. With such passion and such temptation, who could be expected to resist? Acquiescence would unlock all the archives and unfold all the mysteries of the great Bel-worship.

(4) *Flattery.* Not only honored by selection to high privileges, but new names were given Daniel and his companions—distinguished names: Belteshazzar—Bel's prince, that is, a prince whom Bel favors; Shadrach—little friend of the king, or rejoicing in the way; Meshach—guest of the king; Abed-nego—worshiper of Mercury, or interpreter of the gods. (See *Gesenius, Hebrew Lexicon.*) These names would at once bring them into fellowship with the young princes of Babylon, and make them peers, if not superiors, to them all. Thus idolatry would be seen at its best. It would not appear the abominable thing they had been taught to regard it.

(5) *Social Influence.* The long dining-room is thrown open. The savor of the king's meat fills the air. The wine, the ruddy wine, sparkles in the blazing light. Come Belteshazzar! Come Shadrach, Meshach, and Abed-nego! All things are now ready. The king looks for you at his right hand. The Babylonian princes and magi enter. All places are filled. No; four seats are vacant. Daniel, Hananiah, Mishael, and Azariah are not present. Why not? Why so eccentric? Why be the laughing-stock of the court? All the other young men are there— young men who also are "to stand in the king's palace." Does not the king know, and his butler, what is best for the young magi? Have they not brought up and educated young men for these positions before? "But Daniel purposed in his heart that he would not defile himself with the portion of the king's meat, nor with the wine which he drank."

(6) *Friendship—In its Utmost Plea.* Yet another entrance to the heart of Daniel does the tempter seek. It is now upon a higher basis. Daniel had been taught to beware of glamour, appetite, pride, flattery, and society. But friendship was a noble virtue. Who could withstand its plea? A benefactor, a warm personal friend, an ardent admirer, one who loved Daniel, pleads the jeopardy of his life. " Now God had brought Daniel into favor and tender love with the prince of the eunuchs. And the prince of the eunuchs said unto Daniel, I fear my lord the king, who hath appointed your meat and your drink: for why should he see your faces worse liking than the

children which are of your sort? then shall ye make me endanger my head to the king."

"Ah, now I have him, I have him," cries the old tempter; "I have at last laid my hand upon his heart." But "prove thy servants," says Daniel to Melzar; "prove thy servants . . . ten days, and let them give us pulse to eat, and water to drink." So Melzar "consented to them in this matter, and proved them ten days. And at the end of ten days their countenances appeared fairer and fatter in flesh than all the children which did eat the portion of the king's meat." The young prince of God has had his way. Hereafter he may be called Belteshazzar at the court of Babylon, but at the mercy-seat it shall be Daniel.

2. RESISTANCE. We hear of the "man of destiny," but here is the man of purpose. But purpose, to be of any avail, must be backed by something substantial. Many a man has purposed well, but has found himself overcome by outward forces. Daniel with good purposes is well-supported in many ways.

(1) *Both He and His Friends have Good Names:* Daniel —God's judge; that is, one appointed to deliver judgment in the name of the true God; Hananiah—the gift of Jehovah; Mishael—he is what the Almighty is; Azariah—whom Jehovah helps.—*Gesenius.* May there not be something in names? If so, these young men had a good start in life.

(2) *Good Instruction in Early Life.* These young men were already "skillful in all wisdom, and cunning in knowledge, and understanding science."

(3) *A Definite and Lofty Aim in Life.* Daniel looked beyond the day and hour. He sought more than mere existence and comfortable living. He saw the far-reaching purposes of God in his own creation. He grasped the lofty privileges of life. There was no wisdom or knowledge attainable by him that he did not covet, feeling assured that in time all would be serviceable to him. So he studied ever with an aim.

(4) *Pre-occupation.* Daniel did not seem to think himself in this world to receive and be served, but, on the other hand, to fulfill the mission for which he was created: not to be enchanted with the world's show, but to charm others with truth and righteousness; to give heed to those things which best fit for life's duties; to pass by the things that would in any way hinder his highest usefulness.

O young friend, fill up to the full the measure of your being with holy thoughts and holy deeds. When the eolian harp is placed in your window, when the siren song is sung, have your ears filled with other melodies. There is for the lover of men enchantment in the wail of a broken heart, melody in the voice of weeping. Be so busy in binding up the wounds of your sin-bruised fellowmen that you will not perceive the pageantry of royalty as it marches by. Say you that the shadows on such a picture are too deep? Remember Gethsemane! remember Calvary! Only in your efforts to save others is your own present safety and your final salvation assured.

(5) *Good Companions.* A blessed thing it is for the

young to have good companions. "Blessed is the man who walketh not in the counsel of the ungodly, and standeth not in the way of sinners, and sitteth not in the company of scorners, but his delight is in the law of Jehovah, and in his law doth he meditate day and night. . . . And he is like a tree planted by the water-courses, which bringeth forth its fruit in its season, and its leaf withereth not, and whatsoever he doeth he carrieth through."—*Delitzsch's Translation of the First Psalm.* "O the blessedness of the man, etc."—*Spurgeon.*

3. THE REWARD. Did ever so lofty a life as Daniel's fail of a reward? Not where God reigns. Space forbids that we should elaborate. Read carefully the entire Book of Daniel at one sitting, and mark the favors heaped upon this noble prophet.

(1) *Favor.* "God brought Daniel into favor and tender love with the prince of the eunuchs" (chap. i, 9).

(2) *Health.* "At the end of ten days their countenances appeared fairer and fatter in flesh than all the children which did eat the portion of the king's meat" (ver. 15).

(3) *Intellectuality and Scholarship.* "And in all matters of wisdom and understanding, that the king inquired of them, he found them ten times better than all the magicians and astrologers that were in all his realm" (ver. 20).

(4) *Ability to Render Great Service to the King.* He not only interpreted the king's dream, but made known unto the king the dream which he himself had forgotten. (Read chap. 3.)

(5) Daniel saved the lives of the wise men, including his three friends and himself, the decree having gone forth that they should be slain. He said: " Destroy not the wise men of Babylon: bring me in before the king, and I will show unto the king the interpretation " (ver. 24).

(6) Daniel and his three companions were appointed to high positions in the kingdom of Babylon (ver. 49).

(7) Daniel's three companions were saved from the " burning fiery furnace." (Read chap. 3.)

(8) *Growth in Character.* Virtue well practiced is self-developing. " Daniel purposed in his heart that he would not defile himself." It took courage to carry this purpose into effect. This was the test of the youth's courage. Later on Daniel was able to exercise the courage of a man. When he tells the king the facts and exhorts to repentance it was not boy's play. " They shall drive thee from men," etc. (chap. iv, 25). " Wherefore, O king, . . . break off thy sins " (ver. 27).

(9) Given ability to read hand-writing upon the wall.

(10) Daniel is made chief of the presidents.

(11) Daniel is delivered from lions' den.

(12) He is enabled to render great service to the kingdom of the true God by holding up the true light through a long period in an idolatrous land.

(13) Through him is revealed the time of Christ's incarnation (chap. ix, 20–27).

(14) He was permitted to see the restoration of his people. (See *Comprehensive Commentary* on Dan. i, 21.)

(15) Was granted a long life.

"Seest thou a man diligent in his business? He shall stand before kings" (Prov. xxii, 29).

"Her Nazarites were purer than snow, they were whiter than milk, they were more ruddy in body than rubies, their polishing was of sapphire" (Lam. iv, 7).

M. D. HORNBECK.

IX.

NEBUCHADNEZZAR'S DREAM.

Dan. ii, 36-49.

GOLDEN TEXT.—All things are naked and opened unto the eyes of him with whom we have to do. Heb. iv, 13.

Is this true or false? Does God know all things that each one of us does and says? Does he see the crime, the deceit, the cruelties practiced by men? Does he know how intemperance curses our land, destroys human souls, padlocks the lips of some of his preachers in the sacred desk, and hinders the progress of Christ's cause on this earth? Does he know every trial, temptation, want of his children? Does he see us when we pray, when we do right, and when we sin? We often feel that he knows the great crisis-hours in individual experiences and in national history. Does he see the little everyday occurrences which make up so much of our daily experiences and yet which we would hardly think important enough to tell our most intimate friend? He saw me when with terrible heart-hunger I laid in the cold ground my darling child. He hears the bitter cry, "I want her!" sees the burning tears which no human eyes must see. Did he see me when I met my unsaved friend? Did he know that my friend was wishing I would help him find the better life? Did God hear my careless jest of yesterday? Christ has said that not a sparrow falleth to the ground without his notice. Is there nothing too minute to escape his knowledge or too mysterious to be understood by him? Is it true that "all things are naked and opened unto the eyes of him with whom we have to do?" This the lesson of to-day affirms and illustrates, while the religious condition of the human family in every land reiterates its truth.

Nebuchadnezzar in the second year of his sole reign as King of Babylon, about 603 B. C., had a dream which filled him with fearful apprehensions.

When he awoke he could not recall its particulars, although retaining its general impressions, and commanded his "wise men" to reveal to him his dream and its interpretation, on the penalty of death if they failed.

These "wise men" were distinguished for their knowledge of literature, philosophy, science, or priestcraft. The leaders of these different classes of learned men could not obey the king's command, and their immediate execution, with that of their associates, was ordered, when Daniel, whose three years of training had been but a few weeks ended, and who was now considered as one of these "wise men," secured a delay of the execution until with his companions he could ask and receive from Jehovah the information which the king desired.

That night the dream and its meaning were revealed by God to Daniel, who, after declaring to Nebuchadnezzar that his knowledge was not due to his own wisdom, but to the favor of Jehovah, said that the king saw in his dream a great image, whose head was fine gold, breast and arms were silver, belly and thighs were brass, legs were iron, and feet partly iron and partly clay. The king also saw a stone strike the image, which fell into minute fragments which the wind blew away, and the stone grew until it filled the whole earth.

"This is the dream," said Daniel. He speaks with perfect confidence, although well aware that a failure to reproduce the exact dream meant his own death, together with that of all the other "wise men" in Babylon. He knew that he could not be mistaken because "all things are naked and opened unto the eyes of him " who had revealed to him the secret thoughts of Nebuchadnezzar in the night watches. Daniel knew also that the truth had come to him in answer to his prayer, and that it was a proof of the divine favor toward him. This furnished him with the requisite courage to interpret the dream. Men are strong in proportion to their consciousness of the truth of their message and of a divine authority given them in its promulgation. "We"—God the revealer and I his messenger—" will tell the interpretation thereof before the king." Those religious teachers among the ministry or laity, whatever their literary attainments or abilities, are miserable weaklings, who are not sure that their instructions are, "Thus saith the Lord." Daniel felt that he was uttering God's truth with God's help, and feared not to declare the whole counsel of God. Ministers who do likewise to-day, whatever their fields of labor, achieve abundant success. The cause of Christ needs such men—the world hungers to hear them. "Thou, O king, art a king of kings." A general title of Oriental sovereigns and an absolute truth.

Nebuchadnezzar's dominion included Egypt and the whole civilized world of Asia. It was in an important sense a great "world-kingdom," "the prototype and pattern, the beginning and the primary representative, of all world-powers."

Daniel recognizes the lawful authority of his king and bows in submission to it, not with a fawning sycophancy, but as a manly man, as later Christ commanded (Matt. xxii, 21) and Paul enjoined (Rom. xiii, 1). He does not forget his position as a subject while he speaks the message of the great king's King. Nebuchadnezzar is not an irresponsible ruler. He received his kingdom as a gift from Jehovah, and is accountable to him. "The God of heaven hath given thee a kingdom, power, strength, and glory." In thy administration of its affairs he is weighing thee, watching all thy ways, learning whether his authority is recognized. Later, when Nebuchadnezzar ignored this truth, he was sent to feed with beasts in the field until he realized "that the Most High ruleth in the kingdom of men, and giveth it to whomsoever he will," while men to-day may be equally and as signally humiliated and punished who ignore the truth that every good and perfect gift in their lives comes from God, who, knowing all their deeds, will hold them to a strict account of their stewardship. God does not balance his books at each nightfall. He is "merciful and gracious, long-suffering, and abundant in goodness and truth, keeping mercy for thousands, forgiving iniquity and transgression and sin, and will by no means clear the guilty." In the equity of the divine administration, since " all things are naked and opened unto him with whom we have to do," sooner or later men and nations are judged according to their deeds.

"Thou art this head of gold." Eastern courtesy demanded that Daniel should thus speak in the presence of the king and his court. Nebuchadnezzar might be used as a representative of his kingdom since he had conquered Judea, Syria, Phenicia, and Egypt in the establishment of the Babylonian Empire. "And after thee shall arise another kingdom inferior to thee," etc.

In the righteous administration of God as ruler of nations, and because of its iniquity, the Babylonian world-power was supplanted by the Medo-Persian, which fell before the Macedonian under the great Alexander, and, in turn, the kingdom of the Seleucidæ in Syria and the kingdom of the Lagidæ in Egypt supplanted the Macedonian and were finally merged into the Roman world-power. These three world-powers, each in turn supplanting the preceding, were represented in the dream of Nebuchadnezzar by silver, brass, and iron, the latter at last mixed with clay, because each was inferior to the preceding, not in external power, but in morality, manifested particularly in their persecution of the peculiar people of God. " In the days of these kings shall the God of heaven set up a kingdom." While the Seleucidæ, Lagidæ, and the other Diadochi were still reigning—that is, during the fourth world-power— the fifth, the Messianic kingdom, would be established. Or, inasmuch as in Nebuchadnezzar's dream the image of gold, silver, brass, iron, and clay, representing the four great world-powers, was intact until struck by the stone, and each of these powers was characterized by an overthrow because of the same spirit of worldly hostility to God, in the midst of this impiety the kingdom of God would be established on earth (Isa. lx, 2). Both are true.

It was this spirit which animated the Baal-worshipers, wrought confusion in Israel, culminated in the loss of the ten tribes, and in the Babylonian captivity. It constitutes the essence of nature-worship to-day, and enters more or less fully into every modern form of unbelief. "Which shall never be destroyed . . . shall not be left to other people, but it shall break in pieces and consume all these kingdoms, and it shall stand forever."

The Messianic kingdom will never be supplanted by another world-power; it will overcome the worldly opposition of men to the spiritual reign of God, will universally triumph on earth, and endure forever.

"This kingdom cometh not by observation" (Luke xvii, 20), but its effects are seen. "The stone was cut out of the mountain without hands, and . . . brake in pieces the iron, the brass, the clay, the silver, and the gold." The manner of the growth of the stone, until it "became a great mountain and filled the whole earth," as the symbol of the Messianic kingdom is not revealed.

History shows that it moves forward with accelerating power, though subject to retarding influences. Sharon Turner, whom no one would charge with falsifying facts, gives the approximate number of nominal Christians as, first century, 500,000; second, 2,000,000; third, 5,000,000; fourth, 10,000,000; fifth, 15,000,000; sixth, 20,000,000; seventh, 24,000,000; eighth, 30,000,000; ninth, 40,000,000; tenth, 50,000,000; eleventh, 70,000,000; twelfth, 80,000,000; thirteenth, 75,000,000; fourteenth, 80,000,000; fifteenth, 100,000,000; sixteenth, 125,000,000; seventeenth, 155,000,000; eighteenth, 200,000,000; and to-day they are reckoned as 479,000,000, and are increasing more rapidly than ever before. It is estimated that the number of conversions during the fifty years ending in 1850 was greater than during the first sixteen centuries; that the number during the twenty years ending in 1870 was greater than during the fifty years before; that the number converted between 1870 and 1880 was greater than between 1850 and 1870; and that the conversions during the year 1890 were fifty per cent. greater than the number of nominal Christians during the first century of the Christian era. This, together with the rapid increase of the various and powerful agencies which are utilized by the Christian Church for the triumph of the cause of Christ, points to the time when the stone shall become a mountain and fill the whole earth.

" Forasmuch as thou sawest . . . the great God hath made known to the king what shall come to pass hereafter: and the dream is certain, and the interpretation thereof sure." Whoever the author of the Book of Daniel, the events which have taken place since it was written and that are taking place to-day reveal its prophetic character. They could have been made known only by Him unto whose eyes "all things are naked and opened," even the secret thoughts of the heart.

Hence the dream of Nebuchadnezzar was divinely imparted. "Forasmuch as thou sawest . . . the great God hath made it known to the king."

Nebuchadnezzar's worship of Daniel as the representative of the Most High, and his advancement in official rank of the three friends of Daniel at his request, with which our lesson ends, was a royal confession of the omniscience of Jehovah, and illustrates the value of a good man's friendship and of the faithfulness of the divine Promiser toward those who trust him.

NICHOLAS T. WHITAKER.

X.
THE FIERY FURNACE.

Dan. iii, 13-25.

GOLDEN TEXT.—When thou walkest through the fire, thou shalt not be burned; neither shall the flame kindle upon thee. Isa. xliii, 2.

WE are already familiar, from the previous lessons out of this book, with the leading facts concerning the three Hebrews who are the heroes of this lesson. We have seen who they are, whence they came, and to what places of honor and responsibility they have attained. We have had some evidence of their faith in God and loyalty to the religion of their fathers. They are emphatically choice men, still, in all probability, comparatively young.

The incident of the lesson is, so far as we know, the climax of their lives; after this we have no further account of them. Their courage and faith in this fiery trial is crowned by Jehovah with a wonderful deliverance; and the story of this has been for many centuries, in many lands, to many hearts a source of instruction, inspiration, and comfort.

In endeavoring to understand this event and to draw forth some of its lessons we notice:

1. That the incident rests on the solid ground of history, not on the shifting quicksands of legend.

The glory of Babylon and the greatness of Nebuchadnezzar are established beyond question; and the mighty monarch took especial pride in the fact that the greatness of the city in his time he had largely created. "Altogether there is reason to believe," says Rawlinson, "that he was one of the most indefatigable of all the builders that have left their mark upon the world in which we live." The evidences are numerous, also, that he was, like the Greeks whom Paul found at Athens, very religious. It seems a most natural thing that such a man in such a position should determine to set up in his province of Babylon a lofty and splendid image. In Egypt, at an earlier date, Rameses the Great had erected many superb statues of himself as the representative of divinity. Colossal statues of gold were familiar to the Babylonians. Diodorus of Sicily describes three—figures of the three great gods of Babylon which crowned the temple of Bel until it was plundered by Xerxes. A statue of one of the Assyrian kings and others of Nebo and Istar were found at Nimroud, so that Nebuchadnezzar's golden image was in keeping with the fashion of the time, while its gigantic size harmonized with his other creations at Babylon.

The monument as a whole, including, we may suppose, the platform from which it rose, towered to a height of ninety feet, with a breadth in some parts of nine, which would seem to indicate that the image was seated rather than erect, like some of the colossal forms Nebuchadnezzar had seen in Egypt.

Whether it was solid gold, or wood covered with layers of gold, and whether it was a figure of a chief Babylonian deity, or of Nebuchadnezzar himself as a representative of that deity, cannot be positively determined.

It was erected in the plain of Dura, in the province of Babylon. There is a plain retaining this name about five miles from the great city to the south-east. It is marked by dry channels of ancient canals for irrigation, and has a series of mounds called the Mounds of Dura. Concerning one of these, "the squared mound," nearly twenty feet high, Oppert says: "On seeing this mound one is instantly struck with its resemblance to the pedestal of a colossal statue, and every thing leads to the conclusion that it is the base of that of which the Book of Daniel speaks."

The inauguration ceremonies of this huge idol were to be on a scale magnificent even for Babylon; and to the high festival the monarch summoned representatives of all the provinces of his empire, in the persons of those who held high office under him. Let it be remembered that it was the Babylonian custom to leave over each conquered province a prince belonging to the vanquished nation, while they and the people whom they governed were brought under tribute to the empire.

The motive of Nebuchadnezzar in bringing together this great company of officials, and in commanding them to worship the image he had set up, was doubtless political as well as religious. He wished to assert his sovereignty over them in a most royally absolute manner by compelling them all to conform to the idol-worship which he himself preferred. Religion in antiquity was strictly a matter of state; disloyalty to the gods appointed for public worship was held disloyalty to the monarch who commanded the homage. In accordance with this idea it was proclaimed that any who refused to prostrate themselves before the idol when the music sounded should be burned to death in a fiery furnace. A picture on the palace walls of Assurbanipal, at Kouyundjik, shows two unfortunate creatures being burned alive, their tongues having first been pulled out. The narrative of these three Hebrews having been thrown into the burning furnace for refusing to worship the golden image is thus in strict accord with Babylonian usages.

Considerable discussion has prevailed in regard to the list of musical instruments mentioned in this account. The names applied to some of these instruments are Greek—*kitharis, sambuke, psalterion;* " harp, sackbut, psaltery "—and this fact has been urged as showing that the Book of Daniel was written at a much later time than the age of Nebuchadnezzar. But, as Geikie says, " though music occupies a small space in the sculptures of the earlier kings, it became a prominent feature in all religious and public ceremonies in Assyria and Babylon in the beginning of the sixth century before Christ—that is, just before the time of Nebuchadnezzar; and nothing was more natural, when we remember the wide dispersion of the Greeks even at an earlier period, than that foreign instruments should have been familiar on the Euphrates at this time."

Thus we see that all the facts and features of this incident, as presented in the record before us, are in no instance contradictory to, but altogether harmonious with, the best historical knowledge we now have of Nebuchadnezzar and his times.

2. This incident has some bearing on the relation of civil government to religion. The root of the difficulty in this case is that King Nebuchadnezzar had no right to force religious services upon his subjects. It was a seriously erroneous idea of government, then quite universally prevalent, that if a man would not obey the sovereign in matters of religion he was disloyal to the State. The king, however, did not know this; he was simply doing as all other rulers of his time did. It cannot even be reasonably supposed that the three noble Hebrews who were the sufferers had any thought that their rights as subjects and as men were trampled upon by Nebuchadnezzar's command. But in our age and land we notice this fact very quickly. We as a people have learned the great lesson that God alone is " Lord of the conscience," and that all men are entitled to worship him according to their sincere religious convictions. Religious compulsion, exhibited here by Nebuchadnezzar in one of its worst forms, has given place to a religious toleration which seeks to fulfill the divine law, " Thou shalt love thy neighbor as thyself." The development of this change of thought and practice has been slow and pain-

ful, a growth of many centuries; and our present religious freedom has been purchased at a great cost.

While we may not claim for Shadrach, Meshach, and Abed-nego that they were in this instance consciously standing for such religious freedom, yet it is due to them to say that they belong in an important sense in the noble army of Non-conformists, those who felt that they must obey God rather than men, and for whom duty to God was above every other consideration. It is to men of this type that the world chiefly owes the religious freedom it now enjoys.

3. We are thus led naturally to observe that these men were true heroes. They understood the king and the situation in which they were placed well enough to be sure that their refusal to join in the acts of homage to the great image would be fatal. There was much at stake in addition to their own lives—the happiness of their friends, especially their great associate and benefactor, Daniel, and the welfare of the captive people whose chief representatives in places of power they were. It would seem as though the temptation must have been very strong to look at the whole matter in the light of a governmental or political necessity, and to bow to the image in company with the large body of officials as a formal expedient to prevent trouble, preserve peace, save life.

But there was a clause in the holy law of Jehovah which they had known from their youth : " Thou shalt not make unto thee any graven image. . . . Thou shalt not bow down thyself to them, nor serve them." This they could not forget, and they would not violate. So they "said to the king, O Nebuchadnezzar, we are not careful to answer thee in this matter. If it be so, our God whom we serve is able to deliver us from the burning fiery furnace, and he will deliver us out of thine hand, O king. *But if not*, be it known unto thee, O king, that we will not serve thy gods, nor worship the golden image which thou hast set up."

They cherished hope of deliverance; but as true heroes of faith they were unconditionally determined to be obedient to God.

4. We consider the glorious deliverance wrought by Jehovah for his faithful servants. Their faith and obedience did not save them from trial. The king, full of fury at their firm opposition to his will, determined to inflict the prescribed penalty in the severest possible form. Into the midst of the furnace at its intensest heat they were cast bound. The king, looking in, saw four men loose, walking in the midst of the fire and having no hurt. " The aspect of the fourth," the monarch said, "is like a son of the gods." By this expression Nebuchadnezzar indicated his belief that a being of the race of the gods was present in the furnace; it is not to be understood that he recognized in this being him whom we call the Son of God. At the same time many able and devout students of the Scriptures hold that the form of the fourth in the furnace was a manifestation of that " Angel of the Covenant " who appeared many times

during the earlier dispensation, the second person of the Trinity, who in the fullness of time became incarnate for us. By his presence and gracious power his persecuted servants were comforted, preserved, and delivered. And upon them rested the honor of having, by their loyalty to Jehovah, caused his name to be magnified afresh, and their own faith and that of their fellow Hebrews to be vindicated before these representatives of the great world-power, and by the king's decree throughout the range of the Assyrian dominion.

The significance of this deliverance to all God's children in time of severe trial is well intimated in the Golden Text. A little reflection also will suggest the bearing of the incident upon the Hebrew people in this time of their captivity in a strange land. Jehovah would not utterly forsake them, but would yet bring them forth from their trials, and vindicate his name and covenant before all people.

HENRY A. STARKS.

XI.

THE DEN OF LIONS.

Dan. vi, 16-28.

GOLDEN TEXT.—No manner of hurt was found upon him, because he believed in his God. Dan. vi, 23.

ON a clay tablet belonging to the archives of Assurbanipal II. is the following record: "Saulmugina, my rebellious brother, who made war with me, in the fierce burning fire they threw him, and destroyed his life. And the people who to Saulmugina, my rebellious brother, he had caused to join, and those evil things did, who death deserved. . . . One sinner did not escape from my hands, my hand held them. . . . Their tongues I pulled out, their overthrow I accomplished. The rest of the people alive among the . . . lions and bulls, which Sennacherib, my grandfather, in the midst had thrown; again into that pit those men I threw."*

Hardly eight years after that was stamped on the soft clay we have in Bible annals a full-length picture of "the fierce burning fire;" and about forty years later still, in the present lesson, "that pit" is with like vividness depicted. In those forty years the scepter of Assyria had passed into Persian or Parsee hands, and it would have been impious to use the sacred element,

---

* Smith's *Assyrian Discoveries*, pp. 342, 343.

fire, as an instrument of death (*A. R. Fausset*); but aside from this the official " ring " who surrounded the throne of Darius Cyaxares did not scruple to use any trick or cruelty by which they might destroy the incorruptible statesman Daniel. He continually shamed and obstructed, if he did not actually punish, their misdeeds.

Thus it appears that about all that is left of the " state papers " of an empire that endured for at least eight hundred years is enough to show those who will accept nothing merely on the authority of God's word that Daniel is a writer of veritable history and to help the unbelief of doubting Thomases. But while these contacts between sacred and secular annals are sufficient to prove that both belong to the same fabric of real human history, they surely serve also another and still higher end. History has been compared to tapestry, on one side of which can be seen only ends of threads and irregular masses of colors, while on the " right side " there are no ragged thrums and disorderly blotches, but a beautiful picture. Secular annals—the daily newspapers—show us little more than a dreary expanse of conflicts and destructions; and it would be hard to discover any good and worthy plan in them were it not for glimpses of "the right side of things " given here and there in the sacred annals. They show us that God has been working through all the ages and in all lands on a tapestry whose full beauty and extent the universe shall one day see. Or we may illustrate the same thought by a more familiar object—the kaleidoscope. Secular history resembles those bits of broken glass lying in the hand, but as they, when put into that three-cornered tube and held up to the light and turned, flash into forms of amazing and almost endlessly varied beauty, so when we study these inspired histories we find selfish intrigues and deeds of blood, the many weak and base and the few strong and noble characters working out the "determinate counsel and foreknowledge" of God. The sin and wrong are not condoned and glorified; "he that *is* filthy" remains "filthy still;" nothing can change the real moral character of past deeds. Yet as God "turns and overturns till he shall come whose right it is to rule," we are led to adore his overruling providence.

In this kaleidoscopic turning various features of human character and various parts of what may be called scenery in the drama of history strangely appear and reappear. Take, for example, that great prophetic Psalm—the twenty-second. For more than a thousand years its first verse kept words waiting to express the Messiah's agony on the cross, "My God, my God, why hast thou forsaken me?" Yet almost midway in that long period our present lesson shows one of God's heroes passing through strikingly similar experiences. Dr. John De Witt's fine translation of the Psalms, *The Praise Songs of Israel*, shows this a little more plainly than our ordinary version. Verses 11 and 12 read:

> "Mighty bulls have surrounded me;
> The strong of Bashan encircle me:
> They open their mouths against me,
> As if lions were rending and roaring."

And again (vers. 19-21):

"But thou, O Jehovah, be not far off!
O my strength! for my help haste thee!
Snatch away from the sword my life;
My precious life from the power of the dog.
Save me from the mouth of the lion,
And from the horns of wild cattle *thou hast answered me!*"

Whether David had in view the savage deeds of the old Assyrian empire or not his language certainly links together this conflict of Daniel and the supreme conflict and victory of Calvary and the sepulcher. Comparing the historic narratives of these two events, we observe in both hurried and tumultuous plottings, barely veiled by forms of law, fruitless efforts to extricate acknowledged innocence from the net of intrigue, and the official sealing of dark and terrible caverns. Still keeping in mind the resemblances between the sufferings of Daniel and those of Christ, let us see how they combine to reveal some of the great principles of human action.

1. We see in the palace of Darius and the judgment-hall of Pilate, as so often elsewhere, how unfortunate it is for weak characters to be placed in any critical position. To be a king and not be kingly, to move in the first circles and be of a very inferior grade of character, may seem to pass when there is no call for any thing but court ceremonial and official "red tape," or the proper method of using cards, etc., but it is far otherwise when great questions are to be decided. Then to occupy some high station is only to have one's moral weakness the more widely advertised.

9*

2. In Darius we see what possibilities of contradiction and inconsistency human nature has in it. He presents a grotesque jumble of Pilate and those who sought the sepulcher at early dawn. One day he represents those to whom custom and precedent are more sacred than justice, and the next day those who can right wrongs only in wild and lawless ways—a sort of Judge Lynch on a throne.

3. Many a man is as proud of his consistency, of always holding one opinion and doing one way, as the Medes and Persians were of the unchangeability of their laws, and often with as little reason and as poor results. Where it is a mere pride of self-will such are as likely as Darius to be hoodwinked and led by influences of which they do not know the source or aim.

4. In those two judgment-halls of Darius and of Pilate we see how the noblest may come into the grasp of the basest, and may seem to drift helplessly to destruction. In the evolution of the work of redemption it seems to be a law that there can be no great victory for God's cause without the occurrence of such events. Wickedness is generally able to accomplish the temporary defeat of any good cause.

5. God's real champion—every true man—sooner or later comes forth triumphant. Christ was thrust into the grave, but at the very gates of hell triumphantly proclaimed his kingdom, shut with his own hand the mouths of its hungry lions so that they touched not even his flesh, and summoned from glory an angel to

open for him the way back to earth. On a lower plane so it was with Daniel, and is with every man who takes unto him the whole armor of God. Nor shall we have long to stay in the lions' den when the glory of God requires an early release. " Weeping " then " may endure for a night, but joy cometh in the morning." Thus Job found it ; thus did Paul also at first, so that he exultantly wrote : " The Lord stood with me, and strengthened me ; that by me the preaching might be fully known, and that all the Gentiles might hear : and I was delivered out of the mouth of the lion " (2 Tim. iv, 17). Yet even while writing this he knew it would not be so always, and that the hour of his departure was at hand (2 Tim. iv, 6). Sometimes the " hour and the power of darkness " are longer, as many a martyr witnesses before the throne (Rev. vi, 9-11). Yet "deliverance will come " for them, and for all who " do good and keep right on " (Rev. xix, 1, 2).

6. It seems very plain that living harmless and unaggressive lives does not secure men against getting into trouble on account of the service of God. While Daniel's life perpetually rebuked the corruption prevalent around him, there is no record or probability that he was in any active sense a missionary of the true religion. That was not a missionary dispensation, and partly for that reason, probably, God had great difficulty some three hundred years earlier in getting Jonah to go on an errand of that kind. Yet the hour of conflict and trial did not fail to come, and in some form will come to us

all. If we have deliberately evaded the cross and sought a path of ease we will go down in the great conflict of our lives. But if, like Daniel, we have dedicated soul and body to high principle and the service of God, then in that dread hour it will be ours, "having done all," to "stand," and at the great day of deliverance the report will be, There is "no manner of hurt found upon him," "no spot nor wrinkle, nor any such thing," "because he trusted in his God."

JOHN P. OTIS.

XIII.*

MESSIAH'S REIGN.

Psa. lxxii, 1-19.

GOLDEN TEXT.—All kings shall fall down before him; all nations shall serve him. Psa. lxxii, 11.

THE place of this Psalm in Jewish history is probably where David delivers up the kingdom to Solomon. (See 1 Chron. xxviii, xxix.) It was designed as a sort of Church prayer on behalf of the new king. But as the prophets prophesied larger and fuller than they knew, so the singer sang a more exalted strain than he was always conscious of.

Delitzsch tells us that the Old Testament view of the Redeemer of the world unfolds itself something like this: The Old Testament in relation to the New is as night to day. In that night there appeared two stars of promise. The one describes its path from above downward; it is the promise of Jehovah who is about to come. The other describes its path from below upward; it is the hope which rests upon the seed of David. These two stars meet at last. They blend into one. The night waneth and the day appears. The one star is Jehovah and the Son of David, the Redeemer and the King of Israel—in one word, the God-man, Jesus Christ.

Looking at this Psalm more closely, what do we find

---

* No homily is given for Lesson XII, which is a review.

to be the traits of the God-man, according to Hebrew thought at this period of the world's spiritual enlightenment?

1. *That his judgment shall be in righteousness* (vers. 1-5). This is the very first thing that is prayed for in the very first line: Give thy judgments and thy righteousness, O God; while the second verse asserts that in righteousness will be his judgments, and to that extent it will be as if it sprang forth from the very hills and mountains.

How is it that among the great mass of people who have little money and less influence with people in high places there is not only a growing feeling, but also a settled conviction, that there is no justice to be obtained in the courts? We hear this bitterly asserted almost every week, and sometimes see it strikingly illustrated, as in the case of the Mafia trial in New Orleans, where the best citizens arose and deliberately put eleven of the guilty wretches to death. What is the trouble? It is because too many of our judges neither fear God nor regard man, but do have an eye to financial increase and legal political preferment.

The New York press asks over and over again when one of the ward politicians, who is also the proprietor of some of the worst drinking dens and brothels, is promoted, as a reward, to a judgeship, " What man expects that he can get justice done in the New York courts?" These men have absolutely no knowledge of the law; some of them could with difficulty sign their names to a legal document, or even read it; and, besides, all lack any thing like good common sense and every-day honesty. How into these dingy halls, misnamed courts of justice, should come the righteousness of the Messiah, until righteousness should seem to spring forth from bar and bench as in poetic and prophetic vision it rose from the little hill and the great mountain ! Thus the poorest of the poor and the children of the needy could come with confidence, knowing that their oppressors should be broken in pieces. And the respect that is now rightfully withheld from judge and juror would be given as long as the sun and moon endure, while poor, blinded, cheated Justice would hold her scales with a new grace because clothed anew with righteousness.

2. *In the second place we learn that his presence shall be reviving* (vers. 6, 7). As we write there is a spring drought over the land, immense forest fires are raging in Michigan and Pennsylvania, and smaller fires at a thousand different places in almost every State. The morning paper tells us that any two of the dozen counties filled with fire in Michigan are as large as the whole State of Rhode Island, while in Pennsylvania the fires in the mountains are beyond all human control, and nothing but a rain-fall can stop their havoc.

Is not this an opportune illustration of the withering, consuming power of sin ? Have we not seen the withered, stunted growth of humanity—withered and stunted because of a faulty and partial manifestation of Christ, as in Catholicism, and from that all the way down to rankest and rawest heathenism? Have we not seen how error, as a wild-fire, will sweep through a community, leaving blackened and ruined homes and lives? There is scarcely a town in the nation which has not been, or is not now being, burned over by spiritualism or liberalism. These are as bad while they last as the fire of the rum-shop. Just now in our town spiritualism has made bankrupt business men, ruined the reputation and characters of church members, separated husbands and wives, and sent at least one victim into the insane asylum. We have seen how a fire of demoralization will sweep through the young men of a community until the streets are filled with those who were once the pride of the town, but who are now so withered and scorched that none who know them will trust or employ them.

What is needed? Is it not the presence of Him who will come down upon these young and growing lives like the spring rain upon the tender plant, and an outpouring of the Messianic Spirit that will drench these fiery evils which leave only blackened ruin behind them, like a three days' rain upon these burning counties? As the growing plant cannot thrive without rain, so neither can men flourish, nor can there be an abundance of peace without the reign of Christ upon the earth.

3. *We still further see that his dominion shall be universal* (vers. 8–11). Here we strike a glorious note. Or, if this Psalm were compared to a magnificent arch, these verses would constitute the key-stone or turn of the arch as it swings down to its other buttress. Why

could not the teacher illustrate it to the scholar this way: with its seven verses on one side and seven on the other, calling the eighteenth and nineteenth the doxology, as they really are. Then how this mighty arch lifts itself high above the sluggish and factory-polluted river, with its slime and reptiles! Is this a fact or only a poetic license, that the great river of humanity is to flow under the Messiah, as the river, with all its burden of commerce, pleasure, and profits, flows under the bridge which spans it? How little likely it appeared when spoken! Israel, though prosperous, was a small nation among the great nations of the earth. How less likely after one thousand years of wrong culminating in the crucifixion of the God-man! What of its likelihood to-day? But that is not the question. What is the plain teaching of the prophecy? Let us take it for exact truth, though in poetic form, and then under greatest defeat, as well as in grandest victory, in darkest night as in brightest day, there will be the sure, if not swift, word of success.

4. *In the fourth place we are taught that this relationship to the poor shall be gracious* (vers. 12–15). When times are prosperous, and men are making more money than they well know what to do with, then the poor are apt to suffer and the needy to be oppressed. This seems a strange assertion to make, yet we believe history bears us out in it. With this thought turn and read anew the Book of Amos. How hard it is for us to realize that when these prophecies were uttered Israel was in its greatest glory! Never before such an exten-

sive territory, never before such a boom in business or so much money made. Houses of ivory were erected, and beautiful grounds were made. Before this, when a king built for himself a house of ivory, it was thought of sufficient importance to be recorded in the religious annals of the nation; but now such houses were so common that they were not worth mentioning as separate facts. And yet, alas! never so many poor and oppressed. This has been true with other nations— ought we not to say with all nations? We see it in the giant corporations and trusts of modern times. The more millions that are combined, and the more millions that are made, the more the wages of the poor are reduced and the greater is the oppression of the needy.

But how glorious is the contrast in the growing prosperity of Messiah's kingdom! "To whom will I look?" says Jehovah. "To the man of a humble spirit." "Whose cry will I hear?" "The cry of him whose wages are kept back by fraud." Money and blood—the ten per cent. cut-down—both alike cry unto God. But from the oppressor shall the Messiah redeem their souls from deceit and violence, and make even the poor rich with the gold of Sheba, and richer still in spiritual blessings.

5. *Finally we learn that his growth shall be marvelous and his kingship without end* (vers. 16, 17). Rapidity of growth and permanency are incompatible. Jonah's gourd may grow up in a night, but it will wither away in a day. It may tower high enough for a man to find cool shadows from the heat of a burning sun, but

a worm can gnaw its life away, and lay it low. The Knownothing movement, the Knights of Labor, and the Alliance may assume immense proportions in a twelvemonth. Strange sects and doctrines and heresies by the thousand threaten for a little season to annihilate all existing forms of religious belief, but the wind of divine thought passeth over them and they are gone, and the places that knew them shall know them no more forever. What unwise observers are those persons who are captured by the rush and glamour of the Theosophists, or Christian "science," or spiritualism, or exaggerated " faith cures," or any thing else that has not been of the substantial and legitimate growth of the divine seed! This growth has on the whole been comparatively slow and regular. It is the fungus of Christianity which has been rapid in growth, as in the days of Constantine, and not only useless, but offensive. But here is a plant of two thousand years of historic growth, under adverse circumstances, in closest and keenest competition. Shall we not expect it to continue? The figure of its marvelous development is beautiful and strong. On the one side shall the growth be to the verdure line on the mountains, and on the other men shall blossom out of this city and out of that city as the herbs from the bosom of the earth. How rapid, strong, and beautiful should be the increase of the Church of Christ! Where is the grievous something which stands in the way of the swift realization of this prophecy? In some sections it requires close figuring to prove that the increase is commensurate with the population; in others, the advance has been satisfactory, considering the hinderance; while in a third, the increase has been more than could be harvested. How glorious the news which comes from India! The handful of seed sown there is yielding such a harvest that all who might be baptized into the Christian faith cannot be trained and built up in Christ for lack of men and means. One presiding elder, Rev. Hasan Raza Khan, is supporting five scholars, at a cost of twelve dollars a month, out of his own salary, which is only fifteen dollars a month. That leaves a small margin for living. In the short space of two months he baptized three hundred and twelve converts, and says that before the close of the year he might just as well make it four thousand, but dare not baptize them faster than he can train and educate them for Christ. "These people," he writes, "become Christians from the heart." Dr. Scott, of North India, declares that " ten thousand heathen could be gathered in this year, if we had the men and the means for so great a work." Bishop Thoburn says: "This is much too low; twenty thousand could be baptized, if we were able to teach them." Does it not seem as if the singer's song were being most wonderfully fulfilled just now in many of our mission stations?

6. *The conclusion or doxology of the Psalm* (vers. 18, 19). First, let us remind ourselves in a sentence of its teaching. It is of the Messiah, of his character and reign. He shall be righteous in judgment, reviving in his influence, universal in his dominion, gracious to the

poor and needy, marvelous in growth, and eternal in his kingship. Therefore, " Blessed be the Lord God, the God of Israel, who alone doeth wondrous things. And blessed be his glorious name forever: and let the whole earth be filled with his glory. Amen, and amen."

We have here a doxology to be sung. And let the people sing and shout over the victories past, and believe in the victories to come. But the best "Amen" that any can give to this Messianic Psalm of glorious promise is a financial one. Here the amen is doubled. It is "Amen, *and* AMEN." So should it be with a great many men's subscriptions to the cause of the world's evangelization, at home and abroad.

"The prayers of David the son of Jesse are ended." Thus will end, sooner or later, the works and prayers of all as individuals; therefore ought we to work and pray the more earnestly while the day lasts. But may the zeal of God's united hosts never cease until this Psalm of calm conquest and universal victory shall be realized through the whole world. Amen, and amen!

W. G. RICHARDSON.

THIRD QUARTER.

I.
THE ASCENSION OF CHRIST.

Acts i, 1-12.

GOLDEN TEXT.—When he had spoken these things, while they beheld, he was taken up; and a cloud received him out of their sight. Acts i, 9.

THE visible passing of the Son of man from earth to heaven is one of the "hinge-events" of his life. On that event turns the claim of his character and mission.

It is nowhere revealed with what acclamations he was received in the heavens. But whatever the joy, the influence of his ascension on the saints on the earth has been to lead them, like the men of Galilee who saw him taken up from them, to worship him. Thenceforth he was the God-Man.

1. *The Fact.* Seneca said: "The ascent from earth to heaven is not easy." But Seneca was an atheist, if we may believe his adversaries. The atheist will not receive the witness of men. And Jesus said: "How shall ye believe if I tell you of heavenly things?"

The difficulties concerning supernaturalism are all difficulties of disbelief. To the mind of the believer there appears nothing that is difficult to Jesus in his miracles. The disbeliever rejects miracles because he thinks them to be impossible. His disbelief is a form of atheism. Given God in his world, and nothing is more natural than supernaturalism.

The ascension of Jesus, like the resurrection or birth of Jesus, was only natural supernaturalism. It "was a necessary consequence of the resurrection," as it was the consummation of the series of his redemptive miracles. It was natural with him ; it would have been unnatural with his disciples.

The time, the place, the nature, and the witnesses of the ascension all corroborate the supernatural claim. In the way most natural to human experience they furnish indisputable proof that the final departure of Jesus was not illusory, but simply as the disciples represented it to be.

The time was opportune. "After having lived awhile on earth ; after having offered his body as a sacrifice for sin ; after having been raised from the dead ; after having shown himself alive to his disciples by many infallible proofs, *then* he led them out as far as Bethany, and in the presence of the whole Church then collected together he was taken up into heaven."

Equally interesting, fitting, and convincing was the locality of the ascension. Approaching Jerusalem from the Mediterranean Sea along the Joppa road, a low gray ridge can be seen beyond the city, scarcely overtopping the massive castle of David and the higher buildings of the holy hill. It falls away toward the right, revealing the pale blue mountains of Moab in the distant background. This low ridge beyond Jerusalem is the Mount of Olives, or Mount Olivet, as it is also called.

The present depressed and desolate state of the

country indicates no such benignant presence of the supernatural as blessed the home of Mary and Martha. Where now there stand a few olive-trees, and the long ridge is barely sprinkled with fig-trees, other taller trees gave a rich verdure to the holy highlands. In the time of Ezra the people went forth unto the mount to fetch for the feast of tabernacles " pine branches and myrtle branches and palm branches and branches of thick trees." The "mountain before the city" was the public park for the people of Jerusalem. " It was their open ground for pleasure, for worship, for any purpose that it might serve."

But it was not the scenic exhibition of Olivet so much as the sacred associations which befitted the place for this crowning incident of its history.

David, before the temple was built, was wont to worship at the top of the mount. And, as if by painful contrast, he climbed up the same mountain on his flight from Jerusalem at the news of Absalom's revolt ; David fled from his son, Jesus ascended to his Father.

It was over this mountain Jesus made his triumphant entry into the holy city. At another time, here he, when he beheld the city, wept over it. It was from a commanding point on the western side of the mountain that he predicted the final overthrow of the temple. Again, after the institution of the supper, "when they had sung a hymn," he led his disciples " over the brook Cedron," " out into the Mount of Olives" to a garden called Gethsemane.

Moreover, it was the home of Jesus when he was at Jerusalem. There is something beautiful in the tender and pathetic reference to his associations there—" He led them out as far as to Bethany."

The nature of the ascension is evidence of the fact of the ascension. Jesus simply arose from the earth to go into the heavens. He had brought his body from the grave, and it belonged no more with corruptible things. It was not subject to the conditions or limitations of the earth. To go away was all that remained to be done. There was nowhere else to go but into the heavens.

The witnesses of the ascension were not deceived, and could not be deceivers. They were the friends of Jesus.

It accorded with their faith to expect that, like Enoch and Elijah, he should be caught up in the air. There is nothing in the narrative to express either their surprise or their fear. When he had admonished them and instructed them and blessed them they only looked steadfastly toward heaven as he went up.

They had forsaken him and fled when he was taken to his trial. But they went with him cheerfully and with great expectations now. They were overcome with their sorrow when he was crucified. But now they returned to Jerusalem with great joy.

The angels who had announced his birth and proclaimed his resurrection were present to confirm his ascension.

Saul, when he had fallen in his way to Damascus,

heard a voice from heaven saying: "I am Jesus whom thou persecutest."

Stephen, when permitted to answer to the accusation of blasphemy in his apology, uttered in the very article of death, said: "Behold, I see the heavens opened, and the Son of man standing on the right hand of God." And among his last words were: "Lord Jesus, receive my spirit."

And John, from the isle of Patmos, saw in the midst of the seven golden candle-sticks the Son of man, whom he heard saying: "I am the first and the last: I am he that liveth, and was dead; and, behold, I am alive for evermore, Amen; and have the keys of hell and of death."

So also the Holy Ghost, whom God hath sent, is a witness. His presence in the hearts of men is the greatest witness. For, every-where present, he fulfills the prophecy of Jesus: "He shall testify of me." If Jesus had not ascended the Holy Spirit would not be here.

2. *The Doctrine.* The ascension of Jesus was essential to the plan and work of redemption. There could be nothing visionary about it; every thing must be matter-of-fact.

It was necessary to relate again the work which Jesus had come to do in the earth with the world from whence he came. He had accomplished a virtual redemption. He was thenceforth to make it actual. He willed that his disciples should be with him where he was. He had finished his work here; but he must "go and prepare a place for " them, " come again," and " receive " them unto himself. It was thus he brought immortality to light.

It was prophesied that he would ascend on high, lead captivity captive, and receive gifts for men. He himself had foretold that he should go away. The ascension was the fulfillment of prophecy and the verification of his own words.

Without the ascension the world could not have understood him. It was the explanation of his character and work on the earth.

Christianity was triumphant at the ascension. Sin was mastered, death was dead, and man was free.

In the ascension of Jesus there was given to all believers the surety of their ascension. As Frederick Denison Maurice has said : " It was the great witness and demonstration to them that they were spirits having bodies, that they were not bodies into which a certain ethereal particle called spirits was infused." They were to be like Jesus.

The heavens are now the pledge of another advent of the Son of man. The body of Jesus somewhere gives locality to the presence of Jesus. His ascension is presumptive evidence that he is with the Father. His Church has a right to claim him as the ascended Lord who shall come again.

3. *The Results.* There were both direct and indirect results of the ascension. And they were so related and intervolved as to connect it with the dispensation and

entire administration of the Holy Spirit. The ascension was the dividing point between the Gospel and the apostolic histories. It concluded the one and introduced the other.

Jesus had lived a Jewish peasant, enduring the humiliations of poverty, betrayal, and all the sufferings consequent to peril, persecution, and death. But in the very act of separation from his disciples these relations and contingencies are all changed. The peasant becomes a prince. He is given a name which is above every name. He is returned to the honors which he had with the Father before the world was.

The psalmist tells us, "He received gifts for men, yea, for the rebellious also, that the Lord God might dwell among them." He obtained a more excellent ministry, and at once became the mediator of the New Testament. The spirit of prophecy discerns what was transacted above the cloud ; the apostles saw what took place this side of it.

The last act of Jesus as he ascended was to lift up his hands and bless. In the very sight of Gethsemane and Calvary, "with malice toward none and charity for all," he went away blessing the cruel world which had received him not, and dispensing gifts not to his friends only, but to the rebellious also.

Of the great gift, in which all other gifts are included—the gift of the Holy Ghost which came on all men—we are all witnesses and partakers.

When Jesus ascended he gave instruction. His words became the ministry of his disciples, who were to witness to the uttermost part of the earth. "The ages to come were now privileged to know him better than those to whom he spoke."

To the faithful work of the ministry, for the perfecting of the saints, for the edifying of the body of Christ, he gave some apostles and some prophets and some evangelists and some pastors and teachers.

The indirect influences of the ascension have been and are multifarious as the intellections and emotions of men. With the ascension the personal element of the Christ who had gone about doing good was taken from the earth, and it no longer excited malefactors to persecute him. Jesus gained honors soon in the city which had crucified him, and by the Roman government he was made the King of kings.

His disciples were exalted with him. They were raised "into union and fellowship with a higher nature." They were "continually looking up to him, in weakness and dependence leaning upon him," seeking those things which were above. His exaltation had become the "pattern-event" of all their lives. They now "knew a man who knew God," and was God.

The Father and the heavenly world were brought nearer and made dearer to the children of men. It is now the aspiration of all Christians to explore with the Son of man the heavenly spaces. The expectation grows apace that he will come again. Faith even is impatient that he come quickly. "Amen. Even so, come, Lord Jesus." J. W. HAMILTON.

II.

THE DESCENT OF THE SPIRIT.

Acts ii, 1-12.

GOLDEN TEXT.—When he, the Spirit of truth, is come, he will guide you into all truth. John xvi. 13.

THE task which the ascending Lord had committed to the infant Church at the close of his forty days' sojourn in their midst was one of extreme difficulty and discouraging magnitude. They were to preach a crucified, risen, and ascended Messiah throughout Judea, Samaria, and to the uttermost parts of the earth. Even when Jesus was still with them, and was recognized as a miracle-worker and an incomparable teacher, it had taxed their fortitude to follow him through these provinces; but what would it be to retrace their steps without their Master and preach his Messiahship, now that he had disappeared from the earth? They were, indeed, to testify that he had risen from the dead; but who would believe their report? Would the priests, who, as Sadducees, denied the existence of angel and spirit? Would the Pharisees? Would they not rather cite the testimony of the soldiers, who affirmed that his disciples stole their Master's body by night? And could they gain the ear of the multitude? Did the masses hold any less firmly than ever that the true Messiah must be a visible leader

10*

and commander who would break in pieces the rod of their political oppressors? Would not the preaching of a vanished Messiah be to the Jewish people a stumbling-block? And could they ever carry to the ends of the earth a message which had been rejected at home? Would not the cross prove a stumbling-block to the Jews of the dispersion also? And if they could so far overcome their aversion to the Gentiles as to preach to them, would not they, too, consider the doctrine of a risen Messiah as foolishness? The disciples had, indeed, hoped that Jesus would redeem Israel; but what outlook had his cause now but certain and speedy oblivion; what prospect had they, if they should obey his last command, but prison and death? Were loyal souls ever brought into a more trying position?

Two final utterances of Jesus, however, somewhat relieved the rigor of the situation. The one was a command, the other a promise. They were not to begin forthwith the work which would doubtless sooner or later bring them before the Sanhedrin and Gentile tribunals. They were to tarry in Jerusalem. This pause which was to cover several days was doubly welcome—it put off the evil day and afforded opportunity for consultation, meditation, and prayer. The promise was that at the end of the interval they should receive power from on high. Vague as may have been their notions concerning this power and the mode of its impartation, yet the definite assurance that it should soon be given them was peculiarly comforting. They were not to begin their arduous experiment without a new equipment of strength.

We note five features in the gift of power which the exalted Lord sent upon his waiting Church.

1. *The Gift was Supernatural.* The sound from heaven was as loud as that of whirlwind or cyclone, but it was not a sound produced by air set in motion. The tongues of fire shone and glided like flame, but were not flame. The disciples spoke with tongues, but there was something behind their speaking which did not belong to their personality. The effect produced upon the multitude could not be explained by ordinary natural causes. A supernatural factor was present. The mighty wind rushing down from heaven was the outward token of a personal energy immeasurably greater than any which belongs to man, an energy coming down from God to man. The luminous flame about their foreheads, like the Shekinah above the mercy-seat, was an unmistakable sign of the supernatural presence of the living God.

The supernatural force began at once to work within them. The promise of the Golden Text was fulfilled, and they were led into new truth. The incoming Spirit intensified and illuminated their perceptions, as an increase of oxygen brightens the flame of the lime-light. Peter's address, which immediately follows, shows how the Spirit clarified their mental vision. They understood the Gospel now as never before. They saw that their Master could never have become, as they had hoped he would, a merely political deliverer of Israel ; but that he had been exalted to the right hand of God to be the Christ and Lord of the whole world. They comprehended now the mysterious title which John the Baptist had given him when he spoke of him as the Lamb of God. At last they could appreciate the necessity and glory of the death, resurrection, and ascension of Israel's Messiah. They could now enthusiastically preach his Messiahship in Judea and Samaria and to the uttermost parts of the earth. No wonder the multitude heard them proclaiming the wonders of divine grace. No wonder that they straightway resolved that none of their number should suffer from want, and proceeded to divide their goods No wonder that all fear of persecution forsook them, and suffering for the divine Christ was regarded in the light of privilege. New wisdom, new love, and new will-power had been given them from the Spirit of God. The residue of the Book of the Acts is taken up with the sequel of this supernatural gift, and explains how Christianity spread from Jerusalem to Rome.

Supernatural aid is as necessary to the modern as it was to the apostolic Church. Intelligence, wealth, numbers, organization, have value as consecrated instrumentalities, but the indwelling and sanctifying Spirit is the life-breath of the Church.

Above every Christian congregation must tower the pillar of fire ; over every pulpit the Holy Dove must hover ; in every religious gathering the power of the invisible One must be felt ; in every closet of prayer a burning bush must be discovered. Without the abiding presence of the Holy Spirit Christian life is impossible.

2. *The Gift was Providential.* Unwittingly, but in God's providence, messengers had been brought to Jerusalem from the uttermost parts of the earth to hear the disciples' testimony concerning Jesus. They were a selected class. They were devout men, who in spite of heathen influences at home, and the perils and cost of travel, had returned to worship at the seat of their ancestral religion. Doubtless they had already borne testimony to the faith of Israel before their heathen neighbors by their patient endurance of persecution and their proselyting zeal. By their life-long acquaintance with the languages and customs of their Gentile neighbors, they were providentially fitted to carry the Gospel to them, in case they themselves should become convinced of its divine authority. It is easy to see, then, why Christ commanded his disciples to tarry in Jerusalem. These selected witnesses were to carry back the news of Pentecost and the new gospel message to hundreds of scattered Jewish communities; thus preparing the way for the twelve and for the apostle Paul.

God's providence always co-operates with his grace. In the solitary desert a Philip appears for the instruction of the eunuch; a Peter is detained in a neighboring city to open the gate of heaven to a Cornelius; and every Damascus has an Ananias waiting to unseal the blinded eyes of a converted Saul.

It is therefore never in vain to labor in the Lord,

whether in season or out of season. Our heavenly Father not only vouchsafes a supernatural gift to work within, but also sets at work providential forces to cooperate without.

3. *The Gift Recognized the Individuality of the Recipients.* The tongues of fire were divided and sat upon each of the one hundred and twenty. It was not enough that Peter, great as he was, should be equipped for work; James and John also must be similarly and separately qualified. And not the pillar apostles only, but the other nine also required the supernatural gift. Nor were the twelve only, in God's plan, to be illumined and girded; the five-score and eight others needed and claimed the blessing. All of God's people were to prophesy.

Jesus always put emphasis on the experience of the person, whether he talked with a ruler like Nicodemus, or with the sinful woman of Samaria. Paul made every thing hinge on personal faith in Christ. Protestantism has restored to the individual Christian his personal access and immediate responsibility to Almighty God. Methodism has taught every Christian to expect the direct testimony of the Holy Spirit to his own salvation, and to watch with awe and gratitude the ways of God with his own soul.

The miracle of Pentecost shows that the supernatural gift is necessary to the completeness of the human soul. On the divine side, as on the human, it is not good for man to be alone. His nature is as truly organized for a supernatural element as is the eye for the light of day.

Made in the image of God, he has the thoughts, questions, and aspirations of one who is but little lower than the angels. He cannot satisfy himself with effects; he inquires into causes. He demands that he be led to the pillars on which the whole fabric of creation rests. Unconsciously he walks about the world with the demeanor of a proprietor. He was obviously made from the outset to live and move and have his being in God. No man can realize his true self until, like the one hundred and twenty, he is filled with the Holy Ghost and divine power.

4. *The Gift Emphasized the Necessity of Unity.* It was when all were with one accord in one place that the Spirit descended. While their common dangers and common joys drew these disciples together, yet a unity like theirs is the normal condition of the Church in all ages. Christ has not only willed that every believer should be supernaturally joined to himself, but also that he should be mystically united to the Church which is his body. This was the burden of his great passover prayer. This also is the cardinal thought of Paul's Epistle to the Ephesians. No Christian can be complete in himself. He is, as Peter taught, a living stone in a spiritual temple, giving and receiving strength and beauty. The individual needs the Church, and the Church needs the individual. This age of democracy ought to see such a truth more clearly than any preceding one.

The power of the Holy Ghost will not descend upon a divided Church. It is the whole and homogeneous lens that brings the distant heavens near, and not its shattered fragments. The chosen instrument for the conquest of the world is a Church as closely knit together as were the one hundred and twenty when the Holy Ghost fell upon them. The Macedonian phalanx became the means with which Alexander humbled the East. A united Church filled with the Holy Ghost will yet humble East and West.

5. *The Gift was the Reward of their Faith.* The disciples waited for the supernatural gift which had been promised. They did not know when it would come, what it would be, nor how it would fit them for their forbidding task, but they did know who had promised the gift to them. Jesus had told them that in their Galilean mission diseases and evil spirits would be subject to them; and they found it so. He had bidden Jairus, the widow of Nain, and Martha to be of good cheer concerning their dead; and in very deed their dead came to life. He had uttered the astounding prophecy that he himself should be killed, and should rise the third day; and it had been so. When, therefore, he said that after the lapse of not many days power should come upon them, we see that they could feel sure this would come to pass. As a supernatural person he had supernatural knowledge and power; hence his promise of a supernatural gift could not be thought misleading. That was faith. Faith reasons. It makes the known reveal the unknown. Like an astronomer who requires only three clear observations to compute the mightiest

celestial orbit, faith discovers in religious experience principles which encompass the throne of God.

To do Christ's will without supernatural aid is as impossible now as it was in the days of the apostles. Spiritual things are still spiritually discerned ; the world is still unreconciled to God ; the carnal mind still at enmity with God ; and principalities and powers are still to be wrestled with. The armor of God and the sword of the Spirit are not antiquated. We can never go to our Judeas and Samarias without power from on high.

Faith was the condition of supernatural power—that should be laid to heart. Faith is the metal point which draws down the celestial fire. Faith discovers in what God has already been yet greater possibilities of grace and power.

MARCUS D. BUELL.

III.

THE FIRST CHRISTIAN CHURCH.

Acts ii, 37-47.

GOLDEN TEXT.—The Lord added to the church daily such as should be saved. Acts ii, 47.

THIS is fascinating history. It is the account of the first sermon and first day of the Christian Church. The occasion was exciting. Peter had denied the charge of intoxication by making a specific counter-charge. His sermon was a good one, well preached. It was true, scriptural, brave, pointed. It was specific, not general. Peter spoke the truth in love; tenderness tempered his boldness; the Holy Ghost accompanied the preaching; the hearing was pentecostal. That is quite as essential as pentecostal preaching. The people listened; the Holy Ghost made effective the word. The people "were pricked in their heart." It was a sharp pain such as remorse causes. They asked a pointed personal question. There were no inquiries as to the sermon. The question was, "What shall we do?" The people even call these supposed drunkards by a new name—"brethren." In the Christian system there is always something after conviction. Christianity has a message after the doctrine that men are sinners. Peter was not a trained theologian, but he knew what to tell those convicted inquirers. Some great preachers are helpless in an inquiry-room. Peter's sermon had been powerful. His instruction was very plain: "Repent, change your attitude to Jesus Christ, turn about; be baptized, not one of you for the entire party, but every one of you." Does baptism save? Not at all. Christ saves. Baptism is the sign of the faith that takes Christ to be the Saviour from sin just repented of. The repentant, believing man should be baptized.

Christianity has a promise to offer. The Holy Ghost has descended upon Peter. Now, upon the authority of the word, which they have rejected in the case of Jesus, he promises this gift to these penitent murderers, to their posterity, and to their scattered brethren. He was not thinking of the Gentiles. The promise was larger than he knew.

Peter was an exhorter. The people were ready to move. They might not be ready to-morrow. The personal appeal is made on the spot: "Save yourselves." They did. As Peter saw the multitudes coming he must have remembered the early morning when he drew in a full net and heard the promise, "From henceforth thou shalt catch men." Arnot makes this beautiful comment on verse 41:

"In order to understand how they received the word 'gladly,' we must remember that they had been 'pricked to the heart.' They had been wounded, and now the healing is grateful. A little religion is a painful thing, but more religion takes the pain away. The word is both a hammer to break the rock and a balm to heal the broken heart. Its first effect is to convince a sinner that he is lost; its next, to make him rejoice in his Saviour."

How were those three thousand baptized? Nobody knows certainly. President Woolsey says that the absence of helpers and conveniences, if not of water, must have prevented the immersion of the entire body. Canon Cook says there was a great scarcity of water, and that the twelve must have baptized two hundred and fifty each—an impossibility.

On the other hand, a Baptist authority declares that there were some of the seventy present, and plenty of water in and about Jerusalem. Chrysostom and his presbyters baptized by immersion about three thousand persons in a single day in the year 404. It will be easy to waste the hour discussing this old question. They were baptized and added to the Church. Methodism insists upon the thing—especially upon the spirit—and allows the largest liberty as to method. Christ commands baptism. He does not prescribe the amount of water or method of application.

The great ingathering is sometimes pointed to as a sign that those were better days than these. The remark sometimes takes the form of a sneer. "Under Peter's one sermon three thousand were converted; under three thousand sermons now one is converted." Readers of Paul's sermon at Mars' Hill might make the sneer against Paul. It did not have any such result. "Some mocked; but others said, We will hear thee again," and a limited number—only two of them being named—believed. The truth is that the sneer is very unfair. Every circumstance attending Pentecost was exceptional. The gift of tongues might as wisely be looked for every time as the conversion of such a multitude.

These converts were well treated. They were "babes in Christ." They needed instruction and care. So, as Meyer says, "They were perseveringly devoted to the instruction of the apostles—constantly intent upon having themselves instructed by the apostles." New converts must not be left to themselves. Teaching follows baptism and conversion. Training in the Scriptures and the doctrines and principles of the kingdom is the privilege of a new convert. The early Church set the modern Church a good example in this regard. Many of these new converts lived in other towns. They were to be missionaries. This was the time of their preparation and training. Baptized, forgiven, and full of the Holy Ghost as they were, they still needed this season of study, prayer, and fellowship with the older Christians. He who is to teach must first be taught. When these were scattered abroad they had a message.

The whole thing was so unusual, so striking, so manifestly marked by the presence of the supernatural, that fear came upon the multitudes.

The fear does not seem to have come upon the believers. A most astonishing display of supernatural power had taken place. Men in sin are afraid of supernatural displays. Adam was afraid of God after his fall.

The shepherds were frightened when the angels sang. Sin causes fear. Miracles make evil men tremble at the thought that God is present. The perfect man had no fear in the presence of a supernatural display. Christ never was afraid. The perfect relation will be free from fear. Read what John says about it (1 John iv, 18).

What about this so-called communism in the early Church? What was it in nature and extent? The passage describing the community of goods is critical. Social reformers, not always Christian, point to this as the ideal state from which the Church has wandered. For not practicing this custom the Church has sometimes been roundly abused as being unapostolic and unchristian. Let us see what we may reasonably infer from this incident. Chapter iv, 32-37, and v, 1-11, must be read in connection with the lesson. These points appear upon investigation:

1. *The arrangement was purely voluntary.* What any man put in was still his. The sin of Ananias was not that he had kept back a portion of his estate by fraud, but that he lied about it. It was still in his power after the sale as before. The community of property flowed out of the new spiritual life. (See Acts iv, 32-37.)

" In point of fact, their experiment was simply the assertion of the right of every man to do as he chooses with his own; and they chose to live together and help each other. It was a fraternal stock company for mutual aid and protection. No man was bound to come into

into it unless he wished ; but if he did come in, he was bound to act honestly."

2. *It was a spiritual result, and not a social experiment.* It cannot be explained except on the spiritual basis. It must be studied in its true setting. Writers have tried to show that it was borrowed from a custom of the Essenes. Others have attempted to establish a connection between this and Plato's ideal state. The practice of the Essenes would scarcely attract the notice of these people, while the ideal state of Plato included a community of wives.

The Brook Farm, " Utopia," and all kindred institutions have been social experiments. Bellamy's " Looking Backward " Society is allied with them. They have arisen for lack of the Holy Spirit. This sprung up spontaneously because of Pentecost. Says Lightfoot : " The reasonable explanation is that we have an independent attempt to realize the idea of brotherhood— an attempt which naturally suggested itself without any direct imitation."

3. *The community of goods seems to have been a community of use, not ownership.* Nobody said that aught that he possessed was his own. They were of one heart. They were perfectly united. The circumstances were peculiar. Many of the people were away from home. All had to be cared for. No one should suffer. So they put their possessions together—"pooled their issues," as we say—and all shared alike.

4. *The plan was local.* Jerusalem was the only city

where it was tried. No trace of it is to be found in any other church. It is not urged upon any other church, as an example to be followed. No other church adopted it. It evidently did not commend itself to other churches as a wise plan. The other churches took up collections just as now when a case of need was presented. (See 1 Cor xvi, 2; 2 Cor. ix, 6, 7.)

5. *It was temporary.* It lasted while the circumstances in which it arose continued. A great crowd of new converts—many of them away from home—were in training, applying themselves to the instruction of the apostles. When they scattered the community of goods apparently ceased. Exactly how long it lasted is not clear, but it evidently was not continued very long. Paul never inculcates it. He does not refer to it as an institution existing when he wrote his letters. All his allusions to the condition of the rich and poor can be easily understood by us.

6. *It did not relieve poverty.* It was not devised for that purpose. Many writers insist upon seeing a close connection between this incident and the subsequent poverty in Jerusalem. Thus Meyer: "And this community of goods at Jerusalem helps to explain the great and general poverty of that church. It is probable that the apostles were prevented by the very experience acquired in Jerusalem from advising or introducing it elsewhere."

Thus Gulliver: "Under such sublime inspirations it is easy to see that a communism, impossible to ordinary human nature, might temporarily flourish. But it is as easy to see that it would gradually settle to the level of ordinary motive, and would be subjected to the disturbances of inevitable inequalities in capacity and industry, as well as in piety. The Plymouth Pilgrims were, perhaps, the most single-minded men of modern times. Yet it was not till the community of lands and goods which obtained in the early years of their settlement gave place to farms in severalty, and to private property protected by law, that the annually recurring danger of absolute starvation in their colony disappeared. The lesson of such a history is, therefore, not solely the lesson of Christian consecration. It includes the utility and the sacredness of the personal control of property. It places before us the problem of combining the largest Christian benevolence with the strict maintenance of proprietary rights."

7. *It was not modern communism.* Says Gerok: "That Christian communism said, 'All that is mine is thine;' the unchristian communism of our day says, 'All that is thine is mine.' That holy community of goods proceeded from love to the poor; but that which is now proclaimed is the result of a hatred to the rich."

And Van Dyke: "Of late years the communistic doctrine has begun to present itself in another shape. It has laid aside the red cap and put on the white cravat. It invites serious and polite inquiry. It quotes Scripture and claims to be the friend, the near relative, of Christianity. So altered is its aspect that preachers of religion are discovering that it has good points, and patting it on the back somewhat timidly, as one might pat a converted wolf who had offered his services as watchdog. They are careful to disown any sympathy with the old unregenerate, bloody communism. Its method and its spirit were violent and unjustifiable. But, perhaps, after all, its fundamental principle was right. Perhaps our institution of private property contradicts the teachings of the Bible, and ought to be abolished, wholly or partially, to make room for something better and more truly Christian.

"There is a fundamental and absolute difference between the doctrine of the Bible and the doctrine of the communizer. For the Bible tells me that I must deal my bread to the hungry; while the communizer tells the hungry that he may take it for himself, and if he begins with bread there is no reason why he should draw the line at cake. The Bible teaches that envy is a sin; the communizer declares that it is the new virtue which is to regenerate society. The communizer maintains that every man who is born has a right to live; but the Bible says that if a man will not work neither shall he eat; and without eating life is difficult. The communizer holds up equality of condition as the ideal of Christianity; but Christ never mentions it. He tells us that we shall have the poor always with us, and charges us never to forget, despise, or neglect them. Christianity requires two things from every man that believes in it: first, to acquire his property by just and righteous means; and, secondly, to 'look not only on his own things, but also on the things of others.'"

And thus this first Church was characterized by pungent pentecostal preaching; acute, active hearing, hearty repentance and true faith; diligent, inquiring discipleship; apt apostolic teaching; true Christian fellowship, practical, voluntary, self-denying brotherhood; earnest praise; favor with the people; daily conversions and daily additions of the saved.

WILLIAM F. MCDOWELL.

IV.

THE LAME MAN HEALED.

Acts iii, 1-16.

GOLDEN TEXT.—And his name, through faith in his name, hath made this man strong. Acts iii, 16.

Two men—Peter and John—Christians, going together into the Jewish Temple to pray, and that just after the inspirations and ecstacies of Pentecost; preachers, yet penniless, though they had first chance at the bag in which all had just been cast in common—this is the opening picture of the lesson before us. Is it drawn true to nature? No, not to human nature, but it is true to the Christ nature.

1. *The Companions.* This first verse reveals, as by a flash-light, the spirit of these companions. Peter and John *together.* What antipodes! Peter, impulsive, bold, energetic, daring; John, meditative, timid, loving, trustful. What ground in nature for fellowship between them? Yet, like Luther and Melanchthon in the crisis of a later age, they were joined in the strength and beauty of a friendship in Christ that gave to each supplemental grace and energy. Of all the disciples, the Acts reveals them as closest together. It took the passion and resurrection-week experiences with Christ and Pentecost combined, to draw Peter and John into this unity of life and work.

"*Going up into the temple,*" though the vail had been rent and the lesson of the spirituality and universality of worship had been taught them! But were they not yet Jews? Was not this still the "house of prayer," the spot forever consecrated by their God when he said, "I have hallowed this place to put my name there forever?" Peter and John had reverence for sacred places—that reverence which is a mark of depth and spirituality in the religious life.

> "Their heart was full of awe
> And reverence for all sacred things;
> And brooding over form and law
> They saw the Spirit's wings."

These early disciples did not spurn religious custom, though it was a custom of a decadent Jewish Church. To their devout souls history and sacred associations meant something. Character that is strong has roots. These grow deep and take hold of institutions representing thought and life and history. Luther was loth to leave the old Catholic Church, Romanized and corrupt as it was. Wesley always clung to the Church of England. Superstition you may call this clinging to the venerable and historic. Well, if the choice is between irreverence and superstition, give me superstition. Irreverence weakens conscience and blunts the spiritual edge of character. Superstition, as the devout Neander has well said, often paves the way to faith. God's plan was not to obliterate Judaism at a stroke, but to transform it. The new corn of the kingdom only gradually burst and sloughed off the husk of Judaism, that venerable and sacred repository of divine truth. " Going up into the temple," then, is in the spirit of Christ.

"*At the hour of prayer*" went these devout men. But what need had they for prayer, just fresh from the open revelation and spiritual excitement of Pentecost? with hearts all ablaze with the sacred fire, and ears yet tingling with the sound " from heaven as of a rushing mighty wind?" By this act they teach that prayer is apostolic; that special seasons of illumination and sanctification are a special call to prayer. Though men may not need more fire, yet need they more grace. Religion means daily duty, not occasional ecstasy. Such illumination is the occasion of temptation—temptation for one thing, to spiritual pride and presumption. David was wise when in an hour of high visitation from the living God he prayed: Lord, keep thy servant from being presumptuous. " Suspect any inspiration that makes you contemptuous of ordinary religious duties." After your Pentecost be found " going up into the temple at the hour of prayer."

2. *The Cripple.* How often is the hour of prayer the hour of opportunity. It was so now, for they met "*A man, lame, at the door of the temple called Beautiful.*" He was carried to the proper place, this wizened cripple of forty years. The Church stands in Christ's stead. It is the place for the poor and lame and stricken ones to come. If they cannot come—not to be put to shame by those old-time Jews—let Christians carry them, not to some

clapboarded mission station, but "to the door of the temple called Beautiful." "The poor ye have always with you," should ever be true of the Church of Christ.

"*He asked an alms*, expecting to receive some *thing*." How like other poor mortals, weak of faith, asking for *things* when in the open palms of Omnipotence there is life and principalities and powers all for the asking. Yet still we ask for mere things of him who is "able to do exceeding abundantly above all that we ask or think, according to the *power that worketh in us.*"

What amazement strikes us when God, above our asking, gives us life and power instead of the mere things for which we pray.

3. *The Cure.* "*But Peter said.*" Did not stop to theorize, as once before at a door of this same Temple the disciples did in the presence of a *blind* beggar, apparently more interested in the theory of blindness and the problem of evil than in those sightless eyeballs glaring appealingly toward the Light of the world. Peter was more of a pastor now; a curate, with sympathy and love, whose touch of faith meant the cure of sin-stricken souls and bodies.

"*Silver and gold have I none.*" What! "All things in common," and the preacher with empty purse and silverless hand! It would seem that he would get his share. Surely, then, this apostolic communion was no "priest's trick; it was no attempt to enrich the apostolate at the expense of the Christian public." Penniless were these apostles, but not powerless. The day of poverty in the Church was the day of power. How often since has the opposite been only too true. The age of wealth in the Church—the age of weakness! There is deep historic truth as well as keen repartee in the reply of Thomas Aquinas to Pope Clement IV. When seated together as great quantities of gold and silver were being carried into the Vatican treasury, the pope proudly remarked: "You see the Church no longer has to say, 'Silver and gold have I none!'" "Yes," replied the saintly Aquinas, "and she can no longer say with Peter to the paralytic, 'In the name of Jesus Christ of Nazareth, rise up and walk!'"

"*Such as I have give I thee.*" This is the law of the Christian life—*give*. There is no exception. Every man has something. He has himself, a self not his own, but bought with a price for higher service. What the Master wants is not your "silver and gold" merely, he wants you. Your possessions are a mere incident that go with the purchase, as the strings thrown in with the bundle by the shopman.

"*Such as I have.*" This was only a hand, yet a hand with a heart in it and faith behind it. It was human to say, "Look up;" it was divine to stretch out a hand to "lift up." He stretched forth a hand of sympathy and power; a hand linked to a soul through which Omnipotence could flow as through the wire flash the power and heat of the electric fluid. Faith gave connection with the original plant of "all power given in heaven or on earth."

"*He took him by the hand.*" "We need the touch of

Christ's hand upon our literature," wrote Mrs. Browning. Yes, and more; we need the touch of Christ's hand upon humanity—poor, crippled, sin-paralyzed humanity—that men and women, "lifted up" in the name of Jesus, may leap up and walk and enter into the Temple praising God. This is the lesson for charity and mission work. Silver and gold are not enough. Hand and heart are needed. Gold may ease the body, but it cannot heal the broken heart and crippled soul. Personal touch can alone lift up and transform.

> "In vain ye fling alms at the rags that ye meet,
> While souls lie bleeding and crushed at your feet."

Go to them. Give them thy hand, these victims of heredity, often foredoomed to spiritual paralysis from their mother's womb. Is the Church to be, indeed, the "body of Christ?" Then let it be the feet of Christ going out into the highways and hedges to carry the lame ones in. Let it be the ears of Christ, responsive to every wail of distress. Let it be the eyes of Christ, looking with tearful tenderness on all. Let it be the hand of Christ, stretched forth to uplift, to heal, to redeem.

4. *The Crowd.* "*All the people saw him . . . were filled with wonder and amazement, . . . and ran together.*" You see the picture. It fairly breathes with life even on the printed page. It is from an eye-witness. What graphic touches in the description! The lame man— *born* lame—feels the thrill of life like electric fire sweeping along his nerves as he is "raised up." Faith, re-

sponsive to the word, makes for power. How strange and sudden it all is, as "immediately" his feet and his ankle-bones, so pulseless and dead, a limp and strengthless burden from birth, "received strength." Intoxicated with the new life, "leaping up, he stood," and, with unhesitating faith in his new-found strength, "he began to walk." And in grateful consecration of his renewed powers "he entered with them into the Temple." Not home to his kinsfolk did he go, nor to show himself on the crowded streets; but with the apostles he went into the Temple "praising God." He acts as people did at Pentecost, filled with new wine. Yes, the wine of life filled his body; the Spirit of God filled his soul.

The people ran and were beside themselves with amazement. There could be no doubt as to the man. Every body knew the cripple for all these weary years crouched at the door. No one could gainsay the cure wrought before their very eyes. Performed not for spectacular display, but in response to a need, the miracle was a demonstration. Men may answer argument and play with the forms of logic, but in the presence of miraculous love and mercy they are dumb as they see that "the lame walk, the blind see, and the poor have the Gospel preached unto them."

5. *The Preacher.* "*When Peter saw it he answered.*" Peter saw *it*—not the crowd, but his opportunity; he seized it; occupied it. It was one of those rare opportunities that come of providence to the preacher. And here we find Peter not only a pastor—a *curé* with the

THE LAME MAN HEALED.

healing touch; he is a preacher charged with an inspiration and power fresh from heaven. But what has happened? In the late gospel records we have a picture of the denying, lying Peter out in the night weeping bitterly. Now, here is the man with a message from God and a courage that is fairly divine. Who is this preacher? Can it be he who in this same city in weakness and cowardice denied his Lord whom he now defends? who shrank in fear and quailed in lying dread before a simple Jewish maid? If so, the messenger is himself a greater miracle of grace and power than the message or the cure.

The *lame man* is, indeed, healed. The greater miracle has been wrought on Peter. He, so lame and limp of soul, now stands forth in the very strength of God. It is the same Peter, but he has come by way of the empty tomb. It is the Peter who in the daybreak twilight by the sea met his Lord. It is Peter tested by the thrice "Lovest thou me?" Peter fresh from the baptism of Pentecost! Love hath transfigured him! The Lion of the tribe of Judah hath made him courageous! The angel of eloquence hath anointed his lips!

"The testimony of Jesus is the spirit of prophecy." Here is your prophet, the forth-teller of truth. Here is your model preacher. He first directs the eyes of the crowd away from himself: "Why fasten ye your eyes on us, as though by our own power or godliness we had made him walk?" He turns the "eyes of their understanding, being darkened," to the Name; to "His name;" the name that their very hands, perchance, wrote above the cross in fiendish spite and ridicule. It is a happy use of the old Jewishism, "name," for "power." To them the name was the symbol of promise and potency; as the psalmist says, "He saved them for his name's sake" (Psa. cxvi, 8). But faith, the personal condition of salvation, is here brought out. The order of the Greek is expressive: "And through faith in his name, his name hath made strong this man whom ye see and know." It is not the name alone that works the miracle, but the name as grasped and made the channel of supernatural power by the faith of the believer.

There is next keen adaptation of the theme to his Jewish crowd and the making of himself at one with them: "Ye men of Israel, the God of *our* fathers hath glorified his son Jesus." And then with what splendid courage and fidelity does he drive home the message! What flinging into their teeth the awful words of truth! Hear him as he sets forth Jesus, "whom ye delivered up;" "denied before the face of Pilate;" "asked for a murderer;" "killed the Prince of life." He then shows them the Christ "whom God raised from the dead, whereof we are witnesses." Then with infinite tenderness and tact he turns to these murderers with, "Now, *brethren*, I *wot that in ignorance* ye did it." How this flings open wide the great door of hope to these guilty ones. But, mind you, there is no weak sentimentalism in his preaching, for we hear ringing out in firm tones, "Repent . . . be converted, that your sins may be blotted out."

Peter is a model for the preacher and teacher of to-day in (1) Laying the foundation in scriptural argument, setting forth Jesus as the Messiah. (2) Driving home guilt to the heart and conscience; the guilt of rejection and the tragic crime of killing the Prince of life. (3) Proffering salvation to the wickedest man through a merciful, atoning Christ, "through faith in his name." (4) Witnessing and exhorting.

WILBUR P. THIRKIELD.

V.

PETER AND JOHN BEFORE THE COUNCIL.

Acts iv, 1-18.

GOLDEN TEXT.—There is none other name under heaven given among men, whereby we must be saved. Acts iv, 12.

WE have for our study at this time the account of the trial of two men arrested for preaching the Gospel—Peter, the oldest, and John, the youngest, of the apostles. This lesson presents to us the pictures of these men

1. When arrested.
2. When arraigned.
3. When acquitted.

1. *The Arrest.* A man who was over forty years of age, and had been a cripple from his birth, had been brought daily by his friends and laid at the Beautiful Gate of the Temple to beg. He could not walk or stand, for he was "carried by his friends." He could not even use crutches, for the man's limbs lay as dead beneath him. He was a man whom nearly all the inhabitants of Jerusalem knew, for he had been carried there each day for years.

One day, about three o'clock in the afternoon, at the time of evening prayer, as Peter and John were going into the Temple, this lame mendicant asked alms of them. They had neither silver nor gold, yet they gave him more than the richest merchant could have given. From these men he received power to walk and leap, and he followed them into the Temple praising God.

This miracle was enough to draw a great crowd to Solomon's porch, and this was Peter's opportunity to preach the Gospel. Christianity has always had for a part of its work the saving of men's bodies, but this has only been an incident as compared to the greater work of saving men's souls. This miracle of healing served to startle men from their slumbers and summon them to open their eyes and ears to the appeal which was, to be made to them. It served also as a credential for these men, proving they were embassadors from God. The manifestation of God's power in the salvation of men will draw the people together. This leaping and shouting cripple was the best kind of a church bell. Many an eloquent preacher has been compelled to preach to empty pews, but when his church has been blessed with a great revival of religion, and sinners are being converted, then every seat in the house is taken. Peter, perhaps from some elevated position in the porch, preached to them Jesus the Messiah; that Jesus whom they had derided and murdered, God had raised to life and glorified; and that it was he, known by the humble name of Jesus, who was the real cause of this man's wholeness.

While we have only the account of Peter's sermon, yet doubtless John also spoke to the people, for we read "*they* spake," and the addresses were so long that time enough elapsed for the authorities to hear of the gathering and the nature of the doctrines which were being preached. While they were still speaking they were interrupted by the captain of the Levitical guard of the Temple, and by some of the priests, who may have thought that for the apostles to preach was an invasion of the privileges which belonged only to the Levitical priesthood, and by the Sadducees, who were bitterly opposed to the doctrine of the resurrection. The Pharisees during the life of Jesus were his bitterest enemies; after his resurrection the Sadducees were the most hostile.

It often happens that a person is lifted by the power of God from his moral deformity, and no one in the world objects; but when once he begins to testify as to how this came to pass, and to glorify his Saviour, then immediately opposition rises against him. The world is willing you should live a blameless life, but will object if you say that *the blood of Jesus* cleanses you from sin. In this case the people were willing that the cripple should be whole—they could not object to the blessing which had come to this man; but because the apostles preached Jesus as the source of this man's strength the authorities are vexed, and because of their teachings rather than their works the apostles are arrested and lodged in jail. Enjoy your religion if you will, but do not say any thing about it, has often been the demand of the enemies of the cross, but when Jesus has been lifted up by some witness of his power, then opposition has arisen. In spite of all persecution, by the testimony of Christians sinners are led to the Saviour, as, in spite of the imprisonment of these apostles, thousands believed in Jesus through their teachings.

2. *The Arraignment.* The morrow, probably the early morning, brought the arraignment of these prisoners before the Sanhedrin. They are called to face the same judges who had arraigned their Master about sixty days before this. There were Annas and his son-in-law Caiaphas, whom, it has been suggested, " were the head of the Jewish people, the latter as actual high-priest and the former as president of the Sanhedrin." John and Alexander are also mentioned, and if their names had not been given here in connection with this trial no one on earth would have known that such mortals ever lived, for this statement is all that we know of them.

This court of seventy-one judges doubtless sat in its customary semicircle, and nigh the center stood Peter and John with the man who had been healed. At one end of this semicircle was the high-priest, who could question the prisoner and at the same time look into the faces of each member of the court. In this court were the priests and the elders of the people and the scribes. This court was to investigate (1) whether this be real miracle; (2) whether it be truly divine or wrought of God.

These men must have felt that there was very little chance of their receiving a just trial, for they remembered when they went before this same court and saw these very same men when Jesus was being tried. They could not expect that these men, who were filled with such bitter hatred, would allow them to escape when they had sent to the cross Jesus himself. They must have felt that their prospect was dark.

When we think of Peter's record in connection with the trial of our Lord, we can have no hope that he will help the cause of Christ now. Then he was not accused by the judges, he was accused by a maid of being with Jesus, and he, in the most cowardly way, denied that he ever knew him. Weak man! What can we expect of such a man now that he is called to make a defense before the highest court of the nation; when he is not accused by a servant, but he is now the prisoner at the bar. The officer of the court has already asked him the question, " By what power, or in what name, have ye done this?" "Then Peter, filled with the Holy Ghost"— that single clause put after Peter's name tells us that we have a man here that does not seem at all like that weak disciple who denied his Master. He is no more like that man than the dead wire is like the wire connected with some battery through which there is flowing a stream of fire. His defense shows us a new man.

He proves (1) that he and John had performed, "not a misdeed, but a good deed;" (2) they could see for themselves that this man had been healed, for he was there before them; (3) that this miracle was wrought by the power of Jesus Christ, the crucified and risen One; (4) that for men there was no Saviour except Christ.

Peter does not say that this miracle was wrought by

Jehovah, even though this would have been safer for him, for then he could have been regarded as remaining in the bounds of Judaism ; but he combines the highest and humblest epithets of our Lord—Jesus the human name and the man from Nazareth, and yet he was the Christ the Messiah. And then this prisoner, arrested for a good deed, arraigns his judges for a most bloody deed, as he adds, " whom ye crucified, whom God raised from the dead." You said he was worthy of death, but God brought him forth as the Prince of life ; by him does this man stand here before you whole. Moreover, this man Jesus, whom you as the builders of God's spiritual kingdom have rejected and cast out as worthless, has been chosen by God as the corner-stone, even the head of the corner. No building can stand without a corner-stone, so there is no salvation for this world except by this name. To the very men who crucified Christ he preaches salvation through the cross. How wonderfully is the promise fulfilled here which Jesus gave them : " When they bring you unto the synagogues, and unto magistrates, and powers, take ye no thought how or what thing ye shall answer, or what ye shall say : for the Holy Ghost shall teach you in the same hour what ye ought to say" (Luke xii, 11, 12).

3. *The Acquittal.* The apostles are commanded to go aside out of the council while the judges confer together. " What shall we do with these men ? " was the question which they had to settle. Their hearts were filled with prejudice; they knew what they wanted to do, still there

were certain facts which they could not deny and which made a great impression on them.

(1) These two Galilean peasants had stood before this highest tribunal of the nation, and had the courage to turn their very defense into an accusation of their judges. They marveled at their boldness. Whence was their courage?

(2) These men were unlearned and ignorant, and yet they were familiar with and understood the Scriptures. They were but laymen, yet they could explain the Scriptures better than any priest of the Jewish Church. Whence did they get their learning?

(3) The bearing of these men recalled the time when Jesus was the prisoner whom they were trying. With his death accomplished they hoped that they had buried forever that whole system of teaching, and yet here is the same doctrine, and they could not help feeling that these men had been with Jesus. "We never had a prisoner before us like Jesus, and yet here are two men animated by the same spirit that makes us feel that he is almost present again in these his followers."

(4) There stood before them the very man whom they had known, and his very posture, and the joy and gratitude seen in his face showed that he had been wonderfully blessed body and soul.

They could not answer these facts, and yet they deliberately made the plan to suppress the truth. The prisoners were accordingly called again, and they were commanded not to speak to any one in the name of Jesus, and they threatened them with penalties if they disobeyed this order. With one more question at this time Peter probed their guilty consciences as he asked, "Whether it be right in the sight of God to hearken unto you more than unto God, judge ye. For we cannot but speak the things which we have seen and heard." They were then released.

Peter goes from this trial, not as from the previous one, to weep bitterly, but he goes to his own company, probably to some assembly-room where the Christians met together, and there they held a praise and prayer meeting —praise-meeting because of the triumph which had come to the church, and a prayer-meeting that they might all have boldness to stand and to speak his word. While they thus poured forth their supplications with thanksgiving, "the place was shaken where they were assembled together; and they were all filled with the Holy Ghost, and they spake the word of God with boldness."

JOEL M. LEONARD.

VI.

THE APOSTLES' CONFIDENCE IN GOD.

Acts iv, 19-31.

GOLDEN TEXT.—They spake the word of God with boldness.
Acts iv, 31.

THE experiences and example of the apostolic Church, as recorded in New Testament history, have been a storage-battery of power to every Christian generation. We of to-day read the record and find fresh and strengthening stimulus at every perusal. These words are not dead and cold type, but have in them " spirit and life," and because of such power they mold character and determine destiny.

We have an illustration of this in the lesson before us. Who can read this narrative without being profoundly stirred by the heroic spirit and fearless action of these leaders of the new movement initiated and instituted by Jesus Christ ? They had seen their Master overwhelmed, as it must have seemed to them, with an irretrievable disaster, and in consequence of it they had returned to their old channels of life. But re-equipped by the marvelous events of the resurrection, and re-empowered by the pentecostal baptism of the Holy Ghost, they began anew the mission for which they were originally selected, and went forth preaching " Jesus and the resurrection." The new evangel spread with amazing rapidity, and thousands became followers of the apostolic doctrine. The authorities of the Jewish Church, recognizing the fact that, as with their Master, the success of the apostles meant their overthrow, sought occasion to exercise their religious and political power in forbidding the apostles to disseminate their principles. The occasion soon presented itself.

A man lame from his mother's womb had sat for years at the threshold of the Gate Beautiful of the Temple. To this gate he had been borne daily, and in Oriental custom had begged his living from compassionate worshipers. One eventful day, both to him and to the world, Peter and John were passing by and were attracted by the piteous appeals of this long-suffering suppliant. Their sympathies were drawn out. They felt within them the rising of that spirit which appeared in their Master when he healed the sick, cleansed the leper, restored sight to the blind, and made the lame to walk. With the spirit came the power, and with a dignity and glory which must have illuminated even his appearance, Peter said to him: " In the name of Jesus Christ of Nazareth, rise up and walk."

With touch of hand the command was obeyed, and the lame man, healed both in body and soul, "leaping up, stood," doubtless in joyful amazement, " and walked, and entered with them into the temple, walking, and leaping, and praising God." Such a miracle filled the people with wonder and convinced multitudes of the verity and power of the new faith. At the same time it stirred the governing Pharisees to immediate action. They arrested the two apostles and put them in prison. The next day they called them before the Sanhedrin, and heard the defense of Peter, in which he told them the source of such power and boldly preached to them personally the need of salvation through Jesus Christ. After a private consultation, fearing to proceed to extreme measures in view of the public favor which the miracle had given the apostles, they " called them, and commanded them not to speak at all nor teach in the name of Jesus."

But such a command was an unlawful infringement upon personal and religious rights, and as such must be firmly and boldly resisted. It was an order that could not be conscientiously obeyed. It arrayed in opposition a higher and a lower authority, and the higher and the spiritual, not the lower and the ecclesiastical, must be obeyed. God had given these apostles their commission to preach, and no earthly tribunal had right or power to overrule it; and so with calmness, but with unflinching courage, Peter replied, " Whether it be right in the sight of God to hearken unto you more than unto God, judge ye. For we cannot but speak the things which we have seen and heard."

They then departed from the court and sought at once the presence of the other disciples, related to them the events which had taken place, and then unitedly they laid their case before God in humble, earnest, believing prayer. They committed their cause to Him who had the power and who had promised assistance in sudden or anticipated emergency. Their confidence was not misplaced, for as they closed their petition the amen of God came in the form of an earthquake, shaking the place where they were assembled, and at the same time their own hearts were filled with the power of a fearless purpose and an unyielding determination. God vindicated in this both his own truth and their principles, and by this renewed investment of his Spirit enabled them "to speak the word of God with boldness."

The suggestions and the truths which may be gathered from the lesson of to-day are many and varied, for example:

The vanity of combinations and conspiracies against God as affirmed in Scripture and illustrated in history.

The beneficent character of the Gospel of Jesus Christ.

The necessity and value of mutual sympathy.

The power of united and believing prayer as taught in the New Testament.

The care of God over his own.

But the Sunday-school authorities in their selection of this passage have suggested as our theme the Apostles' Confidence in God, as illustrated in the incident of their imprisonment and trial. It was a critical hour in the history of the youthful Church. The members and leaders were confronted and opposed by the organized and properly constituted authorities, political and ecclesiastical. They were condemned in advance by these, and where might makes right they could hope for no mercy when the issue became acute and prejudices became exasperated. The disciples had in a measure been prepared for trouble by the pre-announcement of Christ: " If they have persecuted me, they will also persecute you." But now it was in sight, and under threat of pains and penalties they were charged to keep silence. But, like the three Hebrew children of Daniel's day, they needed no time for considering the question. We find no hint or shadow of one that indicates on their part any wavering of purpose. Their prayer does not even submit the question to God as for a moment debatable. They call divine attention to the facts and pray that " with all boldness they may speak thy word."

.We look for the grounds of this confidence and courage, and find them incorporated in the lesson text. This confidence was based on:

THE OMNIPOTENCE OF GOD, which was (1) *A fundamental element of their religious faith.*

The Mosaic economy had taught them this. The history of their own people, which they still cherished, and the memories of which were dear to them, was full of illustrious evidences of the power and glory of Jehovah. He it was who had broken the yoke of Egypt, had led them through the wilderness, had driven out before them the inhabitants of Canaan, and whose own right arm had gotten them the victory. It was God who had blessed them in all the following years, established them a nation, and made firm the thrones of his servants David and Solomon ; and when through sin they had suffered defeat and disaster, it was God who had delivered them and by his power had vindicated the purpose of their existence as a people. They had not changed in becoming followers of Christ this fundamental faith in the God of their childhood and of their earlier manhood.

This element of their religious faith was further buttressed by (2) *The convincing events of the life, death, resurrection, and ascension of Jesus Christ.*

God had spoken and acted through him. His teachings and his miracles had given indisputable evidence to their minds that he was the Chosen and Sent of God ; that in them God had pledged himself to the new departure and would defend and preserve those engaged in it. The FACTS were then, as they should be now, the unanswerable factors in the propagation of the Gospel. When they beheld " the man which was healed standing with them, they could say nothing against it." The apostles remembered the man with the withered arm, the blind beggars at the gate of Jericho, the ten lepers, the feeding of the multitudes, the devil-possessed daughter of the Syro-Phenician woman, and, greater than all, the triple exercise of divine power by which the beloved daughter of the ruler of the synagogue, the widow's son at the gate of Nain, and His own friend Lazarus had been called back from the realms of death and clothed with mortal life again. More than these, they had seen Him himself die and then come forth again, the Lord both of death and life. With such facts, how could they refrain from testifying " the Gospel of the grace of God ? "

(3) In addition, the Holy Ghost WITHIN them enabled them to make forceful and persuasive the truth they advocated.

It is true they were neither skilled in arms nor trained in schools; they had neither wealth nor social position; but God was with them, and they were invincible. Pentecost had made them all-powerful. With hot hearts and anointed lips "they spake the word of God with boldness," and in doing this they laid the foundations of an empire universal in its extent and eternal in its duration. Pharisees and Sadducees, priests and scribes, ecclesiastical hirelings and state governments, the puny opponents of Christ and his Gospel, have given place to the despised Nazarene; and this Jesus, whom they disowned and crucified, is now recognized to be both Lord and Christ. Irresistible, because of the unction of the Holy Ghost, they made possible the flower and fruitage of a Christian civilization.

Let us emulate their dauntless courage, touch the sources, as they did, of supernal power, make regnant in our lives the principles they enunciated, and then the world will be at our feet as it was at theirs, and we shall go forth, as did the apocalyptic rider, on the white horse, "conquering and to conquer."

JOHN D. PICKLES.

VII.

ANANIAS AND SAPPHIRA.

Acts v, 1-11.

GOLDEN TEXT.—Be not deceived; God is not mocked; for whatsoever a man soweth, that shall he also reap. Gal. vi, 7.

THE contrasts presented by different lives in this world, and those presented by the same life at different times, are very marked. In the Scriptures we have many such contrasts. For example, Joseph at home, the pride of his father, and Joseph sold by his brethren to the Ishmaelites; Moses in the palace of the Pharaohs, and Moses suffering affliction with the people of God; Saul the youthful king, with every inducement and incentive for making for himself a noble record, and Saul disobedient to God, filled with an evil spirit, and ending his life by his own hand; Elijah the victorious prophet, and Elijah disheartened, fleeing the wrath of Jezebel, and asking God to let him die; the three disciples on the mount of transfiguration, seeing Christ's glory, hearing the words of the celestial visitants and the voice of the Invisible, and the other disciples at the foot of the mountain wrestling with a demon.

Our present lesson brings before us another scriptural contrast. From the closing verses of the preceding chapter we get a beautiful idea of the Christ-like spirit which prevailed in the primitive Christian Church. The brotherly love manifested in the oneness of heart and soul, and in the community of goods practiced by the Church at that time, is a striking commentary on the sweetness of spirit which had been imparted by Christ to his immediate followers. The conduct of those disciples is an example in kind of what intimate fellowship with Christ must ever produce in the individual members of his earthly Church. " The multitude of them that believed were of one heart and of one soul: neither said any of them that aught of the things which he possessed was his own; but they had all things common. . . . Neither was there any among them that lacked: for as many as were possessors of lands or houses sold them, and brought the prices of the things that were sold, and laid them down at the apostles' feet: and distribution was made unto every man according as he had need" (Acts iv, 32-35).

Certainly in this we have portrayed a most happy condition of things. Love reigned in the hearts of those early Christians ; and where love is blessings innumerable follow in its train.

In the fifth chapter, however, we have a sad contrast. A dark cloud arises upon the horizon ; into the sweet music a discord is introduced ; the happy family relations are disturbed by an unlovely and an unholy disposition. As Matthew Henry observes, " The chapter begins with a melancholy ' but,' which puts a stop to the pleasant and agreeable prospect of things which we had in the foregoing chapters." We had just been introduced to Joses, surnamed by the apostles Barnabas, the son of consolation. Having possessions perhaps greater than his fellow-disciples, which made his case a peculiarly noted one, and actuated by a divine spirit of generosity, we have seen him selling his land, and bringing the money and laying it at the apostles' feet for distribution among his less favored brethren. We can easily imagine the praise that would be bestowed upon him for his self-sacrificing deed.

Inspired by this example, or, at least, coveting the esteem which this act had won for Joses, Ananias and his wife determined to appear equally generous. And so they sold their possession, and Ananias came with great show of benevolence, bringing to the apostles only a part of the price, but bringing it as though it was the whole. There was every appearance of Christian love and unselfishness in this transaction; but the spirit thereof was wanting.

Had Peter been in the same condition of heart as when, a few short weeks before, he had told a cowardly falsehood to shield himself from the possible consequences of being known as a follower of Christ, he would never have detected the deception which Ananias and Sapphira were now practicing. But God had reconstructed Peter; and he and his fellow-apostles were now for a peculiar and special work by a peculiar and special gift of the Holy Ghost in establishing securely and guarding faithfully the Christian Church.

Can we doubt that as Peter looked upon Ananias, and by the aid of the Holy Spirit read the lie that was in his heart and conduct, if not upon his lips, he must have had vividly and sorrowfully recalled to his mind the lie with which he himself had so basely denied his Lord, and that again, in his soul, at least, he must have "wept bitterly?" And thus in the experience of every Christian how often the conduct of the ungodly recalls the memory of his own past sinfulness, and makes him turn away from his former self in penitence and disgust!

As Peter lays bare the intent of Ananias's heart, that man stands in the presence of the Spirit-filled apostles speechless. In dumb amazement he listens to the terrible accusation, while his own conscience adds its sharpest sting to the words spoken. His sin has found him out *when and where he did not expect it*. God's hand is laid upon him in summary retribution. Falling down, "he gave up the ghost;" "and the young men arose, wound him up, and carried him out, and buried him."

The fate of his wife, who had conspired with him in this deception, was soon sealed. Coming in "about three hours after," possibly to inquire as to the whereabouts of her husband, or perhaps to receive with him the expected praise for their pretended generosity, she adds lying lips to the acted falsehood, and soon her lifeless body lies at the feet of the apostles, and she is carried out to her burial.

The question may be asked, Was not this punishment of Ananias and Sapphira too severe? No time was given for repentance; no opportunity was offered for them to consider their transgression, and to cry unto God for pardon.

We may find answer to this inquiry, I think, in the following suggestions:

1. *Their sin was an aggravated one.* "Thou hast not lied unto men, but unto God," were Peter's words to Ananias. The peculiar enormity of their sin consisted in its being committed against the Holy Ghost. They knew of the pentecostal gift. They had undoubtedly been eye-ewitnesses and ear-witnesses of the remarkable occurrences of that pentecostal day. They knew of the continuance of this divine power with the apostles in the cure of the lame man at the Temple gate, and in their bold utterances before their accusers and judges. And now they come with a definitely settled purpose to deceive the Spirit of God in the persons of God's chosen ones, thinking him to be such a one as themselves. In their thought they had degraded the Holy Ghost to the level of human frailty and human ignorance. Because God had not taken immediate vengeance upon other sinners, therefore he could not know.

The unpardonable sin is against the Holy Ghost; and Peter said to Ananias, "Why hath Satan filled thine heart to lie to the Holy Ghost?" or, as some have translated it, "to belie the Holy Ghost." Dr. Lightfoot supposes that Ananias was not an ordinary believer, but a minister, and *one that had received the gift of the Holy Ghost with the hundred and twenty.* Yet he dared thus by dissembling to belie and shame that gift.

2 *It was a deliberate sin.* It was not committed as the result of a sudden temptation; but these two had consulted together about it, and had entered into a mutual agreement to work this deception upon the apostles and the Church. It was cold-blooded in every respect. There was apparently no necessity laid upon them by outward circumstances. Certainly there was no law of the Church making it obligatory for them to sell and give. " While it remained, was it not thine own? and after it was sold, was it not in thine own power? " asks Peter. " This community of goods, as it existed in the Church at Jerusalem, was a purely voluntary thing. It was not required by the apostles." Ananias shows himself to have been by deliberate choice a hypocrite. He need not have been in the Church at all. He shows baseness at every point of his recorded history. " He was not censured because he had not surrendered his entire property, but for falsely pretending to have done what he had not done."

3. *Sin must have become the settled purpose of their lives.* God does not pronounce condemnation unto death for an initial sin or for a series of sins. It is only when the soul becomes saturated with sin, when there is no longer hope of the man's bearing fruit unto righteousness, that God casts him off. Some single sin may mark this period, and thus stand out as the great and crowning act of a life of wickedness, as was probably this sin in the career of Ananias and Sapphira, proving deadly to their moral manhood and womanhood, from which it

was impossible for their souls to recuperate. It must have been a crisis in their inner lives marking the determination of their souls—a crisis not apparent to men, but open and plain to the eye of God. " As one may receive a saber stroke and live, and yet die if a needle enter a spot in the spine where the nerves start which move the lungs; or, as poisons, taken little by little with impunity, make a cumulative deposit which at last acts as one fatal dose ; so a single sin, apparently venial, may make the climax of sinfulness."

4. *The severity of this punishment may have been due in a measure to the conditions surrounding the Church at that early period.* The Church was in its infancy. The apostles had just been endued with a miraculous gift of the Holy Spirit. If, thus endued, they were not able to discern the motives prompting the deeds of any of their number, then discredit would be thrown upon their endowment. By this awe-inspiring event, recorded in our lesson, however, was made clear to all that the great Discerner of the thoughts and intents of the heart was present with the apostles; and thus those who might wish to unite themselves to the Church through worldly motives, having merely a desire to participate in the proceeds from the goods and possessions sold, would be deterred. The impression made upon the people by this miracle of judgment shows how salutary was the lesson, and would warrant us in believing that it was needed. See the eleventh verse : " And great fear came upon all the church, and upon as many as heard these things."

But whatever reasons may be found for this summary punishment of Ananias and Sapphira, satisfactory or otherwise, we are sure that "the Judge of all the earth shall do right." And that this punishment was of God we cannot doubt who accept the statements of the narrative as inspired.

We may further learn from this lesson:

(1) That those who presume upon security and impunity in any sinful course are reckoning ignorantly and foolishly. They deceive themselves, they may deceive their fellows; but they cannot deceive God. "Be sure your sin will find you out." The words of our Golden Text should ever be a warning: "Be not deceived; God is not mocked: for whatsoever a man soweth, that shall he also reap."

(2) It is useless to bring half of self to God in consecration. God demands the whole heart; and there is too little of us individually to make an offering of less than this. A half-hearted service for God is well-pleasing to Satan; for he knows that it means a sure service for himself.

(3) The wheat and the tares ever grow together in the earthly Church. It was so in the Christ's time. Judas Iscariot was one of the twelve. Joses and Ananias were both members of the same Church. It has been so ever since. It will be so "until the harvest." Then Christ "will say to the reapers, Gather ye together first the tares, and bind them in bundles to burn them; but gather the wheat into my barn." We have not the wisdom for

this separation, " Lest while we gather up the tares, we root up also the wheat with them." It has seemed at times in history as though the tares had almost choked out the wheat ; but God has always had his faithful witness ; and " the foundation of God standeth sure, having this seal: the Lord knoweth them that are his."

Let each one of us build over against his own house— the house of his own character—that it may stand secure and untarnished when the light of judgment day is turned upon it.

God save us from the sin of Ananias and Sapphira ! God save us from all sin !

GILBERT C. OSGOOD.

VIII.

THE APOSTLES PERSECUTED.

Acts v, 25-41.

GOLDEN TEXT.—We ought to obey God rather than men.
Acts v, 29.

IN the earlier chapters of the Book of Acts Luke, the historian, keeps close to Peter as the central figure; in the later he travels with Paul. Whatever the distinctions of Pauline and Petrine theology, we are here in the midst of the facts upon which both are based. We find Peter with a new experience. He had learned that it took less courage to cut off a man's ear than to face the ridicule of a servant-girl; that boasting of superior loyalty to his Master was no security against a swearing denial; that a broken heart was the best preparation for spiritual power. Peter had been converted, and was able to strengthen his brethren. Pentecost had made him the rock that Christ had chosen him to be. He had become a man by being filled with the Spirit of God.

He illustrates here a most important scriptural truth as deep as the incarnation itself, namely, the baptism of the Holy Ghost gives man a fuller possession of himself. We are not surprised at the commotion created by the apostles. Twelve such men, with such an experience and such a message as these men had, were enough to stir any city, and jostle the composure of any rabbi. This new heresy was becoming popular. The lame and the sick were being carried into the streets in full faith that even the shadows of these despised Galileans would heal them. Solomon's porch had drawn a crowd of incurables from all over Jerusalem, and the conviction was rapidly spreading that the kingdom of heaven was at hand.

The apostles did not sneak into the back streets and alleys for their work, but in the most public spot in the city they preached Christ. Such aggressive Christianity was sure to stir up the devil. Easy-going Christians, who are generally going the devil's way, could have escaped serious trouble, but wide-awake, fearless workers could not be left alone. The high-priest, whose revenues had been cut off when Christ drove the money-changers out of the Temple, who had not forgotten the face and name which he thought had been destroyed forever, found this name more popular with the masses than ever. As the Sadducees sought to control the masses, something must be done at once to silence these men who were openly defying their express commands. He and his party "rose up, . . . and were filled with indignation." The bloodiest inquisitor of Spain or Mexico knows how to be "filled with indignation." The apostles were thrown into "the common prison," but prisons could not hold such men. Every healed man and woman in Jerusalem would pray for them.

Healing power was a pledge of helping power. The witnesses of the resurrection had no uncertainty about the supernatural. Three years with Jesus, and three weeks with the Holy Spirit, had made the supernatural seem to them very natural. It had become as unreasonable to deny the reality of spiritual force as to deny the reality of action of the human will upon the body. The keys of that door were not all in the jailer's keeping. The keepers could not determine just how soundly they would sleep. Angels might be expected at any time. It was no greater exhibition of God's power over nature or in nature to open a prison door than to open a rose-bud.

"The angel of the Lord by night opened the prison doors, and brought them forth, and said, Go, stand and speak in the temple to the people all the words of this life"—all the words of this salvation, this new life of God among men, of men with God.

The early comers to the temple-worship or temple-market next morning found the apostles there before them preaching in the very spot where they had been arrested, but with a new illustration of the power of their risen Saviour.

Meantime, the great council had been called to dispose of these preachers so securely locked up. The importance of the case is seen in the coming of the twenty-four chief pri ~, the twenty-four elders of the people, and the twenty-" |rrscribes, all of whom held their places by reason of age, wisdom, and weight of character. Even the great Gamaliel was present. It was an august assembly which filled the circle of seats in the great hall and waited for the coming of the prisoners. But the first news astounded them. The well locked and guarded jail was found empty. Their minds swiftly ran from this event back over all that had happened during the last few weeks, and very naturally "they doubted of them whereunto this would grow." The awkwardness was not at all relieved by the announcement made at this juncture: "The men whom ye put in prison are standing in the temple and teaching the people." The chief watchman of the Temple took a squad of soldiers and very respectfully escorted the apostles to the council hall. Such prisoners, with such a hold on the people, were not to be handled roughly, as there were signs of a shower of stones. No questions were asked about how they got out of the prison or how they healed the sick. There was a disposition to keep close to questions of authority. "Did not we straitly command you that ye should not teach in this name?" and with singular weakening toward the plea of injured innocence: "Ye have filled Jerusalem with your doctrine, and intend to bring this man's blood upon us." How the guilty conscience remembers the day, the deed, the word closely linked with known crime! These men had doubtless started the cry of the crowd which pressed around Pilate: "His blood be on us, and on our children."

The apostles' reply was in substance the same as in their former trial. Then it was, "Judge ye if one should hearken unto you more than to God." Now it is, "We ought to obey God rather than man." Then it was, "We cannot but speak the things we have seen and heard." Now it is a positive charge of their personal guilt in the crucifixion of Christ, the certainty of his resurrection and exaltation, his bestowment of repentance and forgiveness of sins upon Israel, and the unfailing witness of the Holy Ghost to all who obey God. The judges, treated as criminals, were sawn to pieces with rage, and very promptly decided that if such men could not be intimidated into silence nor locked up they must die, and thus the contagion of the new religion would end.

Then stood up Gamaliel, learned in the law, a careful observer of events, broader in spirit than the men of his age, honored of all the people, and commanded that the men should retire while they held a consultation. " His plea was not so much for systematic tolerance as for temporary action. Let these men alone at present. As far as we can see they are only the victims of a harmless delusion. There is nothing seditious in their practice, nothing subversive in their doctrines. Even if there were we should have nothing to fear from them, and no need to adopt violent measures of protection. Fanaticism and imposture are short-lived, even when backed by popular insurrection. But in the views of these men there may be something more than at present appears ; some germ of truth, some gleam of revelation may inspire their singular enthusiasm, and to fight

THE APOSTLES PERSECUTED. 283

against them may be to fight against God. There was time to watch the development of this new fraternity. . . . The advice was too sound and the authority of the speaker too weighty to be rejected."—*Canon Farrar.* The frequency and the failure of rebellious uprisings were enough to account for Gamaliel's tolerance without attributing to him, as some have done, a secret faith in Christianity. Following his advice, the fury of the other members of the council could only express itself in the useless command that the apostles should preach no more in this name, the command being enforced by the strongest argument left to them—that is, beating. They gave them the full benefit of Deut. xxv, 1-3. But the apostles took their punishment cheerfully, and went out from the presence of the council "rejoicing that they were counted worthy to suffer shame for his name." They made straight for Solomon's porch and took up the preaching just where they had left off, and arranged also to preach in every house that was open to them.

This incident is suggestive in every detail. It should be compared with the incident of chapter iv, noting the change in the apostles, the people, and the priests.

We see the courage of humility and the humility of courage, the strength of tolerance and the weakness of intolerance, the failure of unbelief and the victory of faith. We see the kind of testimony that is to overcome and win the world for Christ. The men who have moved the world toward God are those who have believed in his will as the highest possible good, and by every means have sought to know and obey him. To obey God is to find the greatest good his world can work out for us, and to build a character which will feel at home with God in the next world.

We see that historical and experimental evidences of Christianity confirm each other. Spiritual experiences are in line with the providential and miraculous events recorded in Scripture. "We are witnesses of these things, so is also the Holy Ghost whom God hath given to them that obey him." We see that the most zealous Christian faith need not become fanaticism. Fanaticism is the outcome of perverted Scripture, morbid and unenlightened conscience, spiritual pride, selfishness. Faith keeps to the word of God, studies Christian experience, is teachable and loving, and believes that God gave common sense for every-day use. Fanaticism said to Christ, "Cast thyself down" from "the pinnacle of the temple." Faith said, "Thou shalt not tempt the Lord thy God."

Every age has had its councils of bigotry, superstition, and selfishness. Every age has had its fearless, faithful, victorious witnesses to the truth. The Savonarolas, Luthers, Wesleys, have not been few, but many. There are boys in shops, girls in factories, young people in society, young men starting in business, older men in the thick of commercial battles, who are making a stand against sin, often single-handed and alone, which is as heroic and sublime as that of Huss or Knox.

When Philip II. of Spain and Cardinal Granville had determined to rid themselves of William of Orange, after setting forth a statement of his so-called offenses, they published their famous ban : " For these causes we declare him traitor and miscreant, enemy of ourselves and of the country. As such we banish him perpetually from all our realms, forbidding all our subjects to communicate with him, openly or privately, to administer to him food or drink or shelter. We allow all to injure him in property or life. We expose him as an enemy of the human race, giving his property to all who may seize it, and if any one of our subjects, or any stranger, shall be found sufficiently generous of heart to rid us of this pest, delivering him to us alive or dead, or take his life, we will cause to be furnished to him immediately after the deed shall have been done, the sum of twenty-five thousand crowns in gold. If he have committed any crime, however heinous, we promise to pardon him, and if he be not already noble, we will ennoble him for his valor."

William of Orange closes his masterly reply with these words: " I am in the hands of God. My worldly goods and my life have been long since dedicated to his service. He will dispose of them as seems best for his glory and my salvation."

J. A. STORY.

IX.

THE FIRST CHRISTIAN MARTYR.

Acts vii, 54–60; viii, 1–4.

GOLDEN TEXT.—He kneeled down, and cried with a loud voice, Lord, lay not this sin to their charge. Acts vii, 60.

THE lesson opens at a crisis. The day of Pentecost led to the persecution of the apostles because they taught that Christ was the Son of God. Now Stephen comes forward to give a spiritual interpretation of the law, and to present the unfolding of worship according to varied conditions under the old dispensation. This may endanger the Temple rites. Then a great company of priests are turning unto Christ. The Sadducees are alarmed, and the most determined opposition from the Jews follows. Stephen is apprehended and brought before the council. Let us consider:

1. THE MAN. The form of his name would indicate that he was a Hellenist; that is, a Jew born among the Gentiles, speaking the Greek language. His name also signifies a crown. In one sense, being the first, he crowns the list of deacons enumerated in the sixth chapter. He also crowns the long list of martyrs who have adorned the history of the Church. He steps into the path of ecclesiastical history, does his work in a few days, and passes to his reward.

(1) *He was versed in the Scriptures.* "When they heard these things, they were cut to the heart." The reference is to Stephen's defense. It was drawn from the Old Testament with an application to his hearers. Cranmer and Ridley learned the New Testament by heart. They also saw its truths in relation to present duties of life. This was the case of the first Christian martyr. He exposed the false view of the Jews toward the Temple and the law. He would have his hearers draw the inference that Moses refers to Christ in verse 37. These half-suppressed references to Christ and to a larger spiritual force in the Old Testament denote how skillfully Stephen handled the Word.

"They were cut to the heart," or, literally, they were sawn asunder in their hearts. It was not one staggering blow which did the work. The truth, laden with rebukes, was gradually making its way through their hearts. The personal application completed the work. The Scriptures are our defense and also furnish our weapons of warfare. They exposed the guilt of the Jews, and are to-day exposing the false supports of many who have substituted a human plan for a divine one.

(2) *Stephen was spiritually enlightened.* "But he, being full of the Holy Ghost, looked up steadfastly into heaven." We may not all have the privilege of Stephen to look into heaven in this life, but the Holy Spirit furnishes enlightening power. Spiritual breadth of vision follows. That creates confidence. The most earnest and active biblical characters have remarkable composure at times.

Moses at the Red Sea, hemmed in by a hostile army on the one hand and by a barrier of fens and of water on the other, stands confidently and awaits the deliverance. Paul, after having preached in what were once five nations, cast out of cities by mobs and with threatenings unto death, is yet in the storm on the deep calmer than any of the hundreds of sailors and soldiers, saying, " Be of good cheer." Moses endured, seeing Him who is invisible; and the angel of God revealed himself unto Paul, saying, " Fear not."

Here was the basis of Stephen's confidence. Facts of the invisible world were newly impressed upon him. We see things here from a short range. Hence mystery and perplexity arise. But if the truth which God has revealed in his Word were impressed upon us in the right degree, with what great confidence we might stand in the severe trial! Perhaps Stephen did not see any more than had been thus far revealed to him by word. But how positively and vividly it is now realized! Greater light and power spring up from the Word. It would be foolish for him to attempt to run away from his foes, or to meet them single-handed. But he need not stand like a stoic to await their blows. He is sustained by a higher power, and looks with joy to the end.

(3) *He possessed a forgiving spirit.* " Lord, lay not this sin to their charge." This prayer is without a parallel outside of biblical history and its influence. Confucius, Isocrates, Seneca, and other Gentile writers hinted at the Golden Rule in a partial or negative form. But

praying for one's enemies has thus far been discovered only in the Bible and in the line of its influence. The cross first brings it to view. It was something new for the world to record when Christ said, " Father, forgive them ; for they know not what they do." Stephen imitates his Lord and Master. He also kept his word : " Pray for them that despitefully use you, and persecute you." This spirit interprets his bold and pointed rebuke against the Jews. This was intended for their good as much as his forgiving prayer. God's severity and goodness go together in conquering the world for the kingdom of heaven. Stephen's sharp reproof and forgiving spirit raised up new workmen in the early Church. We now notice :

2. STEPHEN'S WITNESSING TO THE TRUTH. (1) *He witnessed that God's presence and favor were not limited to any set place.* This leads us back to Stephen's defense, again involved in "these things" of the first verse of the lesson. He had been charged with speaking " blasphemous words against this holy place and the law." False witnesses said that. The falsity consisted largely in attributing to him a hostile and blasphemous spirit. He evidently declared a higher form of truth than was explicitly stated in the law, or practiced in the Temple. Yet it was a truth developed from these. God has had a history with his people, and it is still going on. This important fact must not be overlooked to-day. We are to read what God's finger is writing in his kingdom now, as well as what it wrote on tables of stone in the past.

Stephen taught that God's presence was not limited to a favored few. This was one link in the chain which drew away Christians from Jewish rites. Peter must yet be taught in a vision that God is no respecter of persons, and Paul will be raised up to declare the same truth in all its variety and picture the liberty in store for the children of God. But Stephen was the forerunner of Paul. This has been denied by some. Yet it is reasonable to believe that the goads of conscience at the time of Paul's conversion were largely drawn from the scene of Stephen's death. Paul at Antioch in Pisidia adopts Stephen's historical method. Then the emphasis he places on the spiritual side of Jewish worship, and the vigorous opposition he makes to God's favor being limited to one place, remind us of Stephen. Augustine says : " The prayer of Stephen gave Paul to the Church."

Stephen's death became the occasion for extending his teaching. Devout men bear him to the tomb. But others are raising the war-cry against Christians. Let victory be complete, is their motto. Soon the church at Jerusalem is dispersed. Its scattered members are carrying life and peace over Judea and Samaria. It was not the swarming out of an over-crowded hive into a new colony. It was the story of refugees. Here was no well-directed plan or skilled leadership. It was the spontaneous utterance of the glad tidings of the Gospel.

It was doubtless necessary that the first disciples should be witnesses of Jesus and the resurrection at Jerusalem. But it was just as necessary that a second step should be taken. That step was to bear witness in Judea and Samaria. Thus Jesus had commanded. There might be a temptation to be in no haste in taking this second step. The disciples loved the Temple. Who could blame them? Here Jesus gave some of his choicest revelations. But lingering amid the incense and smoking sacrifices too long they may bind these practices, only belonging to the past, on the new society, and fetter its future course. They were providentially thrust out into new fields, as we may be, by apparent disasters, to secure in the end the best results.

(2) *Stephen bore witness that Christ had been elevated to glory and power.* " I see the heavens opened, and the Son of man standing on the right hand of God." Stephen was the first to bear witness to the fact of seeing Christ after his ascension. Paul and John were granted such visions later (Acts ix, 3, 4; 1 Cor. ix, 1 ; Rev. i, 12-17). Perhaps such witnessing was needed to encourage the early Church. It made invisible things appear as a positive reality. It also confirmed Stephen's teaching. Christ had taught that spiritual worship anywhere was pleasing to the Father. He predicted that the Temple would be overthrown. He forcibly instructed the Jews by parables that the way of salvation was open to the Gentiles. This was not the talk of an idle dreamer, but of one who now was standing on the right hand of God. If they accepted Stephen's witness there was new and conclusive evidence of Christ's divine mission, and a seal to his Messianic office.

It would follow that a peculiar privilege had been granted to Stephen. Any rabbi might have coveted it. The glory of God had appeared to him as well as to Abraham and to Moses. If his face had shown like that of an angel his words now had a heavenly support. They must be treasured up like those of patriarchs and of prophets. The issue was plain. Turn and accept Jesus. But instead of this they cried out with a loud voice, stopped their ears, and ran upon him with one accord, and cast him out of the city and stoned him. Since the Jews had no legal right at this time to inflict capital punishment, they were disobedient to Roman law. They were also disobedient to the higher law of God. They resisted the Holy Ghost. This sin is in the world to-day. This enlightened age may well hear the rebuke of Stephen, and gain still higher light by walking in the Spirit.

(3) *Stephen bore witness that Jesus receives his people after death.* He did not formally affirm this fact, but prayed to Jesus to receive his spirit ; or, in bold literalness, " Take my spirit by the hand." The idea is not so much the guidance of a traveler as the welcoming of a guest. And are not such as Stephen called to the marriage supper of the Lamb? God longs to dwell with his people. The tabernacle in the wilderness and the Christian Church on all continents are founded on the idea of gathering a people out of the world. In the midst of that people or community is the Lord of all. If the first steps of this union make man a guest with Christ, how gracious and blessed will that reception be when he

gathers his own from the four quarters of the earth, when the last enemy shall be overcome, and the angels shall sing no more of peace on earth, but shall sing a heavenly song of victory!

In all this witnessing Stephen was faithful unto death. He uttered the truth and his foes gnashed on him with their teeth, but God gave him a heavenly vision. Now he has something more to say, like all true disciples when they have received a special blessing. It is said that some Churches are " gone dumb with old age." But if they possessed the spirit of Stephen they would soon renew their youth and teach the world the divinity of their faith.

With him there was no struggle for peace or light at last. All was settled. His last words are for others, even his foes. Livingstone was found in the cold embrace of death in the attitude of prayer on the Dark Continent—a beautiful close of a great life. Stephen is found in the attitude of prayer when, perhaps, from murderous blows he can no longer stand—a sublime ending of faithful service. Life is before us all. It may be earnest with a hopeful anticipation well founded. If it be like Stephen's, at evening time it shall be light.

J. H. ALLEN.

X.
PHILIP PREACHING AT SAMARIA.

Acts viii, 5-25.

GOLDEN TEXT.—And there was great joy in that city.   Acts viii, 8.

WE can hardly appreciate the Jewish feeling of hatred toward the Samaritans. To the Jew they were mongrels, idolaters, outcasts. God's frown hung over them. In the sky of his love and mercy there was an empty place above Samaria.

In the southern hemisphere, if we turn even so small an instrument as a ship's glass toward that part of the sky known as the "coal-sack," or "end of the universe," its awful blackness flashes into clusters of tiny suns. Christ's "dealings" with the Samaritans become, as it were, our glass. Through it we see that over this people the love of God had gemmed itself in promises as bright and beautiful as those which shed such radiance upon Judea.

When Philip went down to the [a] city of Samaria the apostles and the church at Jerusalem had begun to see that the Gospel has no geographical boundaries. Even with this discovery they seemed in no hurry to quit Jerusalem. They had to be "broken out."

It is not improbable that the day of Pentecost had attached them too strongly to one place. They wanted more time to talk over the wonderful things that had occurred. They were more inclined to celebration than to evangelization.

God knew that there was little hope for the Gospel in the shadow of the Temple. The dispersion without doubt had become a necessity. It would probably have come by other means had not Saul of Tarsus appeared. God saw that he would scatter the Church abroad, and he let him do it.

God uses all men, all events, to serve his cause. Saul made havoc of the Church, and, as things turned, helped evangelize Samaria. Philip in Samaria points straight back to Saul of Tarsus in Jerusalem. God turns persecution into blessing. Nero played no small part, though a negative part, in founding the Gospel in Rome. Rough usage in our Master's service often does us good. It makes us more active for him. An occasional cyclone makes better sailors than continuous fair weather. Getting a ship upon her beam ends now and then is the best way of teaching how to keep her off her beam ends.

Driven from Jerusalem, Philip went down to the city of Samaria. Its name at this time was Sebaste. It had been given to Herod the Great by Cæsar Augustus. Herod enlarged and beautified it, and in honor of the emperor gave it the name Augusta, of which Sebaste is the Greek translation.

The first thing Philip did was to go to a city. Somehow the Gospel has flourished best in the city. Our Lord's work centered in Jerusalem. The apostles in their missionary tours always turned toward the great cities of the world. We read of Philip but once outside of a city. He met the chamberlain of Queen Candace in a desert. But here in the person of the eunuch he was preaching to a court and doubtless to a kingdom. Philip was pre-eminently a preacher to cities. " But Philip was found at Azotus [Ashdod] : and passing through he preached in all the cities, till he came to Cesarea " (ver. 40).

There is nothing in the city which the Gospel fears. It is not abashed in presence of intellect, of wealth, of social and political power. It turns them to its own uses. Its history has been chiefly identified with that of the most powerful cities, the best races, the most cultivated languages.

In our day we deplore the decline of preaching in the country. Fill the cities with men like Philip and the contagion will spread (ver. 25). The problem is not how to carry the Gospel into the country, but how to spread and maintain it in the city. The growth of cities is phenomenal and, from the stand-point of Christian work, startling. The country has practically become a suburb. Loudly the city calls for evangelization. The thousand of the city must not give way to the hundred of the country. A multitude of men are needed who, like Philip, will make straight for the city.

Philip knew the shortest road to the human heart. He preached Christ unto them. He evidently did not argue. He uttered no harsh words. He did not take them to task because they had no Bible but the Pentateuch. Their mixed and perverted worship he did not assail. It is altogether likely that he made no reference to the hateful controversy so long raging between Gerizim and Moriah. He preached Christ unto them. He gave the facts—facts resting on the person of Christ and stayed by Christian experience.

In preaching, as in every thing else, nothing can take the place of facts. Every-where the great human quest is for facts. If you are preparing information to be used in a congressional committee room, you will be told not to give arguments, but facts.

Preaching Christ is dealing with facts, central and sublime facts. He is the supreme Fact of the world. And the great fact concerning him is that he is the personal Saviour of men. Grand is he in creation, in history, in knowledge, but grandest is he enthroned in the heart of man.

His greatest joy is in saving the soul. This is the glorious fact of preaching. Every thing concerning Christ turns on this. No better designation of the work of a preacher of the Gospel can be found in the Bible than is contained in the brief phrase, "And preached Christ unto them."

The great message announced, Philip at once began to do good. He worked miracles. He did not do this merely to convince the people that he had told them the truth. He did it to help them. His miracles were of two kinds. The first was to rid many of unclean spirits; the second, to heal diseases.

There is a natural and beautiful sequence of Christian work here. First in importance is the salvation of the soul. There immediately follows moral renovation. Then comes physical benefit.

We cannot cast out unclean spirits or heal diseases. We *can* preach Christ. The two great forces we are to exercise in place of Philip's power to work miracles are those of example and kindness. These are more needed in the Church of to-day than miraculous gifts. Unclean spirits cannot endure moral purity. In its presence they require no exorcism. Of their own will they flee from it. And how does Christian sympathy mitigate suffering and disease? We need not pray for miraculous gifts. As true Christians we wield a power quite their equivalent.

The Gospel had been given to the people in its threefold power—to save, to cleanse, to cure. With sin forgiven, unclean spirits cast out, diseases healed, how could it be otherwise than that there should be great joy in that city?

There was one deeply interested spectator of Philip's work—Simon the sorcerer. It does not appear that he cared much for the preaching. His eye was on the miracles.

In this single particular it would not be difficult to duplicate his case in our day among very good people.

Here was something probably new to him—genuine miracles. There was no trickery in it. By his art he could do some wonderful things. He was helped therein, as we may infer from what the Bible tells us of ancient magic, by the powers of darkness. But he knew himself to be a deceiver, the practitioner of a wicked art.

When, therefore, he saw Philip, without resort to charms, amulets, herbs, incantations, mystical letters, and many other awe-inspiring devices, do what was utterly beyond the power of magic, he was, of course, "amazed." He became ambitious of possessing a like power. It would make him the great magician of the world. We may reasonably conjecture that in order to acquire the secret of Philip's power he believed and was baptized.

It is possible for people of the modern world to come perilously near to believing in Christ in the interest of "signs and great miracles."

And what wrath must fall from heaven upon those who pretend to Philip's gifts, bewitching many for private gain. Removing the coverings from Simon's heart, we see that self-interest was at the bottom of his infatuation with Philip.

But he was to be still more amazed. Christianity is a religion of surprises. The more men see of its working, whether they be friends or foes, the more it moves them to wonder.

Philip had gone as far as he could go. He had done much; but there was one thing he could not do. By the laying on of his hands the Holy Ghost could not be received.

There was no common level of prerogative in the early ministry. Very early God introduced a beautiful and varied order into it. While Peter and John could do all that Philip did, Philip could not do all that Peter and John could do.

It was the "gift of God" peculiar to the apostles that now drew Simon Magus to them. Here was something more baffling, more amazing, than the things Philip had done. Common, plain people who had been baptized with Simon at once, through prayer and the laying on of hands, became the recipients of marvelous gifts. They spoke in tongues they had never learned; they prophesied; they healed; they wrought miracles. What a power was this possessed by the apostles to bring down such gifts (chap. xix, 6; 1 Cor. xii, 8, etc.).

Simon's wonder, at least, was natural. We wonder as did he. God has withheld from us the miraculous gifts of the apostolic age. We do not need them. The Church is planted. Christianity is established. While we are learning a new tongue the Gospel is preached in every tongue. The physician and the hospital are healing while we are acquiring the art of healing. It was not so at first.

The apostles' hands had not been laid upon Simon, his heart had not been touched by Philip's preaching, and he was, of course, open to any temptation that the powers of darkness might suggest.

If God be not with us the powers of evil are. To be saved from the smallest sins as well as the greatest we need to be gathered under the wing of the Almighty. Away from his brooding love and sheltering power we are not a moment safe.

Simon's sin was a deed of awful sacrilege. It does not appear that it was *the* sin against the Holy Ghost; but it was *a* sin against the Holy Ghost. It belonged to that class of sins from which the worst men shrink.

Wicked men reverence the name of the Holy Ghost as they do not that of the Father or the Son. Infidels are silenced when we talk to them of the Holy Spirit ; of his witness in our hearts ; of his guidance in our lives. There is a hush among scoffers when we speak the name of this person of the Holy Trinity. This universal shrinking from irreverence toward the Holy Spirit may be an instinct divinely implanted within us as a specific preventive against the unpardonable sin.

We do not need, however, to commit Simon's sin ; it is not necessary to profane the name of the Holy Spirit to be guilty of sins against the Holy Ghost. Indifference to his pleadings, slighting his calls, are sin enough. In this we all have to say that our hearts have not been right in the sight of God. This is the dispensation of the Spirit. We are peculiarly exposed to sins against him. O, let us watch and pray lest we commit *sins* against the Holy Ghost.

Some of us have stood where Virgil and Dante found imagery that makes men shudder to read of. We have been down into Vesuvius's awful cone ; in the flarings of a single torch we have stood upon the margin of the river Styx. In these places we have recalled the poetic scenes of which they are the dreadful negatives. But Virgil and Dante are unable to furnish a picture so remarkable in its setting, so fearful in its details, as that which Peter now gives us of Simon's heart.

And what is this picture? It is a picture of sin; sin which torments, curses, and destroys us. In Simon sin took the form of a wicked and powerful ambition. In us it may take the form of something else. This picture of Simon "in the gall of bitterness and in the bond of iniquity" is simply a picture of the human heart with God out of it and sin in it.

We trust from what follows that Simon was forgiven. He was alarmed at Peter's revelation of his condition and his danger.

Unless we be conscious of God's favor we ought to be alarmed every moment. If Christ came into the world to save sinners; if the Holy Spirit, the Bible, the Church, the ministry are working for this end, how ought he to feel who is resisting one and all?

May this lesson bring us nearer to Christ; may it inspire in us a deep hatred of sin, which is Satan's magic, and may it awaken us to covet more earnestly those gifts of the Spirit, which, while they may differ from the gifts that came by the laying on of the apostles' hands, nevertheless belong to the same Spirit.

H. H. CLARK.

XI.

PHILIP AND THE ETHIOPIAN.

Acts viii, 26-40.

GOLDEN TEXT.—He that believeth on the Son hath everlasting life. John iii, 36.

WE have before us in this narrative an interesting and instructive picture of mission work in apostolic times —simple, yet graphic, containing all the elements of a pleasing story; at the same time bringing home to our hearts the great truths of communion with God, angelic ministry, divine leadership, and salvation through Jesus Christ.

This story of Philip and the Ethiopian is so rich in practical suggestions that the teacher will find it difficult to select the most important for the hour with the class. Your attention is invited to the consideration of four important features in the lesson:

1. *God's Providential Direction in Individual Life.* "And the angel of the Lord spake unto Philip." This meeting of Philip and the Ethiopian was not the result of mere accident or chance. A species of pre-established harmony existed between these two souls before they were conscious of each other's existence in this world. An angel messenger gives the directions by which they were to be brought together. Many times the oppor-

tunities of life seem purely accidental, but if we could follow all the steps by which these opportunities were prepared we would find the deep, well-laid plans of God's purposes: "Behold, I send an Angel before thee, to keep thee in the way, and to bring thee into the place which I have prepared" (Exod. xxiii, 20).

Frequently we speak of accidents determining a man's destiny, forgetting that in the vocabulary of God there is no such word as chance. It seemed a mere chance that Moses was discovered by Pharaoh's daughter—a chance river current, as a fitful morning breeze, bringing him to the bathing-place of the princess. "But eternal choice that chance did guide."

In that basket floated the destiny of God's chosen people. In that babe the providence of God was to furnish the human means of Israel's deliverance from the bondage of cruel Egypt. A sleepless night in the life of Ahasuerus, an imperial whim to pass away the weary hours by having the records of the kingdom read; but back of that sleepless night was a providence working to bring Mordecai to a position of influence, where he will be able to foil the malignant plot of Haman.

A dusty pilgrim overtaken on a desert road by the chamberlain of a pagan queen, that is all the world's wise ones see in this incident of our lesson; but in this chance meeting there is the hidden fire of a divine purpose. In that meeting the treasurer of Ethiopia receives the message of the Gospel into his care-worn heart, and with an anthem of joy goes forth a saved man to plant in far away Africa the seeds of saving truth :

> "Thou camst not to thy place by accident,
> It is the very place God meant for thee;
> And shouldst thou there small scope for action see,
> Do not for this give room to discontent."

Behind all life's varying scenes—its joys, its sorrows, its social positions and its political ambitions, its individual cares, its national crises—there is the guiding hand of God. It is the privilege of the Christian to rely on other forms hovering, guiding, arranging, and inspiring the events of life, so that redeemed man may co-operate with the purposes of God : " For he shall give his angels charge over thee to keep thee in all thy ways."

What comfort to short-sighted, burden-bearing pilgrims, to think that God's angels are ministering spirits marshaled under King Jesus to guard and defend us against the assaults of our great adversary, the devil, who is continually striving for our destruction.

2. *The Willing and Obedient Servant.* Notice the nature of the directions given by the angel and what was involved in obedience thereto. Verse 26 gives us the text of the angel's commission to Philip: "Arise, and go toward the south, unto the way that goeth down from Jerusalem unto Gaza, which is desert." In a sense Philip is to proceed under *sealed orders.* The directions are simple in terms so far as they go. Go to a certain road. Yet in a sense they are vague and indefinite. Sixty miles of desert highway, with the haughty, wicked city of Gaza

at the southern terminus, was a command seriously requiring some more definite statements as to what duty was to be met and where the field of future work was to be found. The angel had revealed to Philip just enough to indicate some of the difficulties in the way. No point or place is mentioned in the message, no time or duty is indicated. To ordinary human nature such directions would make room for two or three questions of a very practical character just here. It looks like a journey, but it may end in a jaunt. Natural, indeed, would have been the questions, Why limit the sphere of my ministry by taking this unfrequented way? Here I am in the populous city, multitudes are being stirred with the gospel message, converts coming every day. I am in the midst of a gracious revival; unclean spirits are crying out for fear, and are leaving the possessed ones clothed in their right mind. Because of this there is great joy in the city. Why, then, must I be side-tracked? why leave the city appointment to take the country charge? That was the voice of *expediency*, and we will always find crouching somewhere in the near neighborhood of that voice the cowardly tempter. And thus the tempter speaks: A long desert journey on foot, a lone pilgrim, prowling wild beasts, night coming on, and no shelter! Philip, there is danger ahead, "lions are in the way." Besides, if you reach Gaza, and it is revealed to you that there is your new field of work, consider what difficulties and dangers await you. Gaza is hardened in crime, bitter in its rebellion against God. It is one of the most ancient cities of the world. Joshua could not subdue it. It was assigned to Judah, but even that warlike tribe could not retain its possession. What an opportunity for another Jonah experience if there had been an iota of physical or moral cowardice in the heart of Philip! Yet to have yielded to his fears, to have doubted the divine wisdom, would have been to have lost the opportunity of meeting the man for whose conversion Philip was the divinely appointed instrument: "Only the willing and obedient shall eat of the good of the land."

We have heard inspiring sermons on that word "*come*" of the Gospel, and truly it is a blessed word, inviting weary hearts to the sweet asylum of rest found in Jesus Christ. Through its tender tones many a prodigal has found his way back to home. But, dear reader, as believers in the cross of Christ, have we realized the blessed privilege of that other great word of the Gospel, that small yet mighty word, "*Go?*" "Go out into the highways and hedges, and compel them to come in." "Go, work to-day in my vineyard." And when falling for the last time on human ears from the lips of our Saviour it was from the spur of Olivet, where the chariot of his Father was waiting to take the Redeemer home: "Go ye therefore, and teach all nations, baptizing them in the name of the Father, and of the Son, and of the Holy Ghost. . . . And, lo, I am with you alway, even unto the end of the world."

It was the inspiration of that great word that moved Philip to obedience. In the sweet harmonies of soul that

united his life in loving obedience to the command of his
Master, all the harsh voices of selfish expediency, all the
lower voices of fear and doubt, were hushed, and like
Abraham at Mount Moriah, like Moses at Sinai, and
Elijah at Carmel, in filial obedience he walked the seemingly desert pathway of duty, making it to bloom and
blossom as the rose.

We dare not leave this thought of loving obedience to
the commands of God without emphasizing another fact
in this connection, namely, that in proportion as we obey
present revelations of God's will, future and fuller revelations will appear. Through obedience God makes a
broader and deeper manhood, and then gives a broader
and deeper truth to fill that enlarged manhood. Philip
had plainly revealed to him the direction he was to take:
" Arise, and go toward the south, unto the way that . . .
is desert." This command was sufficient for prompt
action at that hour. Philip had capital enough at that
moment to go right to work for God in the new field.
When the hour of opportunity came for other work than
walking a desert highway, verse 29 informs us that another revelation was given. Philip is on the journey, he
is overtaken by the chariot of the Ethiopian : " Then the
Spirit said unto Philip, Go near, and join thyself to this
chariot." An angel directs Philip to leave the city and
go southward on the desert road, but in this new scene
of duty the servant of God is brought into close quarters
with a sin-burdened soul. That work can be done by no
angel. The Holy Spirit, the third person of the Trinity,

is to take the truth as it is in Jesus and bring it home to the Ethiopian's soul with saving power. This higher revelation was given to Philip through obedience to the former revelation. God always furnishes revelations of duty in installments according to the necessities of the hour and the measure of our faith. The way at first may seem dark. The commands of God may seem foolish to the demands of expediency. Human reason may stagger and fall and refuse to go farther. But to the eye of faith the "inventory of the universe is in heaven." God will furnish himself a lamb for the burnt-offering. He will reveal place and method when the hour of opportunity strikes:

> "Lead, kindly Light, amid the encircling gloom,
>   Lead thou me on!
> The night is dark, and I am far from home;
>   Lead thou me on!
> Keep thou my feet; I do not ask to see
> The distant scene; one step enough for me."

3. *A Bible-reading Traveler.* Not a novelty, perhaps, in those days of religious pilgrimage, but certainly somewhat of a novelty to-day. The soul is not much advantaged in the scenes of modern travel. Ocean steamers and vestibule-trains have little to conserve spiritual thought. How seldom do we see the Word of God in the hands of travelers to-day! If you want to be conspicuous and regarded as a little "cranky," take your Bible and read it on the railroad train. The newspaper, the sensational novel, the card-table—these are the monopolists of the time of the American traveler to-day.

"Sunday is the dullest and gloomiest day of the whole

week," said a commercial traveler to the writer not long since. What a dearth of *soul-health* such a confession reveals! With free churches in all our cities, with good singing and able preaching and hearty invitations to the house of God pealing from church-bells, Sunday ought to be the refreshing oasis in the care-burdened life of the traveling man. A Sabbath day in a strange city to such a man as the Ethiopian would have been regarded as a day of privilege, a day of worship; for just such a purpose he had come a very great distance to worship in Jerusalem, and his religious spirit he carried with him out into the duties of the secular week. He had gone "to behold the beauty of the Lord, and to inquire in his temple." His soul had thus been stirred to a sense of deeper need, and he now searches the Word of God to see with spiritual eyes the profound meaning of those words of the prophet: "He was led as a sheep to the slaughter; and like a lamb dumb before his shearer, so opened he not his mouth," *et seq*.

This Bible-reading traveler offered Philip a better chance to preach the Gospel to him than the average hearer furnishes the preachers of to-day. He was prepared for the message. It is a significant statement in the lesson that Philip "opened his mouth, and began at the same Scripture, and preached unto him Jesus." The eunuch had come from a period of profound meditation on the Word of God to hear the gospel sermon. Philip had not to contend with a hearer who had come from the perusal of the Sunday newspaper to hear the sermon.

The latest scandal rehearsed at the Sunday breakfast-table presented no obstacle to the preaching of the Word. How differently modern audiences would listen to the words of teacher and preacher if they were to come to the sanctuary fresh from a personal study of the Word of God. Many times have we heard the casual remarks dropped from the lips of the careless hearer as he retired from church: "The preacher did not strike me to-day." "He did not reach my need." "I don't think he prepared that sermon with his usual care." Dear friend, what about your preparation as a hearer by an hour's thought on the Word of God, or a few moments' earnest meditation on the interests of your soul before you heard that sermon? You come from the wild clamor of the stock-exchange; you come from the cankering cares of the business week; you come from the late Saturday evening pleasure-party; you come from a six days' constant contact with mad efforts to gain that which perishes with the using, and expect the man in the pulpit to banish all this influence in the short hour of service, and feed you with the "bread of life" without one moment's preparation by earnest prayer or devout reading. Shame, O man of gospel privileges and open Bible! Let this man of Ethiopia rise up and rebuke your wicked presumption.

Again, this Bible-reading traveler had some difficulties in the way of his receiving the truth as it is in Jesus. He had his doubts, as we all have. But he did not make an idol of his doubts and set it up as an object of worship. Honest doubt is to be respected, and when it is honest

God will provide a way for its removal, as he did in the case of Thomas: "Lord, I believe; help thou mine unbelief," will be answered in full when the soul ventures to exercise its *little faith*, seeking thus to prove God rather than by sending his doubts out as a picket-line, and demanding the Saviour to come through challenged before he can enter the heart.

Almost in the same breath whereby the Ethiopian expressed his doubt he uttered the words of his confession of faith, "I believe that Jesus Christ" is the Son of God, and that moment the recording angel wrote his name in the Book of Life. That faith he sealed in baptism, thus uniting himself with the followers of Jesus in the Church, and bearing back to his home the first-fruits of faith in Jesus Christ as Saviour and Lord.

4. *The Rejoicing Christian.* Our Bible story ends well. The Spirit of the Lord caught away Philip, and the eunuch went on his way rejoicing. Philip had been the instrument of converting the eunuch to Christ, not to the preacher. The soul that truly finds Christ does not backslide when the evangelist goes away, or when the minister changes his appointment. He is in possession of the divine Comforter as companion. The man has entered a life of trust whose elements are joy and peace in the Holy Ghost. He sees divine things, a new heaven and a new earth, bluer skies than even the Orient shows, greener fields than ever greeted his vision before. O, the hour never to be forgotten in the life of the believer, is that hour when the sorrowing, sighing, sinning soul is

PHILIP AND THE ETHIOPIAN. 313

christened in the experience of regeneration with the new name in the "Lamb's Book of Life."

Reader, we have not truly found Christ unless we find joy in his service. A cool critic stood before one of Turner's gorgeous skies all ablaze with the glories of sunset, and said to the artist: "I never see such colors of cloud as you paint." "Don't you wish you could?" said Turner. "As for me, I never can begin to paint the glories I see."

So with the Christian. " Eye hath not seen, nor ear heard, neither have entered into the heart of man the things which God hath prepared for them that love him." Friends of Jesus, if we are ever to be happy in heaven, the basis of that holy joy must be laid in our life with Christ in this world.

The eunuch had come from far-off Ethiopia with his burden of sin; he was going back home very much in the same condition. The Holy Spirit turned his attention to salvation through the cross of Christ. He accepted the sacrifice, he received pardon, he went on his way rejoicing. Christian teachers, many scholars will gather in our classes for the study of this lesson. The prodigal will come leaning on his broken staff. The gay young lady will come with the look of feasting in her face, but with famine in her soul. The indifferent pleasure-seeker will be there. The tempted and fallen will be there. Must they go away as they came? May each one of us be the instrument in the hands of the Holy Spirit of so showing some souls the Cross that they may go down to their homes rejoicing in the Lord. E. M. TAYLOR.

XIII.*

THE LORD'S SUPPER.

1 Cor. xi, 23-32.

GOLDEN TEXT.—Let a man examine himself, and so let him eat of that bread, and drink of that cup. 1 Cor. xi, 28.

WE cannot read Paul's account of the first celebration of the Lord's Supper without being impressed with the wonderful simplicity of the ordinance as administered by Christ himself. How different from the pomp and ceremony with which it is attended in some modern churches! Who, for instance, would recognize in the celebration of the Mass in the Church of Rome the commemoration of that simple yet expressive feast which Jesus instituted with his disciples in the little room at Jerusalem on the night of his betrayal?

It is surely a painful evidence of the weakness and corruption of the human heart that the beauty and simplicity of this divine institution should have been so distorted and mystified in subsequent ages of the Church.

In seeking to study this important ordinance of the Christian Church it is well that we can do so in the light of,

1. ITS FIRST INSTITUTION. Paul takes us back to

---

* No homily is given for Lesson XII, which is a review.

the original sources of knowledge on this subject. What he teaches on this matter he "received of the Lord." This is much better than human authority. Just when and in what manner he received this information he does not tell, and we need not waste time in idle conjectures concerning it. He simply states the fact.

(1) *The time of the supper* was "the same night that he was betrayed." Hence the ordinance is properly styled the *Lord's Supper*.

The early disciples also chose the evening hour as the time for administering this ordinance. Just why the Church has so generally fallen into the custom of having the communion at a morning hour is not very clear; but it is safe to conclude that the particular hour of the day is not a matter of importance, the simple command, or request, being "As oft as ye do it," "do it in remembrance of me," nothing being stated as to the particular time of celebrating the eucharistic feast. As to the frequency of its occurrence as suggested by the words just quoted, it may be noticed that the early Church observed the ordinance every Lord's day, and possibly more frequently. There is no hint that it was to be annually observed, like the feast of the passover, nor, on the other hand, need we conclude that the practice of the early Church in celebrating the ordinance every Sabbath is binding upon us. Those Churches that make it a monthly observance may be regarded as keeping the spirit of the New Testament injunction.

(2) *The elements employed* were simply the bread and

the wine as used in the passover feast. The bread and the cup are referred to again and again, with no hint that these simple elements were changed into the body and blood of Christ, as taught by the Romish Church. This monstrous doctrine, which offends the sense and contradicts the reason, arose in the ninth century, and received the official sanction of the Church of Rome in the thirteenth. It has been the fruitful source of a multitude of errors and superstitions. It changes what was intended to be a beautiful memorial of Christ's passion and death into a sacrificing of Christ. Instead of his being the sacrifice *once* offered for the sins of the people, they would have us believe that he is being perpetually offered as a sacrifice at the hands of the priest. Hence has followed in that Church the custom of elevating the host to receive the reverence of the people, the worship of the elements, as the real worship of Christ, bearing them in public procession through the streets and into the country as a means of dispensing some mystic blessing among the inhabitants; and so on to the end of this sad chapter of perverted doctrine. In what striking and beautiful contrast with all this are the words of the apostle: " As often as ye eat this *bread*, and drink this cup, ye do shew the Lord's death till he come."

(3) *Thanksgiving.* Another thing that we observe in connection with Christ's institution of this ordinance is the *thanksgiving.* In the matter of "giving thanks" at meals Jesus has set us a commendable example, and by

his conduct in this respect administers a severe rebuke to those graceless souls who sit down to their well-loaded tables without a single recognition of the Giver of their daily bread. But the thanksgiving on this occasion was somewhat out of the usual order. It occurs at the close of the passover meal, at which time he goes on to institute for his people a new feast with a new meaning, and to commemorate a more glorious deliverance than that from Egyptian bondage. It was for "the remission of sins," and deliverance from its cruel thraldom, that the Lamb of God was slain. The thanksgiving, therefore, may properly be regarded as a grateful recognition of the " true bread" which came down from heaven, of which, if a man eat, he shall never hunger.

It is just possible that the modern idea of "consecrating the elements" is a perversion of Christ's act and meaning—a sort of inheritance which we have received from the "*Mother Church.*" Christ simply taught us to *give thanks* in connection with the receiving of the bread and wine which represents his broken body and shed blood.

2. THE DESIGN OF THE ORDINANCE was (1) to keep ever before the minds of the Church the great fact of *Christ's death* for us. The command is, "Do this in remembrance of me." The ordinance, therefore, is commemorative, and not sacrificial. It is a beautiful memorial of this the greatest event in the world's history. The desire to commemorate events that are related to us is strongly implanted in the human heart. We see this in all eyes

and among all peoples. Jacob set up his rude pillar of stones at Bethel to commemorate the wonderful nightvision; Samuel gratefully raised his Ebenezer between Mizpeh and Shen, saying, " Hitherto hath the Lord helped us." The passover feast was another memorial to keep alive in the memories of Israel their wonderful deliverance out of Egypt. The history of God's ancient people is full of these reminders of divine mercies and blessings.

So likewise the Lord's Supper is designed to keep ever before the minds of his people the fact of the great love of Him who loved us unto the death. " As often as ye eat this bread, and drink this cup, ye do show *the Lord's death* till he come." It points us backward to the cross, and forward to his coming again. We shall do well, therefore, to keep this simple view of the ordinance in in mind. It is thus that it becomes:

(2) *A precious means of grace.* It is a visible sermon which makes its appeal through the eye to the heart. It preaches Christ, and him crucified. Properly celebrated it makes a powerful impression upon the unconverted. Albert Barnes has said that it is not designed nor adapted to be a converting ordinance. But I am not so sure of this. I was present once at a very solemn and feeling administration of the Lord's Supper. During the last invitation to the table the minister referred in a touching manner to the fact that the bread and the wine represented the broken body and shed blood of the Lord Jesus Christ—the atoning death of our Saviour.

He then said, "If there is any one present who desires personally to receive the benefit of his death and passion, and is willing to confess his faith in him and love for him, do so by coming forward and partaking of the emblems of his sacrificial death." At once an intelligent young lady arose, and, bursting into tears, came down the aisle weeping, and bowed with others, and received the holy sacrament. Nor did the Lord turn her empty away, for she was instantly and beautifully saved in that act of appropriating Christ, and continued a devoted Christian. The invitation of the preacher and the prompt action of the young woman were, no doubt, somewhat out of the usual order, but the incident serves well to illustrate the important fact that the ordinance may be so administered as to be a most effective way of preaching Christ, and him crucified, and to become a real means of grace not only to saints, but to perishing sinners as well.

And who will say that such occurrences might not be much more frequent if this central fact of the ordinance were made more prominent?

The grace, of course, is not communicated through any supernatural power inhering in the elements, nor in the person administering them, nor yet in the sacramental rite as a whole. It is simply a natural and rational means of grace. As the ordinance serves to set forth in a lively and impressive manner Christ's sufferings and death for us, it becomes a powerful means of awakening and stimulating our love toward him. When we intelligently receive the elements of bread and wine, we by faith appropriate Christ to our souls.

3. WHO SHALL PARTAKE OF IT? This is a question that needs some consideration, especially in view of the well-known practice of the Church of Rome in withholding the cup from the laity.

The plain inference from the record of the first institution of it by Christ is that all of the disciples (with the possible exception of Judas) received the bread, and in regard to the wine, the express words of Jesus are, " Drink ye *all* of it." In view of such a command the practice of the Romish Church appears very strange indeed. They attempt to justify it, it is true, by saying that as the bread is by the consecrating act of the priest changed into the real body of Christ, it necessarily contains the blood, and hence the laity receive both kinds when they receive the wafer. But consistency would require that the priests receive the blood of Christ in the same manner, and thus dispense with the cup entirely. The fact that they do not shows that it is a mere subterfuge for disregarding the unmistakable command of Christ. The plain words of our Lord, as well as the practice of the early Church, teach us that this sacrament is not only for the priesthood, or ministry, but for all of his followers. The same conclusion is reached from the analogy of the paschal feast. All of the families of Israel and all of each family partook of the paschal lamb. Christ is our passover, and the conclusion by analogy is plain that all the members of the true Israel should partake of the slain Lamb. Again, as the Lord's Supper is a means of grace, all alike should share its blessings, as all alike need them, and would naturally desire to express their love for the Author of these mercies.

But the very nature of the ordinance is such that the sinful, the ungodly, the irreligious, and the impenitent should not come to the communion-table of the Lord. For such do not in the proper sense "discern the Lord's body."

The ordinance is an outward expression by the participant of faith in Christ as his personal Saviour, of obedience to him as his Lord, and of loving gratitude to him for his saving mercy. These are the essential elements of an evangelical faith, and they are all wanting in the class of persons to whom I have referred. For the unbelieving, disobedient, and unthankful to come to the Lord's table is to profane this holy ordinance and crucify the Lord afresh. Such, the apostle tells us, are "guilty of the body and blood of Christ."

He who approaches this table, therefore, should do it with great thoughtfulness and reverence, lest he come into judgment and condemnation. Let him "examine himself" that he may know that he is worthy to come to so solemn and sacred a feast. But let not the timid and self-distrusting Christian be thus deterred from coming to the Supper of the Lord for fear of eating and drinking unworthily, for such are usually among the most worthy. Those who are charged with the responsibility of administering this holy ordinance should exercise great care and wisdom not to discourage the morbidly conscientious, while trying to arouse the careless to thoughtfulness and self-examination.

> Come, all who truly bear
>   The name of Christ your Lord,
> His last mysterious supper share,
>   And keep his kindest word.
> Hereby your faith approve
>   In Jesus crucified:
> " In memory of my dying love,
>   Do this," he said—and died.

R. C. GLASS.

FOURTH QUARTER.

I.
SAUL OF TARSUS CONVERTED.

Acts ix, 1-20.

GOLDEN TEXT.—Except a man be born again, he cannot see the kingdom of God. John iii, 3.

SAUL of Tarsus was on the road to conversion long before he entered the road to Damascus. Though living in the atmosphere of "threatenings and slaughter," he was not removed from the region of divine conviction. The seeds of spiritual suggestion had entered the persecutor's heart at the stoning of Stephen, and they came to full fruition during the long silence and loneliness of that memorable six days' journey. Bethel, Shiloh, and Sychar, where were Jacob's well and Joseph's tomb; Mount Gilboa, where his great namesake was slain; Tabor, wooded to its very top, from which centuries before Barak's hosts had descended in battle, and "the stars in their courses fought against Sisera;" Carmel, where God answered Elijah by fire, were associations on his way which may have furnished the spiritual heat that tended to hasten the growth of these seeds in this young man's soul.

It will not do for us to underestimate the power of little things in the soul's conversion. The chance word of a friend, a suggestive passage of some book, the consecrated life of a Christian mother, have been the beginnings that have caused many a spiritual desert ultimately to blossom like the rose.

Genuine conversions are never sudden conversions in the sense that they are suddenly wrought by the divine hand upon some soul which has never had previous spiritual enlightenment. It is true that " as he journeyed . . . *suddenly* there shined round about him a light from heaven;" but it would be far from the truth for us to affirm that up to this time Saul of Tarsus had had not been taught of God.

Neither is it true that his was a mind unsettled and uneasy in its intellectual and moral beliefs. On the contrary, he was an ardent Jew, inheriting and taking pride in all the traditional beliefs, historic glories, and Messianic hopes of the Jews. His judgment about things could not be easily moved and radically changed at a bound. Clear and analytic, cool and logical, we expect such minds to move slowly and reach decisions deliberately—above all, when such a decision changes entirely all previous views and feelings, as it did with Saul of Tarsus.

The zeal which sent Saul to the high-priest, desiring of him letters to Damascus, was not that of a Peter who drew his sword and smote off the ear of the high-priest's servant. The one was but the blazing forth of a sudden excitement, the other was the deep-bedded furnace-heat of profound conviction and sense of duty. " I verily thought I *ought* to do many things contrary to the name of Jesus of Nazareth."

Now, although Saul was the possessor of these qualities of mind and heart which we have mentioned, his conversion was not out of harmony with the circumstances of the case. God comes to different men by different methods of approach. The Ethiopian eunuch, quietly reading the words of Isaiah, needed the calm instruction of a Philip. But a Saul, "yet breathing out threatenings and slaughter," could be reached only by a special manifestation of the power of God. With *such* a man it were impossible to *reason*, therefore God strikes him to the ground. But he strikes him to the ground that he may raise him up again, in every sense a new and better man.

In that crisis-hour of his existence this man, like every other genuine convert to divine truth the world has ever seen, was overwhelmingly surprised to find himself sought after by the very Truth he ignorantly fought against; and, trembling and astonished, he said : "Lord, what wilt thou have *me* to do?" It is the first marvel of every seeker after God that long before he began his search God was seeking him out from among the children of men. The divine love runs out far ahead of even our first impulses toward the truth, and is waiting to reveal itself unto us.

Whatever else may have been true about this Judean rabbi, this is certain, he was honest in what he did. The essential element of honesty, which Jesus ever seems to demand of every convert, lies in the spirit of readiness to inquire for some new hint or suggestion of service for Christ which the individual may follow out in his every-day life. The heathen may be honest in his devotion as he bows down to blocks of wood and stone, but once convinced of the truth of the God of the Bible, he cannot remain an honest man if he persists in clinging to his idolatry. No more can any soul convinced of its own sinfulness and of its need of a Saviour remain honest if it does not at once ask the question, " Lord, what wilt thou have me to do ? "

Christ becomes a terrible bar of judgment when we come face to face with him, listen to his teachings, understand what he asks of us, and turn our backs on his claims. Unconditional surrender is the first demand after we realize that Christ is the Saviour. The sincere persecutor must become at once the sincere repenter, for it takes a sincere repenter to make a sincere seeker after God. How long does it take a sincere seeker to become a converted individual? Not an instant. The honest seeker after God must first be "turned about " before he can even begin his search for God. Saul of Tarsus was "turned about " when he recognized the Lord whom he had persecuted, and asked what he would have him do. But was Saul of Tarsus then a Christian ? The answer to this will depend on what is meant by being a Christian. If "despair of self and trust in God," with the purpose of doing his will, whatever that may be, makes a Christian, then Saul was a Christian when he groped his way through the Damascus streets, led by the hand of an attendant. But if a Christian is only one who has been filled with the Holy Ghost, then was Saul not a Christian till three days later, when, in answer to the word of Ananias, he "received his sight forthwith, and arose, and was baptized." While we would enter into no hair-splitting discussion of this point as to just where Saul's Christianity began, we are among the number of those who believe that whenever any soul sick of sin looks into the Word of God with the high purpose of being mastered by the Christ there revealed, just there its Christian life begins. It is doubtless true that there are blessings of Christian experience on the wing for that soul from that very moment which it may not realize for some time to come. Thus it was with Saul. He must needs *wait* for this special *blessing*. Why, we cannot tell. There are mysteries of grace as well as of other realms which surround us every-where. To those who are willing to *wait*, continuing steadfast in prayer, the blessing of *full* salvation is sure to come. It came to Saul when "there fell from his eyes as it had been scales" and from his soul the darkness of sin. From this moment he was "a new creature in Christ Jesus." Old things had passed away; Saul the sinner now becomes Paul the preacher.

Thus Wesley, the zealous legalist, though not the persecutor, "going about to establish his own righteousness," had not submitted to the righteousness of God until that hour in Aldersgate Street. Suddenly, while listening to instructions drawn from the great epistle of this very Paul, he felt his heart strangely warmed, felt that he did trust Christ for all and was saved. Thus the boy Spurgeon, in a little Wesleyan chapel, heard the words, " Young man, look! Look to Jesus and live ! " "And I looked," said he, " and was saved." Thus always the day dawns and the day-star arises in human hearts.

> " Faith lends its realizing light,
> The clouds disperse, the shadows fly ;
> The Invisible appears in sight,
> And God is seen by mortal eye."

The work suddenly wrought in the soul of this man who traveled that Damascus road so long ago was evidently intended by God to be the most striking example in all history of his converting power. But we must not forget that the processes of conviction, repentance, and pardon, and the saving of a soul under the discipline and training of God, are the same in every age. Different men are led to God by different circumstances ; for the providences of God are never the same in two lives. But when the soul once opens itself to let in its Maker, he enters, and that soul is regenerated in precisely the same manner as was the soul of Saul of Tarsus.

It is not given unto us, as unto him, to have a personal vision with the natural eye of the personal Christ. God does not need to teach the resurrection to every age as he taught it to that of Paul, but unto every one of us is given the opportunity of realizing the power of his resurrection by being born again.

Let us not, then, concern ourselves about the way along which God shall choose to come to our souls. Let us only ask in sincerity that he come.

A. W. TIRRELL.

II.

DORCAS RAISED TO LIFE.

Acts ix, 32-43.

GOLDEN TEXT.—This woman was full of good works and almsdeeds which she did. Acts ix, 36.

IF Dorcas was raised from the dead in answer to the prayer of faith, why may not many other saints be similarly raised through prayer on the part of consecrated disciples of Jesus Christ? Would the same faith exercised by the same parties during Dorcas's illness have prevented death and accomplished the restoration of the sick? These questions are intimately connected with a subject much discussed in church life—faith-healing. Many thoughtful Christians are interesting themselves in the relations of disease to drugs on the one hand, and to prayer on the other. Some think that they discern general promises in the Scripture that cover all classes of sicknesses, and that warrant the believer in dispensing with all the remedies of the materia medica; faith, and faith alone, is sufficient for recovery from bodily ailments. Others, who are not able to read into the general promises that which is claimed by the "faith-healers," ask: If faith be potent for the healing of disease, why should holy people be sick at all? and if a sickness is unto death, why should not the prayer of those who believe in faith-healing be able to raise the dead?

As many have confused ideas on this important topic it may be profitable to define the boundaries beyond which faith may not go, and to state the area within which God performs miracles upon the bodies of his saints. The character, sickness, death, and resurrection of Dorcas afford an admirable opportunity for a fresh study of this phase of church life.

The state of the Church at the time when this incident took place needs to be rehearsed.

The persecution of which Saul of Tarsus was the recognized leader had terrified the people, and many who felt the claims of truth were afraid to avow their convictions, or even seem to be interested in the new religion. The few converts who stood the test of imprisonment and threatened death were refined like silver in the fire, but the work of propagating the truth went on slowly. But when the chief inquisitor became a disciple of the Nazarene, and with great power taught from the Scriptures that Jesus was the Christ, the reign of terror was broken, and men breathed freer. "Then had the church rest throughout all Judea."

Mere quietude, however, is not the law of progress; something was needed to overcome the timidity of the church at Joppa, and to awaken the attention of the money-making people of that sea-port town. God had his own way of encouraging the faithful and arousing the careless.

Dorcas was the instrument by which he accomplished these ends.

The faith of this woman was of the highest type. Her belief was more than a theological assent to the truth; it was more than a conviction that God is able to perform all he has promised; it was more than the repetition of some formula of doctrine that she and those associated with her might have used as a watchword; her faith worked by love and purified the heart. "This woman was full of good works and almsdeeds which she did." The Christian who is abundant in mercies has the sympathetic soul of the Master. A heart of love toward God and man is the best proof of the very highest development of faith. "There is none other commandment greater than these." "If ye fulfill the royal law according to the Scripture, Thou shalt love thy neighbor as thyself, ye do well."

Notwithstanding the faith of Dorcas, "It came to pass in those days, that she was sick, and died."

There are several considerations that press upon us in view of these facts. Sickness is not necessarily an indication of sin on the part of the individual attacked by disease; some of the holiest people are those who have struggled through years of pain, and who though suffering intensely have always been in a triumphant frame of mind.

Neither is illness to be attributed to a lack of faith. It is presumable that Dorcas used the ordinary remedies, and that she asked God's blessing on the means; but neither remedies nor faith availed; she died.

It is God's purpose to let the physical forces of the universe take, in most instances, the natural courses he has made; he has good reasons why diseases should be allowed in the majority of cases to develop through the various stages of their natural history. Sometimes we can see the good that comes to us from illness; not unfrequently it brings forth the fruit of a new purpose; even by death good may come to those who live, and the individual, like Samson, slay more in his death than in his life.

There are times, however, when for his glory God interferes with the natural order of things, and brings to pass supernatural results. Such was the case in the resurrection of Dorcas's body.

When loving hands had performed the customary rites, the body was "laid in an upper chamber." Great was the sorrow in that stricken household; no hired mourners were necessary when widows gathered to weep together over a common loss, and rehearse to one another the good deeds done by her to their fatherless children, "showing the coats and garments which Dorcas made, while she was with them."

As the church members turned their faces heavenward, God put it into their hearts to send for Peter, a dozen miles away at Lydda. Others had died at Joppa, but God had not put it into the minds of their friends to send for an apostle. The Lord himself moved the friends of Dorcas to do this; and when Peter heard the request of the "two men" sent, the Spirit moved him to respond. " Then Peter arose and went with them."

Perhaps Peter had not the slightest idea what he would be called upon to do, but he started out. It would be very interesting to us had Luke recorded the conversation between the apostle and the two messengers as they walked back to Joppa; perhaps they conversed about the details of the sickness and death of this excellent lady, spoke of the grief of the family, deplored the great loss to the Church, and magnified the opportunities for good had she been spared. As they journeyed, convictions sent by the Spirit of God formed in Peter's mind; he saw the possible mission of such a woman raised to life and proclaiming the power of Jesus in covetous Joppa; her known worth would make her experience more striking to the public conscience. By the time he had reached the city he had received divine illumination as to the course that ought to be pursued. Entering into the house, " Peter put them all forth," that his mind might not be distracted from any suggestion that the Spirit might make to him, and he "kneeled down and prayed."

Others equally deserving a resurrection had died and were buried without a word of prayer for their resurrection. Stephen, "a man full of faith and of the Holy Ghost," was not called back from the spirit-world. It was for the glory of God that the first martyr was taken by "devout men" from the bloody stones that had been hurled at and upon him and carried "to his burial." It was for the good of the kingdom of God that Peter was inspired to ask for the return of Dorcas to her work, and Christ heard the petition he had himself put into his servant's heart. Without especial illumination the apostle would not have had the intelligent faith to pray; but with the direct prompting of the Holy Ghost, "turning him to the body," he said: "Tabitha, arise!" The same Voice that commanded Peter to pray ordered Dorcas to return to the earth and re-animate the waiting dust. Obedient to the call, she re-entered the cold form, "opened her eyes: and when she saw Peter, she sat up." The apostle, pursuing the same policy he had followed from the first, and using all natural means in addition to the supernatural power bestowed, "gave her his hand, and lifted her up; and when he had called the saints and widows, he presented her alive."

The Results. There was joy in the household of Dorcas; the night of weeping had passed and the morning of joy had come. As the people heard of the wonderful work that had been wrought it became a sign to them that the Lord was in the midst, "and it was known throughout all Joppa." Men who scoffed at the name of Jesus accepted him as the Messiah, "and many believed in the Lord." The revival spread, work came to Peter in abundance, "and it came to pass that he tarried many days in Joppa." Prejudices were overcome—even tanners were given a standing—and no fault was found with the apostle because he accepted the hospitality of "one Simon a tanner." Cries of mercy were heard among the convicted, and hallelujahs among the delivered. Lydda, Joppa, Cesarea! As Eneas walked about Lydda and the surrounding country telling the story of his being raised by Peter from the bed on which he had laid for eight years, "Saron saw him, and turned to the Lord;" Joppa was thrilled with spiritual life at the resurrection of Dorcas; and Cesarea was visited with blessings in the conversion of Cornelius and in the gift of the Holy Ghost that " fell on all them which heard the word." The results abundantly justified the exhibition of miraculous power in these three cities.

The inferences drawn from the healing of Eneas and the raising of Dorcas, so far as the topic in hand is concerned, may now be stated:

1. Holiness is not a bar to disease, although a Christian life tends to health and longevity.

2. Remedies are to be used under the advice of skilled physicians.

3. God usually permits diseases to run through the varied stages of their natural history. Sometimes medicine arrests the development of disease, and the vital forces effect cure; at other times disease reaches its climax, subsides, and recovery is reached without either prayer or medicine. Again, diseases terminate in death. These things happen alike to saints and sinners; yet God works them all into his beneficent plans, and makes them " work together for good to them that love " him.

4. There are times, however, when it is for the glory of God's kingdom that the Head of the Church should arrest disease by the direct action of his own Spirit.

5. When it is the purpose of Christ to "bear our sick-

nesses," he illuminates the minds of certain faithful disciples, impressing them with the belief that a petition offered for healing will be granted.

6. Faith exercised upon the gift of especial illumination will be honored.

7. No person has been raised from the dead since apostolic times; therefore no illumination has been given for this purpose; supposed illuminations have been hallucinations. In the cases of healing, trustworthy examples are not wanting; yet the instances are comparatively rare, and great care is necessary to distinguish between the illumination of the Holy Spirit and the hallucination of our own spirit. In the vast majority of diseases it is the will of God that we should ask him to bless the remedies used, and then be resigned to the result.

8. The highest type of faith expresses its needs according to the best knowledge at the time, and trustfully leaves the outcome to Him who has said, "Your Father knoweth what things ye have need of before ye ask him." It often requires more faith to resign one's self calmly to death, and commit orphan children to the care of the Lord, than it does to claim a supposed general promise, by the belief and appropriation of which recovery is anticipated.

J. M. DURRELL.

III.
PETER'S VISION.

Acts x, 1-20.

GOLDEN TEXT.—Of a truth I perceive that God is no respecter of persons. Acts x, 34.

THE record of the advance of the young Church gives in quick succession three typical conversions: first, that of the eunuch, a foreigner, but a proselyte to the Jewish faith; secondly, that of Saul, born and bred a Jew; thirdly, this of Cornelius, a Gentile seeker after God. Within the range of these experiences the whole world was compassed. When the Holy Spirit fell upon the household in Cesarea a great question was finally settled, for none could doubt that the Gentiles were to find Christ without carrying over into the new kingdom of peace the now useless ritualism of the Jews.

"The conversion of Gentiles was no new idea to Jews or Christians, but it had been universally regarded as to take place by their reception into Judaism."—*Alford on Acts* x, 1. But, further, there were some disciples who were already shaking themselves free from the prejudices of their fathers. The Cyprian and Cyrenian missionaries had preached Jesus, free from Judaism, to "Greeks" (Acts xi, 20) before Peter reached Cesarea. But the probable conflict between old prejudices and new-found privileges would shake the young Church into embittered sects. The highest apostolic sanction for an unfettered Gospel was the need of the hour.

1. *The Vision of the Roman* (vers. 1-8). The home of Cornelius lay thirty miles north of Joppa. Built by Herod the Great in honor of Cæsar Augustus, the seat of the Roman rule in the land of the Jews, a city of splendor, with spacious artificial haven, having a temple erected to the emperor that held his statue as Olympian Zeus, and lying, as it did, within the sacred territory, yet a center of Grecian influence and plagued by the corruptions of a pagan worship, Cesarea afforded every possible phase of contrast to the age-long intolerance of Peter's countrymen.

The gap between the fisherman and the soldier is widened by every added ray of light that falls upon the scene. The soldier's name calls up the Cornelian *gens*, none nobler in Rome, " borne by the Scipios, and by Sulla, and the mother of the Gracchi." Rome's wide empire flashed before the eye of this true-born Italian, nor could he dream that faith in a Nazarene peasant would give the Cornelian name its truest honor.

Yet he was one of those rare souls of whom not a few have illuminated the darkness of heathenism, whom heart-hunger leads to the truth. He was a " devout " man. He " feared " God. The second word is simply a closer definition of his religious character. His " fear " was not a superstitious dread of the wrath of God, but a brave man's dread of failing to do the will of God. Furthermore, his piety had power in it, and this, mingled with peace, won over to his faith "all his house."

No man's religion can, without great hurt, fail to set forth the two sides of the character of his God. In the man who orders his household in the fear of God "mercy and truth are met together, righteousness and peace have kissed each other." The home of the truth-seeking, alms-giving, praying pagan captain shames many a so-called Christian home circle, wherein parental authority is discounted, and lax control has masked itself under the name of love.

Cornelius, constant in alms-giving and prayer, draws near to the kingdom of God's Son. For him "prayers ardent open heaven." While observing the Jewish hour of afternoon prayer he saw with his bodily eyes, not in trance, but "evidently," an " angel of God," and heard his name called. In his very natural fear of the heavenly messenger he asks, "What is it, Lord?" He is quickly reassured. His faith and his works have, in the striking figure of the angel, made a hand-in-hand pilgrimage to the throne, bearing between them a "memorial." They had offered no sacrifice. "Intrinsic merit or efficacy is no more ascribed in these words to the good works of Cornelius than to the oblations from which the figure or comparison is taken."—*Alexander.* The kingdom is about to be entered. The order is, "Now send."

The time had come. The outlying Gentile world had

grown sick at heart. The "middle wall of partition" was falling to the ground. Cornelius, for the pagan world, was to learn that the cross was the center of the circle, and Peter, for the Jewish world, that the circle was as big as the globe. The divine direction is very exact. Both of the apostles' names are given. The location of the house, the occupation of its owner, his name, all fall into place to show how well God cares for the little things in great crises. " Now send. I am discharged. The man you need is in Joppa."

Whether Cornelius knew it or not, Philip, a resident of Cesarea, might have been called to his side within an hour. But Philip was not the man for the occasion. Of all men Peter was best fitted to preach Jesus to Cornelius, of all men the one most needing the results of his preaching.

" He will tell thee what thou oughtest to do." These words emphasize two important truths: (1) They point to the value of human agency in the salvation of men. Angelic is less than apostolic ministry. '" The former directed Cornelius to an apostle, the latter directed him to Christ."—*Grotius*. Not even the Holy Spirit could safely take the place of a plain man who had seen and known and loved the incarnate Christ.

The value of human testimony to a historic fact was never lost sight of in the foundation of the Church. The answer to Hume and Strauss may be found in the meeting of these men. A man not a myth has entered our world, and God has committed to men first of all, not to books, nor papers, nor tracts, the publishing of the Gospel. The true witness of true men is the surest way of redeeming China to God. A ship-load of Bibles sent to Africa will, unaided, amount to little. Ten holy men turned loose will leaven it for the twentieth century. The man and the book together are invincible.

(2) They point to Jesus as the consummate revelation of God. When he can be found all else is insufficient. And it was because he could be found that Cornelius was not, could not be, allowed to remain where he was. His devoutness was not enough. He had outstripped the mass of his heathen fellows, but he needed the cross to enter his life. No one dare teach that faith in specific doctrines of Christianity is superfluous. The opening words of Peter's sermon cannot be bent to prove that all religions are of equal value or that faith in the Redeemer is needless. Cornelius was "acceptable to God" —that is, he was to be received into Christian fellowship without being compelled to conform to extraneous legalities—but he was not "acceptable" outside of the redemption of Jesus Christ. (So Meyer, Whedon, and Hackett.)

2. *The Vision of the Jew* (vers. 9-20). God's providences make a perfect fit. Through a great door "on golden hinges turning" the Church was about to pass out into all lands. The shining halves of this hinge reflect the wise care of the Master. The messengers reached the tanner's door not an hour too soon, not a moment behind time. Was the man on the house-top

ready? A great thing was about to happen. A huge prejudice had come to its death.

Let us pause to scan the past life of the fisherman. He had been in part prepared for the nearing duty. A more scrupulous Jew would not have entered a tanner's house. Peter lodged there. He had not been without much glorious training. He had been taught, tried, had fallen, had been forgiven and restored to honor. Yet he was not ready for a world-wide need. Not even three years' closest contact with Christ will give a man all wisdom. The words of Jesus never took the place of the educating activities of after life.

Peter had been called to be a "fisher of men" (Matt. iv, 19). He had heard the centurion commended (Luke vii, 7). He had learned how meats defile, and how they do not (Mark vii, 18). Near the tragic close of his Lord's life he had seen that certain Greeks sought Him (John xii, 20), and that in them the Gentile world was welcomed. For it was then He said if men would lift him up he would lift up the world. Then he remembered those last words, "Teach all men" (Matt. xxviii, 19). Had not Pentecost left its high-water mark in Jerusalem? (Acts ii.)

Yet he was not ready. Like his fellows, he saw in the direction of his prejudices. "It required the surgery of events to insert a new truth into their minds."* Yet he was God's best man for this hour, for, as Bruce has well said, " Every thing may be hoped of men who could leave all for Christ's society." †

---
* *Training of the Twelve*, p. 495. † Idem., 14.

To learn that spirit is more than form, and that God is not partial, was a great lesson.*

The noon hour finds Peter on the flat roof of the tanner's house,† praying and very hungry. The "trance" into which he fell was a "peculiar mental state in which he was enabled to discern objects beyond the apprehension of man's natural powers" (*Hackett*), though there was no actual reality in the things seen.

Through the opening in heaven a "great sheet" was let down, held "*by four rope-ends*" (*Alford*), or "*attached with four ends*, namely, to the edges of the opening which had taken place in heaven" (*Meyer*). In it were all kinds of animals without exception, clean and unclean. From these Peter was told to choose. With old-time bluntness he refuses. He knows not who speaks, but calls him "Lord." Then, while the vessel hung before him, a second time and a third time the voice repeated the order, and as the vision left he remained alone with the words ringing in his ears that he was not to call "common" (so the verb) what God had cleansed.

What did it mean? Little wonder that he was "perplexed." The very most outward mark of difference between Jew and Gentile had been set at naught. He

---

* The traits of the religion of Jesus, as admitted by the Tübingen school, are (1) universality, (2) spirituality. The two elements in Peter's life to be changed were (1) Jewish narrowness and (2) ceremonialism.

† The site of the house now shown may be the same. "The house itself is a comparatively modern building, with no pretentions to interest or antiquity."— Stanley's *Sinai and Palestine*, p. 269.

15*

knew why these regulations had existed. (See Lev. xi and Deut. xvi.) The descendants of Abraham were not alone in making distinctions of animals. Yet none others were so thorough as those of the Jews. "The ordinance of Moses was for the whole nation. It was not, like the Egyptian law, intended for priests alone; nor like the Hindu law, binding only on the twice-born Brahman; nor like the Parsee law, to be apprehended and obeyed only by those disciplined in spiritual matters. It was a law for the people, for every man, woman, and child of the race chosen to be a 'kingdom of priests, an holy nation' (Exod. xix, 6)."*

He "thought" on. Was the "hedge" between races to be destroyed? Possibly. Was the vision meant for his own enlargement of privilege? Surely not.

The sight, the order, shocked his sanitary creed, his patriotic sentiment, his conscience. The lesson of devotion to "the land" he had well learned from earliest years as he grew skillful in making nets and managing boats and relieved the tedium of the fisher's toil by reciting the words that had a double meaning for him: "If I forget thee, O Jerusalem, let my right hand forget her cunning" (Psa. cxxxvii, 5). It was hard for a Jew to yield even to a command from the skies.

His "thought" may have taken in the city spread below. He looked to the west. There lay the sea.†
Its shores embraced representatives of nearly all hea-

---
* *Speaker's Commentary*, note on Lev. xi.
† The Hebrew "yam" is the same for "sea" and "west."

thendom known to the Jew, and far beyond the visible horizon it widened out to mingle with seas unknown that compassed the world. He knew not the future. His past life had been spent on a tiny lake. These two—the lake, the sea, the sea, the lake—pictured the struggles in the mind of the man whose training had been provincial, whose future—what? Would Judaism go westward with Jesus? He strained his gaze westward. Out yonder Ephesus, Athens, Rome, were rocking in sin's tumult, like the crafts he had steered on the stormy inland sea. Would his Master say "Peace" to the fury of the waves that were beating down their hopes? It might be. He knew his people's history and how God had mercy on Nineveh. Could he, the Jonah of the new times, repeat the prophet's disobedience?

At the bidding of the Spirit he turned to go down to see what the men wanted. He was to go with them, "doubting nothing." They were sent of God. So to the idolatrous capital he will journey with the vision clearing up each step of the way. The world for the cross, the cross for the world. Judaism is not big enough for Jesus.

To get to Gentiles with "Jesus only" has been and remains the highest duty of every true disciple. Cost? None knew better than Peter. It is not hard to follow Livingstone to his burial in Westminster Abbey; but to go back into Africa, and from the spot where his heart lies to describe a great circle of hope for black pagans, that is quite another, yet quite the nobler, thing.

R. T. STEVENSON.

IV.
PETER AT CESAREA.

Acts x, 30-48.

GOLDEN TEXT.—Through his name whosoever believeth in him shall receive remission of sins. Acts x, 43.

THIS is one of the most dramatic chapters in the Bible. It is the record of a new epoch in the development of the Christian Church. Up to this point the apostles had preached only to Jews and Jewish proselytes, and all the converts to the new faith were Jews, either by descent or adoption. The Gospel here crosses the boundary of the Hebrew race and is published to the Gentiles. Next after the day of Pentecost and the conversion of Saul we find nothing in all the Book of Acts which exceeds in grand historic interest this sermon of Peter to the Gentile world.

The previous lesson has made us familiar with Cornelius. Cesarea, his home, was the civil and military capital of Judea, and the "Italian band" probably served as the garrison of the city and the body-guard of the governor. He seems to have been an intelligent and conscientious man who had outgrown the superstitions of idolatry and polytheism. Living among Jews, he saw the superiority of their religion, and had abandoned his old faith and worshiped the true God without, however, submitting to the ceremonial law.

The account of the two visions—that of Cornelius, and that of Peter—came more legitimately in the last lesson; though it is remarkable that each is given three times over in the Book of Acts. When Peter and his companions arrived at Cesarea Cornelius "fell down at his feet and worshiped him." The word used need not mean religious homage. It often denotes civil reverence. Considering the character already given to Cornelius, it is difficult to suppose that he had any intention of rendering to Peter the "worship" due to God only. It was but natural for him to think that one so pointed out by an angel must be deserving of the highest respect. Yet Peter, knowing how likely such honors were to be misinterpreted, said, "Stand up; I myself also am a man."

The words of Cornelius, "Now therefore are we all here present before God, to hear all things that are commanded thee of God," present to us a picture of a model congregation. Every word is emphatic. It is a beautiful expression of entire preparedness to receive the expected divine teaching. The sentence is worthy of being written over every pulpit in Christendom.

Peter commences his discourse by saying that he perceived—what had always been true, though Jewish prejudice had never realized it till now—that God was no respecter of persons, but that in every nation he that feared him and wrought righteousness was accepted of him. He does not mean that all religions are of equal value, for the conversion of Cornelius and his admission into the Christian Church is the main point of the whole transaction. He means, rather, that Jew and Gentile are alike in the eyes of God, and that one could be saved as easily as the other. No man was accepted because he was a Jew; no man excluded because he was a Gentile.

Peter assumed that Cornelius had some knowledge of Christ, but proceeded to teach him the way of the Lord more perfectly. He preached "peace by Jesus Christ," the glorious sum of all gospel truth. He gave an account of some of the leading events of our Lord's life, declaring that he "went about doing good." What single sentence could better describe his earthly course? He went about Judea, Samaria, and Galilee, not for gain or fame or pleasure, but to "do good." He told of his death on the cross, his glorious resurrection, and in conclusion presented him as the Judge and Saviour of all men.

Suddenly Peter's words were interrupted by the rushing descent of the Holy Ghost on all present. By visible and audible manifestation the miracle of Pentecost was wrought afresh on these converts from heathenism. Indeed, this has been appropriately called "The Gentile Pentecost." They "spake with tongues"—they had new thoughts and emotions, and they required a new language. "The old dialect will not express the new life." This miraculous outpouring of the Spirit certified at once to the truth of Peter's words and the genuineness of the faith of these first Gentile converts. It solved Peter's remaining doubts. No one had hitherto been admitted into the Christian Church without having first entered the Jewish communion. Now it is shown that Gentiles may come direct to Christ without passing through Judaism on the way. The Church could not refuse to recognize those to whom God had given the certificate of his Spirit. Hence Peter commanded them to be baptized. Is it any wonder that the delighted Gentile converts "prayed him to tarry certain days" with them? "Golden days," as Bengel suggests. This lesson is full of most practical and helpful teachings. Among them we may notice:

1. *Circumstances do not make men.* There is a great deal of unexpected goodness in the world. Some of the noblest characters have been developed amid unfavorable surroundings, with no godly example to copy, no friend to counsel, no monitor to warn. Josiah in Jerusalem, Daniel in Babylon, and Joseph in Egypt are examples of exceptionally good men amid exceptionally bad surroundings. So we would hardly have looked for a devout man among the officers of the Roman army. Yet it is worthy of note that of each of the four centurions mentioned in the New Testament something commendable is written. One had built a synagogue, another testified to Christ's righteousness even at the cross, another preserved Paul's life when he was shipwrecked, and Cornelius was, as we have seen, a devout, God-fearing man. All this shows that piety *can* flourish under most unfavorable circumstances.

2. *Welcome new truth.* The multitude of unsolved problems ought to make men modest. But many seem to have made up their minds on every subject, and to

have left no room for appendix or supplement. It is astonishing, when Christianity is such a broad thing, on what a narrow platform many are contented to stand. It required a miracle to uproot Peter's prejudice—to shake off the yoke of Jewish exclusiveness, and win him over to a world-wide Christianity. The universal fatherhood of God and the brotherhood of man were twin truths, neither of which he was prepared to accept. Let us allow old prejudices to die under the light of new truth. While the Gospel cannot be improved, men's understanding and interpretation of it may be indefinitely improved. Not all new things are true, and certainly not all true things are new; but mere antiquity is no evidence of value. A thing may be very old and very worthless. Give a warm welcome to all new light, and remember, "there is no such thing as a dangerous truth." In reading this chapter barriers give way and the horizon widens. "One feels as if sailing on a great ship, under a bounding breeze, out of a narrow harbor into a wide sea; every moment the shores withdraw and the waters broaden."

3. *Providential preparation of hearer and preacher.* There is a beautiful connection and interplay of divine providence seen here. These two visions were needed to remove the prejudice of both Jew and Gentile; that the one might teach, and the other hear. May we not believe that God thus often makes ready both the sower and the soil? That he prepares the hearts of hearers for the reception of the truth, making them like moist and

mellow soil; and then guides the steps and hands of the sower and directs each falling seed of truth he scatters?

4. *God has no favorites.* This was not a new truth, though now, for the first time, it dawned upon Peter in all its fullness. He might have found it in the Scriptures. (See Deut. x, 17; 2 Chron. xix, 7; Job xxxiv, 19.) The outpouring of the Holy Spirit upon the Gentiles taught him that they were, in all that is essential to salvation, on a level with the Jews. God does not limit his favors to any particular class. He made special revelations to the Hebrew people, but he did not neglect the Gentiles.

> "There's a wideness in God's mercy,
> Like the wideness of the sea."

He hears the prayers of all men, and grants them equal access to himself and to his heaven.

5. *Visions and tasks are never far apart.* Special divine manifestations are given to men not for their own delight mainly, but for the good of others. The value of any vision of glory lies in its power to give fitness for work and endurance. The vision is but the vestibule through which we are to pass to the greater glory of sacrifice and service. We must make our experience help us in our work, and be able to say after any rich disclosure of divine light to our souls, "Whereupon I was not disobedient to the heavenly vision."

6. *Men, not angels, are to preach the Gospel.* When, after long and earnest prayer, the angel appeared to Cornelius, doubtless he thought his request for light and

instruction was to be answered then and there. This is what he has waited for, and he listens to hear the glorious words of life. But the angel speaks not a word about the way of salvation. He teaches Cornelius nothing. He is simply the celestial guide to a human teacher. The angel bids him send for Peter, and adds, "He shall tell thee what thou oughtest to do." Angels, while they joyfully herald the advent of Christ, and direct men to his apostles and ministers, have no part in the direct ministry of the Gospel. Man preaches to his brother man—the sinner saved to the sinner lost. No doubt Cornelius was directed to send to Peter for Peter's good as well as his own. There is ever a blessed reflex influence in the faithful preaching of the Word, but it was especially so in this case.

7. *The Holy Spirit crowns obedient labor.* While Peter was preaching the Holy Spirit "fell on all them which heard the word." Power with man is God's gift. Apart from the help of the Holy Spirit the work of the Christian preacher or teacher is as much beyond him as the creation of a world. His work is often called arduous, but the word is not expressive enough. We have a work to do which is impossible to us unaided. It is quite out of the region of human power. But if in answer to our prayer and faith the Holy Spirit falls on teacher and class to-day, our poor powerless words will thrill with a divine energy, and these lessons will be written on our hearts.

GEORGE W. BROWN.

V.

THE GOSPEL PREACHED AT ANTIOCH.

Acts xi, 19-30.

GOLDEN TEXT.—A great number believed, and turned unto the Lord. Acts xi, 21.

How frequently the enemies of truth overreach themselves! It is inconceivable that any of their persecutors, who leveled their insane rage against the followers of Jesus, expected by so doing to advance the very cause they hated.

Yet so it was. The dispersion was the very best thing that could have happened to Christianity at this time. God used the fanatical and cruel outburst for the extension of his kingdom. As the wind scatters the sparks of a great conflagration throughout the city, setting innumerable fires in its tracks, so the scattering abroad of the disciples at this critical time was the means of kindling the fires of Pentecost upon new altars. We seem to see in this passage three pictures of the apostolic age, centering respectively in Stephen, Barnabas, and Agabus, and all of them well worthy our careful study.

1. *The first picture centers in Stephen.*

(1) Great in his life, he was surpassingly great in his death. The grim monster was unable to check the majestic stream of his influence. In that hounded, despised,

persecuted company who escaped from Jerusalem with their lives, " taking joyfully the spoiling of their goods," the great protomartyr lived again upon the earth.

(2) The fugitives went north into Phenicia, a little country comprising the eastern coast of the Mediterranean, one hundred and twenty miles long by about twelve broad, including Tyre and Sidon, and extending from the inner Eleutherus to a little south of Carmel; and to Cyprus, an island lying off the coast of Phenicia, and within sight of it, which had been early colonized by the Phenicians, and included at this time many Jews among its inhabitants; and to Antioch, the capital of the Greek kingdom of Syria, situated one hundred and eighty miles north of the northern frontier of Phenicia, having a population of nearly half a million, and reckoned the third city in importance in the whole empire.

(3) What an opportunity presented itself to these persecuted followers of the Nazarene! And they embraced it to the full. At first they seem to have confined their labors to the Jews. They were still bound by the shackles of the old faith, and so to them even the glorious Gospel must be confined within proper limits. If any man would embrace the new truth he must first go through the gate of Judaism. But these men in the company of dispersed ones, "men of Cyprus and Cyrene," having been saved as Gentiles at the pentecostal outpouring in Jerusalem, saw no reason for withholding the Gospel from all nations. Accordingly, when they reached Antioch and found it peopled with Greeks, they

began " preaching the Lord Jesus " to them. They believed that the " middle wall of partition " had been thrown down, and henceforth there was to be one fold and one Shepherd.

(4) And the result justified their faith. Great success attended their efforts. " The hand of the Lord was with them: and a great number believed, and turned unto the Lord." And soon it became apparent to all hearts that Christianity is not a " local lamp, but a universal sun," which pours its beams of light and heat impartially over hill and dale, over lake and forest, tipping every foam-crested wave of the sea with fire, and tingeing every cloudlet of the summer sky with amber and gold. While luxuries grow in a few sheltered spots of earth, necessities abound every-where ; and because Christianity is a necessity, and not a luxury, it is fitted to be the universal religion.

2. *And now the second picture is flashed upon us, centering in Barnabas.*

(1) Back over the way the dispersed ones had come. From Jerusalem went the news of their success to the Church, producing a startling effect. By reading between the lines one can observe the haste with which the leading members were gathered for consultation, and the eagerness with which the strange story was rehearsed. Their action in sending forth one of their number to investigate has been variously interpreted. Some see in it a meddlesome bigotry that would interfere with the glorious work, and forbid even

the spread of the Gospel, except by their sanction. Others declare that Peter's defense (recorded in the first part of this chapter) had opened the eyes of the Church to the fact that "God is no respecter of persons," and their action can only be viewed as a kindly desire to encourage and help forward the new movement. Taking into account the effect produced by Peter's speech (ver. 18), we are inclined to the latter view. They really rejoiced that a "short cut" to the heart of the Gentile world had been found.

(2) The messenger they sent would indicate this. Barnabas "was a good man, and full of the Holy Ghost and of faith." Such a man would be in sympathy with the work, and so we think the temper of the Church in Jerusalem is reflected in the character of the man they sent to represent them. It must not, however, be inferred that Barnabas was a fanatical, rattle-brained enthusiast. He shows himself a cool, level-headed man of affairs in this crisis, and only after he had thoroughly examined the movement did he give it his sanction and lend himself to its continuance. "He saw the grace of God." That settled it with Barnabas. No doubt he saw many other things inseparable from such a work that he could not commend. But this one thing, the manifest presence of God, rising like the white lily above a stagnant pool, was enough for him. There is no mistaking the real flavor of a genuine revival of religion. Nothing is like it in the heavens above or in the earth beneath. And when the true child of God sees it he

recognizes it instantly and glorifies God. So Barnabas was glad. Nor did he spend his gladness in an ebullition of emotion. He went right to work, exhorting them all that "with purpose of heart they would cleave unto the Lord." Is it strange that a great impetus was given to the work? Would we not naturally expect as a result that "much people was added unto the Lord?"

(3) And now the revival began to assume such proportions that assistance was required; and Barnabas bethought himself of that little, but mighty, man who had been driven by persecution from Jerusalem to his native city of Tarsus—Paul, who was yet to be named the apostle to the Gentiles.

Hastening thither, the overburdened servant of God succeeds in enlisting the sympathy and co-operation of Paul, who accompanies him back to the scene of action. Can it be that there was given to Barnabas at this time some conception of what it meant to open the door of opportunity for such a man? Probably not; but now that the "great apostle's" course is run, and the two friends have met in heaven, it must be a continuous source of hallowed joy to the "Son of Consolation" that he was God's agent in lifting the veil of obscurity from such a man, and setting him in the front rank of the world's greatest. For a whole year the two apostles carry on the work at Antioch with signal success. This was the teaching time. The fruits of the great revival were being conserved—the converts confirmed in the faith and plans laid for their further discipline and development.

(4) And here the disciples were lifted to the dignity of a name. Hitherto enemies had called them "Galileans," or "Nazarenes." They spoke of their own teaching as "the way," and themselves as "disciples." No one knows how the new name, "Christians," came to be used. Perhaps it was given in derision, as " Methodist " and " Puritan." But no one can doubt its appropriateness. "Christ-ones" puts the great Saviour above every other consideration—a personal pre-eminence entirely fitting.

3. *And now the third picture rises before us, centering in Agabus.*

(1) As to the prophet himself we know very little. He is mentioned again in Acts xxi, 10, where he predicts the arrest and imprisonment of Paul, dramatically symbolizing the act by binding himself with the apostle's girdle. But the order of prophets was, we know, already recognized in the Church. Whether he was sent by the Church in Jerusalem, as Barnabas was, or whether he came of his own accord, we can only conjecture. At any rate, his mission was of great importance.

(2) His prophecy was very specific. Unlike the oracles of mythology, there was no ambiguity in the prediction, a " dearth " (or " famine ; " see Revised Version). The expression " throughout all the world " was the common term for the Roman Empire; and it may be that this must be interpreted as hyperbolical, inasmuch as Josephus declares that this famine was confined exclusively to Judea. And yet Eusebius, in his ecclesiastical his-

tory, speaks of it as having prevailed "over the world." But the point is not important. It is only essential to observe the wonderful precision of the prophecy, and the accuracy of the statement—"which came to pass in the days of Claudius Cæsar." Their points are abundantly corroborated by history, some of which was written by those hostile to Christianity.

(3) But the practical effect of the prophecy is the main fact to be emphasized. No sooner did it fall from the lips of Agabus than the new disciples resolved to aid the church in Jerusalem. They saw the great need instantly. Judea was poor, Antioch rich. The wealth of the one should be made to serve the poverty of the other. Thus they reasoned. Could better evidence of the genuineness of the work of Antioch be asked for than this practical benevolence? And what an exemplification of real church unity is here! The need of Jerusalem, the response of Antioch, drew the one Church of Jesus into a beautiful and loving fellowship, "Every man according to his ability." That is absolutely ideal! All giving something. All giving as much as they could. The contributions went to the elders by the hands of Barnabas and Paul. That shows that this company of Antiochene Christians was not a lawless mob, but men who had respect for authorized methods, and recognized regular church officers. "Let all things be done decently and in order."

4. *We have time only for a few practical lessons.*

(1) Christianity is never content to remain at home.

It migrates and emigrates. Indeed, it may be questioned if it has a home—whether there is any country on the globe that can claim it as its own.

Its spirit is to compass all lands in its efforts to reach the race. Nor does it ever wait until all are saved in a given place before moving on. It sounds the trumpet, offers the blessings, and then goes to other lands. One says: "In proportion as we sit at home we disown Christianity." We are needed in the regions beyond, and until the last believer is gathered, and every pilgrim safe in heaven, the Gospel must *go*.

(2) Let us learn to strike for the centers of population. According to the teachers of social science the cities are the "storm centers," especially in our republic. Here the multitudes gather, here vice flaunts itself on every street corner, here the great social upheavals occur, and here wealth is accumulated. Obviously, to capture these centers is to conquer the strategic points of the country for Christ. " From Jerusalem to Antioch."

(3) Notice, too, that this was a ministry of the laity. At first neither Paul nor Barnabas were present. The work was carried on by those who had been prepared for their calling, not by the laying on of authoritative hands, but by the pentecostal baptism. Such a ministry is absolutely disinterested, and in all ages has been successful. One great need of the Church to-day is not more professional workers, but more men and women aflame with love for souls to enter into personal missionary labors. The world never can be evangelized by a few

ordained preachers. The mass of believers need to enter personally, and not by proxy, into the toil of the great harvest field.

(4) How simple was this ministry. They preached the Lord Jesus. Not speculations, not theories, not philosophy, but facts concerning a real person, were relied upon. It ought to teach us that colossal church buildings and elaborate music and high-sounding ritual and learned and elegant discourses are not the essentials of Christianity. These are but the fringe at best, and often are so many barriers between the soul and God. While we despise no instruments nor organizations nor accessories of worship, let us not forget "the simplicity that is in Christ."

(5) Last of all, see the Christian comradeship of these two men. Barnabas, without a shade of envy seeks out Paul, and cheerfully resigns first place to him. And Paul modestly remains in Tarsus until called for, that he may not interfere with the work of his brother. A beautiful spirit is here exhibited, and both earn thereby the title of great men. In honor they prefer one another. Let us learn to co-operate not with God only, but with our brothers also, sinking all personal feelings and ambitions in the greatness of the work.

H. H. FRENCH.

VI.

PETER DELIVERED FROM PRISON.

Acts xii, 1-17.

GOLDEN TEXT.—The angel of the Lord encampeth round about them that fear him, and delivereth them. Psa. xxxiv, 7.

WE come to-day to one of the most interesting events in the history of early Christianity, a story which illustrates the power of prayer, the protective providence of God, and the rapid extension of the Gospel.

The honor of first martyr of the Christian faith belongs to Stephen. The honor of first martyr of the apostolic college belongs to the apostle James. The story of Stephen we remember. He was condemned by the Sanhedrin in Jerusalem to be put to death by stoning, was dragged outside the city walls, and the executioners who had the matter in charge did their work well. We are told that they "laid their garments at the feet of a young man named Saul." It was a novel and strange experience that was beheld that day—a man under a shower of stones pleading for the cruel men who smote him: "Lord, lay not this sin to their charge." Saul looked on and had his own thoughts. He saw and heard too much that day for a Pharisee. A mysterious conviction seized him which became a fire in his bones and which burst into a flame "on the way to Damascus."

"The Church," says St. Augustine, "owes the apostle Paul to the prayer of Stephen."

There is good reason to believe that the young persecutor who put Stephen to death was in Jerusalem at the time of the death of James, and that he stood by and saw the head of the great apostle stricken off by a Roman sword. In the narrative of St. Luke immediately preceding our lesson (xi, 27-30) we are informed that there was "a great famine over all the world in the days of Claudius," and that the wealthy church in Antioch, the capital of Syria, sent "relief unto the brethren that dwelt in Judea." These alms were conveyed to Jerusalem by Barnabas and Paul. The date of this event is well ascertained to be the spring of the year 44 A. D.

"Now about that time Herod the king put forth his hands to afflict certain of the church." The first four words of this passage are rendered by Meyer in his commentary, "But at that juncture;" and these words he tells us fix the story of our lesson as contemporaneous with the visit of the two apostles to Jerusalem. Archdeacon Farrar holds the same opinion, and writes: "It is clear that they arrived shortly before the passover, or toward the end of March, 44 A. D."

The great apostle never forgave himself for the part he took in the death of Stephen. Again and again, with ever fresh repentance, he recurs to it in his letters and writes himself down as "the least of the apostles, not meet to be called an apostle," because he persecuted the

Church of God. We can imagine the intense emotion with which he would behold this fresh outburst of persecution.

Let us dwell for a moment on the first martyred apostle. James was brother of John, author of the fourth gospel. He belonged to the honored trio, Peter, James, and John, the three permitted to enter with their Master the sacred chamber where the daughter of Jairus was raised from the dead, who beheld the glory of the transfiguration, and were present at the tragedy of Gethsemane. It was the mother of James who requested for her sons that they might sit on his right and left hand in his kingdom, and we can understand how on this fatal day in the year 44 that mother would recall, were she then alive, her foolish request and the Lord's reply: "Ye know not what ye ask. Are ye able to drink the cup that I am about to drink? They say unto him, We are able. He saith unto them, My cup indeed ye shall drink" (Matt. xx, 22, 23). And they drank it, loyal, heroic, loving disciples of their Lord—James by the martyr's death, and John, the greater sufferer, by the martyr's life of a hundred years.

This tyrant king who slays God's prophets to make a Jewish holiday, who was he? There are four Herods conspicuous in New Testament history: Herod the Great (Matt. ii, 1); Herod Antipas, son of Herod the Great, who beheaded John the Baptist, and was ruler at the time of the crucifixion; Herod Agrippa, grandson of Herod the Great and Mariamne (of the family of the

Maccabees), son of Aristobulus and Berenice, born 11 B. C. and deceased 44 A. D.; and another, a son of Herod Agrippa, called by St. Paul "King Agrippa" in Acts xxvi, 2. These princes were all petty despots, frivolous, treacherous, and cruel, but were not wanting in a certain brilliancy and personal beauty which were marked features of the founder of their dynasty. The Herod of our lesson, known as Herod Agrippa, spent his youth in Rome, where by lavish expenditure and excesses he won the favor of the royal princes. In 37 A. D., at the death of the Emperor Tiberius, we find him in a Roman dungeon for treason, but the new Emperor Caligula gave him a chain of gold for his iron fetters, put a crown on his head, and sent him to rule in his native country. In 41 Caligula was murdered and another favorite of the wily Agrippa succeeded to the empire. Claudius extended the dominions of Agrippa, so that at the time of our lesson he was one of the great sovereigns of western Asia and governed a territory equal to that of Herod the Great.

This Agrippa was a singular mixture of the profligate and the devotee. In Jerusalem he affected the religion of Moses; in Rome he was a pagan. Josephus relates that he was found weeping in the Temple because he was only half a Jew (his grandmother was a Jewess), while at Cesarea he was the patron of the theater and the pagan games, and in Italy he was the boon companion of the unspeakable princes of the house of the Cæsars. We can readily understand, therefore, the words of the author of the Acts: "Because he saw it pleased the Jews he proceeded further to take Peter also."

Man proposes, God disposes. The sacredness of the passover saved the life of Peter. What a mixture of superstition, conscientiousness, and depravity is human nature! The young man who put Stephen to death "verily thought he ought to do many things contrary to the name of Jesus of Nazareth." The priests who before Pilate's hall of judgment uttered the historic cry, "Crucify him!" refused to cross the unholy threshold of the pagan ruler. And now, since there is not time for the trial and execution of the apostle before the passover, he must be kept in prison till after the feast. Peter is therefore committed to four "quartettes" of soldiers, that there may be a quartette for each of the four watches of the night. This ringleader of the pestiferous sect must not be suffered to escape. The order is given: "Guard the prison well; let him be chained; keep a patrol; look to the gates." The seven days of the feast move slowly by. The last night has come. On the morrow this successor of Pontius Pilate, "willing to content the people," will take Peter from the dungeon, exhibit him before them, and publicly put him to death.

Two scenes attract us on this last night. Look in first at the house of Mary, the mother of Mark. It is a gathering of the Christians for prayer. Peter must not die. He is their leader by appointment of the Master, the bravest of the brave and tenderly beloved by all. They have met daily behind bolted doors through the fearful days of the feast. And if Paul and Barnabas were in the city we must believe that they, too, were at that meeting on that fateful night. " But prayer was made without ceasing of the church unto God for him." O, the power of faithful prayer!

The rulers cared little about the prayer-meeting; if they knew of it they would have despised it, just as the Sanhedrin in Jerusalem and the Senate in Rome would have despised the assembly of the followers of the Crucified in the upper room. But history has ways of its own. The might of final conquest is in the realm of the spiritual. Behind all things is God.

> "O where are kings and empires now,
> Of old that went and came!
> But, Lord, thy Church is praying yet,
> A thousand years the same!"

Look now into the prison. It is past the middle hour of the night. Peter sleeps on his bed of straw. The two soldiers, chained to his wrists on either side, sleep also; the monotonous foot-falls of the guards in the prison courts have lulled them to slumber. The huge " iron gate " is bolted and barred. The dungeon is dark and silent, and without, under the starry sky, the great city also sleeps.

Peter has been called " the apostle of hope." Did he fall asleep hoping for deliverance, or did he fancy that the end had come, as he recalled the words spoken by

Galilee, "When thou shalt be old another shall gird thee and carry thee wither thou wilt not?"

And now a marvel takes place. "Behold, the angel of the Lord came upon him, and a light shined in the prison: and he smote Peter on the side, and raised him up, saying, Arise up quickly!" Let us note that God only did for Peter what he could not do for himself. The angel roused him. The mystic light revealed to him his situation and the sleeping guards, and perhaps recalled a similar glory once witnessed by him on the mount of transfiguration. Tenderly the angel raised him up, bending and helping the dazed apostle to his feet. We notice the same word is used here which tells us how Jesus "raised up" the demented boy whom he healed after the transfiguration.

Peter co-operates with the angel, and as he struggles to his feet " his chains fall off from his hands." Now in quick succession the angel gives his brief commands. "Gird thyself, bind on thy sandals. . . . Cast thy garment about thee, and follow me." The apostle obeys. Out through the prison courts they pass in single file. Some spell is on the Roman guards, called in our text "the first and second wards;" they reach the "iron gate," which opens "of its own accord." They pass out and are under the stars. That the angel led the course toward the prayer-meeting we may be sure; and then with an intimation that yonder his friends were praying for him, God's messenger is gone.

We are dealing with history, but is this not also a

parable? Have we not here the process of the escape of a sinner from the prison-house of sin? Most men have been in Peter's dungeon, and sin's chains have been upon their limbs. To break the chains, to rise up, to escape, is impossible in their own strength. They find a law that " when they would do good, evil is present with them," and they are "in captivity to the law" of sin and death (Rom. vii, 23). This is readily recognized as to the drunkard, but it is equally true, and perhaps more dangerously true, concerning respectable (?) sins, such as selfishness, dishonesty, worldliness, pride, unbelief. It is true concerning the liar, the profane man, the libertine. " His own iniquities shall take the wicked himself, and he shall be holden with the cords of his sins" (Prov. v, 22).

But God seeks his lost ones. There comes a moment when an angel smites the prisoner on the side and cries, "Arise up quickly!" And as Peter found gracious arms about him, so the sinner finds a power within him that helps him to his feet. So John Newton was lifted up on the deck of the slave-ship. So the young midshipman, afterward Admiral Foote, when on board a United States war-ship. The duty of such a moment is obedience. Peter did not parley or apologize. A resolution to be good does not make us good. The renewed nature is God's work, and it is granted *while we are obeying*.

And the frequent half-conversions of our churches, the Ephraims who are " cakes not turned," are they not like

Peter when he was standing upright, with his chains off, but in the prison still?

"Cast thy garment about thee; follow me." The angel led him to perfect liberty.

> "Long my imprisoned spirit lay,
>   Fast bound in chains and nature's night;
> Thine eye diffused a quickening ray,
>   I woke; the dungeon flamed with light;
> My chains fell off, my heart was free,
> I rose, went forth, and followed thee."

JOSEPH PULLMAN.

VII.

THE FIRST CHRISTIAN MISSIONARIES.

Acts xiii, 1-13.

GOLDEN TEXT.—That repentance and remission of sins should be preached in his name among all nations. Luke xxiv, 47.

IN the past few years we have often been invited to read new books of history with very suggestive titles, such as *The Making of England, The Building of a Commonwealth,* etc.

We have been glad of these departures from older forms, for they indicate to us an effort on the part of the writers to trace out certain great laws or influences under which and through which the succession of events took form. The result has been to give us a clearer understanding of history, and many excellent lessons for our own onward course as a people.

Although a new departure in modern book-writing the method itself is as old as the Bible. God, whenever great movements were to be inaugurated, and great advances to be made along the line of his kingdom, has always laid bare the powers behind such movements, and made clear the factors that have led to success.

The present lesson is not an exception. In it are revealed the elements that gave Barnabas and Saul their success as the first Christian missionaries, and the power that sent them forth. The order of thought before us will be as follows:

The Three Elements of Success in the First Christian Missionaries:

1. Earnestness.
2. A Holy Ghost Commission.
3. Obedience.

1. *These Men were in Earnest.* It is no dead Church on which we are permitted to look as the chapter opens before us.

In the persecution that arose from the death of Stephen the followers of Jesus were scattered abroad and journeyed as far as Phenice, Cyprus, and Antioch, preaching the Gospel of Christ with such power and fervor that at Antioch a great number believed and turned unto the Lord.

Hearing of this success of the Gospel, the Church at Jerusalem sent them, as their preacher, Barnabas, a "good man," "full of faith" "and the Holy Ghost." His ministry was crowned with marked results in gathering converts; and, wishing for help, he sought out Saul and brought him to Antioch.

As the lesson opens we are introduced in this earnest church to an earnest company. Day after day these men "ministered" at the altars of God, leading the people toward a better life, preaching Christ to them as the hope of the resurrection and eternal joy, "fasting" as a means of bringing themselves into closer communion with the Holy Ghost, and doubtless *praying* for direction in the work that was opening before them.

This picture given us by the Scripture is in itself a prophecy of greater things.

Out of such times and such gatherings the great forward movements of the Christian world have come.

Luther read his chained Bible, fasted, prayed, and ministered as best he knew until his soul's vision grew clear, the old restrictions of his life fell away, and the great and effectual door of the Reformation swung open. Wesley, in the midst of "ministry," "fasting," and "prayer," felt the warming touch of the Holy Ghost and transformed the religious thought and practice of the eighteenth century. A poor shoe-maker, busy with lapstone and leather, finds time to inquire of God, and through William Carey the modern missionary movement is born.

God has not changed in our century, and when Booth, amid the slums of London, repeated the history of Antioch, there came to him the message of "Darkest England," the key-note of a movement that will mile-stone the line of Christian progress as did Methodism and the Reformation.

God gives no message to the lazy. *Samuel* was *awake* when God called him; *Pentecost* was a time of work and prayer before the coming of cloven tongues of flame; and when we look upon this busy hive of work and worship we are like men who stand amid the shadows of an April night and hear the crash of ice in the river, the sighing of the wind, and the steady drip of rain. *They* know there are *answering forces* in the earth that will lift the summer banners of the grass and weight the autumn with abundant harvest. *We* know that God has answering powers for earnest souls, and look for that which came as the second factor of success, the message of the Holy Ghost.

2. *These Men were Spirit-commissioned.* "The Holy Ghost said," etc.

Sometimes in our Western mountains the traveler discovers a stream of sparkling water leaping from the bosom of the cliffs and making its way toward the plain below. As he follows its course it suddenly disappears beneath the surface, indicating its channel, if at all, by here and there a tree growing among the heaped-up bowlders; miles below he finds a quiet pool edged with rushes and starred with lilies, and from its lower rim a river flowing to the sea, and the traveler comes to understand that the spring in the mountain, the clear lake in the dusty plain, and the river with its ceaseless current moving oceanward are all parts of one great nature-plan of God.

So in the lesson before us, when the Holy Ghost said, "Separate me Barnabas and Saul," *it was a step in the fulfillment of a divine purpose toward which the Spirit had been moving for years with untiring power.*

Fifteen years before this gathering at Antioch Jesus Christ appeared in Palestine, made plain the essential relations of God to men, unfolded the course of the coming kingdom, submitted himself to the death of the cross, arose from the dead, and ascended into heaven, leaving as his farewell message the *missionary commission for the conquest of the world.*

The evangelists give the message in varying language. " Go, teach all nations," says Matthew. " Go into all the world, and preach the Gospel to every creature," says Mark. " Repentance and remission of sins should be preached in his name among all nations," is Luke's form of the message.

With this difference of language there is perfect unity of thought.

God's purpose, the Gospel for the whole world, through the preaching of Christ's followers.

When the disciples returned from the Mount of Olives on ascension day *world-wide* triumph or *world-wide* defeat was before them. The new teaching was not to be *a* religion, but *the* religion of the world.

This was the visible fountain-head of the missionary movement, which was quickly hidden from view by the local interests of churches, giving only here and there tokens of its presence. It had touched Peter and forced him over the Gentile line to preach the Gospel to Cornelius; it had mingled in the message that came to Saul after he had seen the light above the brightness of the noonday, but on *this day at Antioch* the hidden current comes forth, " Separate me Barnabas and Saul for the work whereunto *I* have called them."

So while this Spirit-commission occupies but a single line of the chapter, it is the greatest factor in the preparation of the first missionaries. It reaches back to the springs of God's purpose, it is the clear lake out of which flows the current that is *still* on its way to the eternal sea.

It has been said, "Find out God's plan for the age in which you live, and then sail with its current." These men had found the current of the *ages*. An embassador in their time carried a commission from his king; they had *their commission*—" the Holy Ghost said."

When there comes to *us* some great blessing from the presence of God, there will come with it the open door toward helpfulness, and we will hear, if we listen closely, the old message, "Separate me" something of thine for service.

With these two factors before us let us note the *third*, which includes the remainder of the lesson.

3. *These Men were Obedient.* Having waited for direction from God, the Church received it willingly, and because the communication had come in the midst of prayer they *continued* in prayer; because fasting had brought them nearer to God, they fasted *still;* and, laying their hands on the chosen ones in token of blessing, sent them forth.

As they departed, note the *divinely human way in which they went about their work.*

The exercise of *common sense* in religious matters is always a token of the presence of the Holy Ghost.

They went *directly* to the nearest sea-port, Seleucia, and took ship for the nearest heathen island, Cyprus; and, hastily touching its most important cities, made directly for the main-land of Pamphylia, a place where the various races met and mingled. Phenicians, Jews, and Syrians filled the cities; Greek culture had touched the life and thought of the people while Roman government and Roman roads held them with bonds of steel to the imperial city.

God always directs missionary effort to *centers* of *dispersion* or *centers* of *power*. Saul, preaching in the cities of "all tribes land," was in centers of *dispersion*, far from whence the Gospel would be carried to Athens and Rome.

With this wisdom of choice there was an intensely *human element*. This journey was a *home-going*. Cyprus was the home of Barnabas, Pamphylia bordered close on Paul's native land; the message spoken years before to another, "go home and tell thy friends," re-echoed in this new revelation. This is the normal outcome of the two preceding factors, earnestness and the Holy Ghost.

In its simplest forms it is the impulse to help some one that is near and dear to us. In its missionary form it is the world-enlightening impulse of the kingdom of God, just as acquisition is the race impulse of the Anglo-Saxon.

As they went forth, then, obedience was sanctioned by a victory over the powers of superstition. The work at Paphos, which occupies so large a part of the lesson text, is but an incident by the way in the great movement that, starting at Antioch, is to reach the ends of the world. Gospel *earnestness* and gospel obedience came face to face with superstition, and the touch of the Spirit drove the pretender into disgrace.

Such has been, and always will be, the history of normal missionary work.

Brother of mine, whose eye may have rested upon these pages, this is not a far-off and unusual action of God that has passed before us. As the image of the sun is mirrored in a drop of dew, so in every soul that meets the conditions something of the work and power and blessedness of this lesson will enter.

If you wait before the Lord in service and prayer and interest that brings to men the true fast of the soul, these things will come to you in their nineteenth century garments, the Holy Ghost will be present, the message will come, " Separate me a portion of money, of service ; go tell the good news of the Gospel to the nearest Gentile," and as you obey you will be in touch with "the first missionaries."

If men would listen with the devout attention of Saul, the world would hear the Gospel within the next fifty years.

M. F. COLBURN.

VIII.
PAUL'S FIRST MISSIONARY SERMON.

Acts xiii, 26-43.

GOLDEN TEXT.—To you is the word of this salvation sent. Acts xiii, 26.

BY a missionary sermon in these modern days we generally mean an attempt to arouse in the hearts of lukewarm or imperfectly-informed Christians an interest in the spread of the Gospel. Of Paul's first missionary sermon in this sense we have no record. There was less need of such exhortation then, in that the heathen were all around mingled with the Christians, and nearly all labor for "those without" was missionary labor in the strictest meaning of the term.

Nor is this sermon which we are called to consider a missionary sermon in the sense of being addressed to the heathen, for it is directed exclusively to the Jews and to such proselytes present ("those among you that fear God") as were so closely associated with the men of Israel that they could be reached by the same arguments. It was not until the following Sabbath that the apostle, having failed to make any extensive impression on the Jews, deliberately turned to the heathen and adapted his teaching to their needs. In the ten years since he was converted Paul had no doubt spoken to the

Jews in Damascus, Jerusalem, Tarsus, and Antioch hundreds of times, but this is the earliest of his discourses preserved at any length, and as it occurs during what is very properly called his first missionary journey it is sometimes given the title of this lesson.

It is an excellent specimen of what must have been the usual line of argument adopted by him when pleading with his fellow-countrymen in the synagogues. Its striking similarity to the sermon of Peter on the day of Pentecost (chap. ii), and the discourse of Stephen before his murderers, so far as it was suffered to continue (chap. vii), shows that this was the customary course of thought. Nothing, indeed, could be more natural or more suitable. God's marvelous and gracious dealings with the nation are recounted—always a grateful subject in the Jewish ear, well adapted to catch their attention and win their good-will. Then Jesus is shown to be the predicted seed of David, the promised Messiah or Saviour fulfilling the prophets and meeting the requirements of the law. His resurrection, so well attested by competent and reliable eye-witnesses, is triumphantly proclaimed as a complete vindication of his claims; and the salvation from sin which can be procured in no other way is earnestly pressed upon their immediate attention as their clear privilege and duty in him.

It is instructive to note how different the course he took with the barbarians of Lycaonia (chap. xiv) and with the Athenians on Mars' Hill (chap. xvii). Paul was an orator of the first class, and never made the mistake of forgetting to study his audience and to speak to each man in his own tongue—that is, with such words as he would be most likely to understand.

The sermon, as a whole, is an excellent model for preachers and teachers every-where. He uttered bold and thrilling thoughts that went straight home to the hearts of his hearers. He was faithful and fearless. He begged no one's pardon for the truth. None could misunderstand his meaning. He stated the central facts of the Gospel with great directness and simplicity. His sentences searched the souls of the sinners before him. He was plain and personal, loyal and logical, skillful and scriptural, and, in a measure, successful.

Paul rings out with abundant vehemence the solemn warning word, Beware. Should not every true preacher, every earnest gospel worker, do it? Persistent unbelievers who despise the mercy of God, he said, shall be destroyed. And in another place he writes, with his own hand to give it special emphasis, " If any man love not the Lord Jesus Christ, let him be Anathema." The gospel of gush and mawkish sentimentality, of which we have more than enough in some quarters at present, is not that which either Scripture or nature declares. Men such as Paul would spew it with vehemence out of their mouths.

But, of course, we are not to be all severity all the time. And we find in this sermon no lack of gentleness and sympathy, courtesy and comfort. There was clear announcement of good tidings (ver. 32) and remission of sins (ver. 38). There was full recognition of the fact, too often forgotten, even at present, that there were those of Gentile or heathen stock who nevertheless truly feared God (ver. 26); recognition also that the guilt of the Jews who killed Jesus was mitigated by their ignorance (ver. 27).

Paul was the very one to remember this latter important point with all its consolatory implication, because it was just the direction in which he himself had found a door of mercy (1 Tim. i, 13). May we not say it is the only door of mercy that any one can find? Christ's prayer on the cross, " Father, forgive them ; for they know not what they do," assumes that had they known what they did they could not have been forgiven. Where there is willful, deliberate, open-eyed rejection of truth by those who have been fully " enlightened and made partakers of the Holy Ghost " (Heb. vi, 4 ; x, 26) it is manifestly impossible to renew them again unto repentance, and there remaineth no more sacrifice for sins, but only a fearful expectation of judgment and devouring fire. This is taught clearly in many parts of Scripture, and also by reason, since there can be no repentance or change of mind except by the accession of new light, and hence if all possible light has been received and rejected there will inevitably be persistence in evil with its accruing punishment.

Yet no one can go free or be absolved on account of his ignorance alone, it should be remembered, so long as that ignorance is not complete and unavoidable.

Neither in Paul's case, nor in that of any of the Jews to whom he or the other apostles preached, was this true. They might have known had they with entire honesty and sincerity investigated. They suffered themselves to be blinded by their prejudices and passions, their self-interest and self-will—which is just what happens now. There is always truth enough for him who is thoroughly in earnest to know it. But there is not enough to compel conviction where there is a disposition to avoid it. He who seeks an excuse for gratifying his own perverse nature can always find one that can be made to answer; and he who seeks the light with his whole heart will sooner or later find that.

Another point of which much is made, both in this sermon and Peter's, is that the death of Jesus was in no sense a divine defeat, but a victory of Providence in spite of men, a fulfillment of prophecy and a confirmation of Scripture, even though much wickedness was mixed up in the event. They fulfilled the prophets by condemning him (ver. 27). Though lawless men slew him, yet he was " delivered up by the determinate counsel and foreknowledge of God" (chap. ii, 23; iii, 18). There is here one of the mightiest consolations for all who are persecuted and afflicted at the hands of men that can possibly be brought forward. The designs of men are one thing; those of God, who uses the former, taking them up into his plans and turning them to good account, are quite another. It has been well compared to the difference between the purpose of the leech who sucks human blood, intending only his own gratification, and the higher, beneficent purpose of the physician who applies the leech for the relief or cure of the patient. Joseph's brethren thought evil against him, and tried to do him harm, but God all the time meant it for good to save much people alive. Precisely so is it in all the so-called calamities which come to God's people. They may spring in one sense from human mistake or malice, since God does not (indeed, cannot so long as men are free agents) interfere with their volitions ; but since he can and does, whenever he sees fit, interfere with the carrying out of those volitions externally in the realm of matter, in the truest sense *he* is the author of whatever reaches us, and he does not permit it to reach us unless he perceives that it will work us good. With this sure foundation for our faith, disappointment is destroyed and calamity robbed of all power to harm.

At least two other great doctrines were treated with more or less fullness in this wonderful sermon of which, of course, we have only a sort of abstract, a brief outline. In verse 30 we have the thrilling announcement, "God raised him from the dead." Nothing is more prominent in all the apostle-preaching than the resurrection of Jesus. It is the central truth with which they were specially charged as witnesses. And the reason for their thus insisting on its vital importance it is not difficult to understand, since had the Christ not come out of the tomb his mission would have been a proved and confessed failure. It is the one pivotal miracle which makes all other miracles natural and easy to credit. "Dost thou believe that Jesus Christ rose from the dead?" is the infallible test-question which exposes the rationalist or discovers the true believer in supernatural religion.

In verses 38, 39, a second great doctrine—justification by faith—the chief theme of Paul's epistles, stands out clearly to view. The marked superiority of Christianity to Judaism is here fearlessly proclaimed, so far as we know, for the first time. Stephen had begun to develop the doctrine, but Paul, convicted by Stephen's death, was the chosen vessel appointed to take up and carry on Stephen's work. He made it the grand aim of his life to set forth unmistakably in the presence of all who would give him a hearing the only answer to the great question, How shall man be justified with God? And that answer was, Through this Man of whom David and the prophets spoke, and whom the people of Jerusalem slew, but whom God raised up.

This lesson presents plentiful material for study. Let the Scripture quotations that are imbedded in it be examined. There are at least seven, besides an extract, in verse 25, from what may be styled the oral gospel, not at that time anywhere yet written down. It is instructive also to note the parallelisms between some parts of this sermon and special verses in Paul's epistles, for the same shades of thought are brought out in one as in the other —an incidental confirmation of the genuineness of both. With verse 33 compare Rom. i, 4; with verse 34 compare Rom. vi, 9; and with verse 39 compare Rom. vi, 7, and viii, 3.

What was the effect of this sermon? Truth is always a test, disclosing the heart. In this case many of both classes of hearers, Jews and proselytes, received the word with gladness and entered into the grace of God. And such was the excitement produced, as the matter was talked over during the week, that almost the whole city came next time to the preaching. How rejoiced the apostles must have been! But, like many later evangelists, they were forced soon to lament the speedy turning against them of some that seemed zealous for the truth. It would seem that practically all the Jews, urged on by bitter bigotry, fierce jealousy, and obstinate pride of race, eventually judged themselves unworthy of eternal life. But it was not the fault of the sermon nor of the preacher.

The human heart is ever the same from generation to generation. And if we modern preachers or exhorters meet often with scant or ephemeral success we can certainly find some comfort in the thought that Paul the apostle, and even Jesus the Christ, had the same experience in their time. To deserve success is the limit of human responsibility. To award it in his own good time—at the last great day, if not before—is God's supreme prerogative.

JAMES MUDGE.

IX.
THE APOSTLES TURNING TO THE GENTILES.

Acts xiii, 44-52; xiv, 1-7.

GOLDEN TEXT.—I have set thee to be a light of the Gentiles. Acts xiii, 47.

WE are struck that in the year 46 of our era the word of the Lord was magnified. St. Paul, accompanied by Barnabas, was on his first missionary journey. It was in the above year, according to Mr. Lewin, that they were at Antioch in Pisidia, Iconium, Lystra, and Derbe. We read in the lesson: "Came almost the whole city together to hear the word of God" (ver. 44); "a great multitude believed" (xiv, 1); and "there they preached the gospel" (xiv, 7). All this amounts to both a faithful presentation of the truth as it is in Jesus, and an encouraging reception of it. These facts bring joy to all Christians. We know that there is no instrument more powerful in lifting one into the life of Jesus than the Word of God; we are pleased to perceive its power in these early times.

We must not fail to look for the CAUSE of the apostles' turning to the Gentiles, for the reason why these magnified the Word of God more than the Jews. One element of the explanation is that these Jews of Asia Minor had dropped into the Hebrew habit of stubbornness. It did not take a very great provocation to bring the Jewish people to a point of contradiction, and when they had established themselves in it it was almost impossible to dislodge them. They helped to undermine their claims on Paul and Barnabas by contradicting (ver. 45).

Another element in the apostles' turning was the blasphemy of the Jews. Associated with their habit of stubbornness was their foolish and uncontrolled speaking. Stubbornness with many peoples is accompanied by sullenness. But it was not so with the Jew; when his opposition was aroused he became sad, and he also became fiercely demonstrative in word and action. He would call down the most profane curses upon the heads of others, and even upon himself. Thus the Jews of the cities in the lesson no doubt shocked the ears of the apostles with their outrageous language.

The chief component of the sinful condition of the Jews, which ultimately caused the alienation of the apostles from them, was envy (ver. 45). They were an intolerant people; they could not brook seeing other nations enjoying privileges superior to their own, especially if these were of a religious character. They would forget that an utterance of a choice spirit among them had been, "Thy way may be known upon earth, thy saving health among all nations." The mass of the Jews were ready at the slightest suggestion to fly off into the most extreme envy. Possibly this is a disposition that has not been entirely outgrown.

There is no doubt that in the plan of God's grace the Jews had the first claim on the Gospel. They were the original custodians of the oracles of God. Any development that human salvation would pass through might be expected to occur in their race. Indeed, this was the manner in which the supreme work in Christ began. John the Baptist, the *avant-courier*, was a Jew of the purest blood; one phase of Jesus's glory was that he was of the seed of David. But the time came when the whole world were brought in as heritors of the gospel promises, and it is no wonder that the natural order of things seemed reversed.

In this connection we wish to notice the ACT of the apostles' turning to the Gentiles. The matter had come to an issue; the Jews had cherished sin until as a nation they were past hope; the great, needy world stood waiting; what else could the apostles do but go to the relief of the Gentiles? Paul and Barnabas, representing the spirit of Christianity, with courage to decide in the emergency, said, "Lo, we turn to the nations of the world " (ver. 46).

We should not fail to mark emphatically the MEANS by which the turning of the apostles was necessitated. These were certain acts of the Jews themselves. They were envy, blasphemy, and contradiction, and they were self-chosen acts. The responsibility of having lost their claims on the Gospel rested on themselves. Hence the apostles use the incisive words found in verse 46, " Seeing ye put it from you, and judge yourselves unworthy of everlasting life." Jewish peoples, if at any time during the Christian centuries they have felt themselves abased temporally or spiritually—and so they must have felt themselves when they have seen the glory of Christ's kingdom—have had this thought to reflect upon, that they brought the condition upon themselves.

Further, we should notice clearly THAT TO WHICH the apostles turned. It was to "Christ for the whole world." Paul and Barnabas wanted to be sure of their position, and so looked back to the prophet Isaiah and heard him saying, in harmony with the broadest spirit of Judaism, "I have set thee to be a light of the Gentiles" (ver. 47). These apostles did not thereby become renegade Jews. They in the first place fulfilled the highest conception of Judaism, and in the next place became Christian men. Their sympathies now were bounded by no nationality; their vision ranged over the earth and took in all lands and peoples, even nations yet unborn.

It does not do violence to the prophetic spirit of these two representative apostles to say that their joyous thought of their work comprehended individual men and women. They rejoiced to think that we all would have personally a part in the salvation of Christ.

Then there is the EFFECT of the apostles turning to the Gentiles. As respects the native residents of these cities in the lesson, at least those receiving the Gospel, there was joy. We cannot help but think that those too callous to open their hearts to the truth felt a sensation of gladness that the way to Christ was offered to them.

Verse 48 is explicit on this point. They rejoiced not only over the general truth that the apostles had turned to them, but with that same personal joy that we all have realized as Christians. So great was their gladness that they and the apostles saw that these saved Gentiles were among those whom God's great plan of salvation contemplated.

Just what the basis of church life was in these very early times we do not exactly know. We are informed of it sufficiently, at least, to be sure that there was a substantial basis. We know that as far back as the day of Pentecost following Jesus's ascension the disciples were adding to the Church. We may be certain, therefore, that these Asiatic converts, as well as the Jews, were gathered into Christian churches. There is in this a lesson for many in modern times. They are willing to acknowledge the value of Christianity; they confess possibly a personal relation to Christ, but they hesitate about coming into full communion with the Church. Not so were the actions of the early Christians!

We are somewhat surprised at the position assumed by the influential women of Antioch as indicated in verse 50. We are accustomed to see women have power in religious matters, but it is usually power for good. The explanation here seems to be something like this: There were certain Antiochian women who had become proselytes to Judaism. These were turned by the Jews against the apostles and their work. These women were of influence, or else they persuaded other women of influence to assist in prejudicing the men of the city against the Gospel. We see in the case of these women of honor how much harm influence can accomplish.

Things soon reached a point in Antioch of Pisidia that rendered it unwise for Paul and Barnabas to remain there any longer at that time. It was hard, no doubt, for them to go. They had collected a church there which would have been much benefited by further ministrations of theirs. To have attempted to stay would probably have been for them to incur death, and to bring still more persecutions on the Church. So, with heart bursting and soul strong, they followed the Master's command to shake off the dust of their feet, and departed.

And yet the apostles were not without joy at the moment of their departure, a fact that would have seemed strange to those persecuting them. "We are destroying their work, and are causing them to suffer," the persecutors would say. But they were mistaken. Paul and Barnabas knew that the seed they had sown could not be stamped out by man; their physical pain they counted as nothing that their Lord might be magnified. So, with a reality that only the child of God can understand, "the disciples were filled with joy and with the Holy Ghost."

So the two apostles left Antioch and struck out south-eastward, conquered but conquering messengers of God. The next place the sacred record tells us of their stopping at was Iconium, fifty or seventy-five miles away.

Here their preaching was accompanied with the same power. Here again they found human nature was marked by very bad lines. Many Jews and many Gentiles were gathered into a church; their duty to the Greek and other elements in the native population was no longer a doubt in the apostles' minds. Again fanatical enmity, fomented by the Jews, and probably also by Satan, compelled them after a time to flee.

Chapter xiv, 3, tells us that at Iconium the apostles performed miraculous deeds. We are interested to note the preservation of this power among the disciples of our Lord; it continued also for some time after this. In the abounding zeal of the apostles miracles were as natural as eloquent words and warm thoughts in others. There was some danger in the exercise of this power. At Lystra Paul and Barnabas barely escaped being worshiped. Miracles are not always the best credentials of religion.

Again a weary journey on foot for the two apostles, twenty miles to Lystra; later, forty more to Derbe. Probably these wanderings were broken to some extent by private presentations of the truth in houses, or somewhat publicly in villages (ver. 6). After all, the work was not as dreary as it might look. Two cities, and many hamlets and homes, were receiving the Gospel. There was the inspiration of the personal contact of the truth with men.

Christianity is a vastly different thing to-day from what it was in the year 46 A. D. But the germs of the present gigantic growth were beginning to sprout then. The same principles of progress and retardation have always prevailed. Oftentimes yet stubborn, Jew-like obstacles will stand in the way; we must then turn to broader Gentile forms of life. The Gospel then advanced; it has always advanced; it will advance until it shall permeate every nation and every form of life.

J. D. SPRIGGS.

X.
WORK AMONG THE GENTILES.

Acts xiv, 8–22.

GOLDEN TEXT.—In his name shall the Gentiles trust.
Matt. xii, 21.

THE apostles were on their final missionary tour. Called and separated to the work of proclaiming the gospel message to the Gentile world, they had gone forth on their great errand of evangelization. Several important places had been visited with marked evidences of the adaptation of the Gospel to all who heard and would receive their message. Persecuted at Antioch in Pisidia, and also at Iconium, they heeded the Master's injunction, " When they persecute you in one city, flee ye into another." They have come now to Lystra, a city of Lycaonia, the exact site of which is unknown. Here, as they enter upon their ministry, they encounter one of those cases of physical need which always appear to the true Christian worker. While the apostle was addressing the crowd, gathered possibly in some one of the public thoroughfares of the city, and while unfolding the Gospel of power he had come to proclaim, there was one face at least which lighted up with heaven-born hope. Life-long disease had prepared the way for the message of life. The apostle was not slow to recognize the springing up of faith in the heart of the poor cripple. That penetrative look which once before on this apostolic journey had revealed such power of discernment discerned the one condition on which help could be granted. A single word, and deliverance comes. None could doubt the presence of extraordinary power. Like the lame man at the Temple gate in Jerusalem, his bonds being broken, he leaps and walks.

The effect of this miracle was to attract immediate attention to the apostles. The city was under the tutelage of Jupiter, whose statue stood just outside the city's gates. The worship of this deity was a regular feature in the life of the people. According to the tradition which prevailed among them, it was not uncommon for the gods to assume human form and appear among men. There was even a story that not far from their own city such an occurrence had actually been witnessed, and Jupiter and Mercury had really appeared in human form. It is not so much, then, a cause for wonder that the apostles were looked upon as divine visitants and worthy of being treated with divine honors. According to the early custom of "making the tallest king," they identify Barnabas as Jupiter, and Paul as his winged messenger, Mercurius.

The common dialect of the people being unknown to the apostles, the preparations for such honors are well-nigh matured before their purpose is apprehended. Headed by the priest of their idolatrous worship, the procession, with the oxen and garlands for sacrifice, has already begun to move toward the gates of the city. Paul and Barnabas are to be worshiped! But no; the proceedings are interrupted. Paul and his companion discover now the meaning of this pageant. Horrified at the indignity which such an act would cast upon Him whose servants they were, they protest with earnest words that they are but men of like passions with those who would do them honor. With well-directed words they are exhorted to turn from the vanities of heathen worship to Him who is the living God, the Creator of heaven and earth, who, though seemingly unmindful of the nations who have gone astray from him, is yet the beneficent source of all good.

The address of the apostle only served to intensify the superstitious regard which they feel toward their strange guests. Hardly are they restrained from offering the sacrifice due to celestial visitants. Popularity, however, is often but short-lived. But a few hours pass and a complete revulsion of feeling occurs. Unbelieving Jews who have come all the way from Antioch and Iconium find it no difficult matter to persuade a superstitious and fickle-minded people that the apostles are emissaries of Satan and worthy only of death. Paul is stoned in the streets of the city and carried forth apparently dead outside the city's gates. The faith, however, which had sprung into existence at the stoning of the first martyr, Stephen, could only gain strength by such persecution. Paul is not dead. As the few faithful disciples who gather about him gaze upon his seemingly lifeless form, lo! his spirit revives, and, rising up, he boldly enters the city to suffer still further, if need be, for the truth's sake. The next day, with his companion, he visits Derbe, which marks the extreme limit of his first missionary tour. At this point Paul was not far from his early home. The temptation, if such there was, to visit these old scenes was easily resisted, and they decide to return again by the same route they had followed thus far. Truth planted must be watered. The few disciples who had been gathered must be comforted and confirmed. And so they return to exhort them to continue in the faith and to teach that we " must through much tribulation enter into the kingdom of God."

So much for the narrative. Let us notice several things.

1. *The Gospel, Whenever and Wherever Preached, is a Ministry of Helpfulness.* The weak and helpless are confined to no single locality. Alike under the shadow of Jupiter's statue at Lystra and the Temple of Jehovah at Jerusalem, suffering humanity appeals for help. Fettered limbs, sightless eyes, and deaf ears invite sympathy and power. To all such the Gospel is a message of hope. " Then shall the lame man leap as a hart, and the tongue of the dumb sing." " Go and show John again those things which ye do hear and see: the blind receive their sight, and the *lame walk*, the lepers are cleansed, and the deaf hear, the dead are raised up, and the poor have the gospel preached to them."

But what are fettered limbs compared with souls that are bound and cramped with evil appetites? The greater help is needed by those who are spiritually lame and helpless. If miracles of physical healing in the early time prepared the way for the reception of spiritual truth, much more do those wrought in the souls of men to-day. The proof that Christ is come is seen in the men and women who are placed upon their feet. The Lystrians were right in their inference. The lame man leaping and walking before their very eyes was an indisputable proof of a divine power operating among them. So are men and women restored to spiritual soundness to-day.

2. *The Sincerity and Loyalty of the Apostles.* The healing of the lame man fixed the attention of the people upon Paul and Barnabas. They became at once the most popular men in the city. The priest of Jupiter vies with the people in paying them honor. What an opportunity to observe the character of the men who were chosen to proclaim first the Gospel of Christ to the world! How easy at such a time for selfish motives and the lack of a true devotion, if such existed, to be revealed! More than one messenger of truth has proved himself unequal to resist the influence of popular favor. The apostles, however, were true MINISTERS. There was nothing of the priestly cast about them. Called to be servants, they were only satisfied when their Master was honored. All undue attention given to them would only detract from the homage due their divine Lord.

They became thus fit examples to all who are seeking praise of men and fail to remember whose they are and whom they serve. We may well rejoice that the cause of truth has been served by so many who have been content only as Christ has been honored by their service.

3. *The Proper Adaptation of the Truth.* Different people demand different presentation of the truth. The readiness of the Lystrians to see in the apostles divine impersonations proclaimed *their* desire, and as well the profound desire of all heathendom, for an incarnation of Deity. There is much in heathen mythology that points toward the truth. The speech of the apostles was suited to the occasion. It was thoroughly Pauline. There is much in it, both in sentiment and language, that reminds us of his teaching at other times. There is a bold proclamation of God as the living One, in whose incarnate life their heathen tradition was more than realized. For proofs of his living presence in the world they are directed to those evidences of his creative power which were all about them. The heavens and the earth are the work of his hands.

Though it was true that special revelation of his power and goodness had been granted to a single nation only, yet no nation had been left without some witness to his beneficent love and goodness. Rain and fruitful seasons, significant blessings to the people living in such a barren district as Lycaonia, proclaimed his thoughtful care and presence. Idolatry had no place under the teaching of natural religion. "The invisible things of him from the creation of the world are clearly seen, being understood by the things that are made, even his eternal power and Godhead; so that they are without excuse." Such teaching was eminently fitted to the people addressed. We read that at Iconium "they *so* spake that a great multitude both of the Jews and of the Greeks believed."

4. *The Worthlessness of Religious Feeling Unless Supported by Intelligent Convictions of the Truth.* Human nature in any of its phases is an interesting study. In nothing, however, is this more true than in those religious changes through which it passes. The sudden change of feeling toward the apostles would seem strange indeed were it not repeated so often in the experience of religious life. From superstitious reverence to the bitterest and most deadly persecution, and that in a single day! Stoned in the same city where but a few hours before you were hailed as a god! Ah, this is not so unusual, after all. More than once did this same apostle encounter such fickleness of purpose. At Melita he is accounted first as a murderer, and then as a god. Of the Galatians he writes: "If it had been possible, ye would have plucked out your own eyes, and have given them to me. Am I therefore become your enemy, because I tell you the truth?"

Such changes are encountered by every religious teacher in the prosecution of his work. The certainty of their occurrence and the proper way to meet them constitute part of a true preparation for religious service.

It is not strange that the emotions are so often the first to be stirred in the beginnings of the religious life. Some one has said that the New Testament is "surcharged with emotion." Certain is it, the feelings must be aroused if the truth ever seizes upon the life forces. But none were wiser than the apostles to lead the people from mere religious feeling to an intelligent faith in Christ. Natural temperament is no insurmountable barrier here. The Gospel of Christ is designed not to destroy, but to direct and control natural impulses. The soul must be led from all secondary causes and agencies to Him who is himself the truth. Only as it centers in him is it safe. A superstitious reverence for Church or creed, for book or minister, cannot survive the tests through which each religious life must sooner or later pass.

5. *The Impotency of All Opposition to the Truth of Christ.* The triumph of the Gospel was not to be an immediate or an easy one. Persecution followed and follows the true heralds of the cross. More than once did these early missionaries, and later ones too, have occasion to remember their Master's words: "If they have persecuted me, they will also persecute you." How often, as the stones fell thick and fast upon the apostle's head in the streets of Lystra, did the image of the suffering Stephen pass before his mind. And then that memorable journey undertaken for the express purpose of destroying the early disciples! How it came back to him as he found himself suffering for the same blessed

cause! But the powerlessness of his own opposition prepared him to meet with courage the opposition he found in every place. The truth could not be stoned to death. Though seemingly dead, it would revive and go boldly forward on its errand of light.

When this first missionary tour was over, and the apostle rehearsed the story of his labors, there was no tone of disappointment in his words. An effectual door for the Gospel had been opened among the Gentiles. Disciples had been gathered in nearly every city. At Lystra, even, one had become a believer who was destined to fill an important place in apostolic history. The conversion of Timothy, which seems to have taken place on this first visit to Lystra, was itself a signal trophy of the apostle's success.

Thus did this first missionary tour become itself a prophecy of the future triumph of the Gospel. "And in his name shall the Gentiles trust."

RAYMOND F. HOLWAY.

XI.

THE APOSTOLIC COUNCIL.

Acts xv, 12-29.

GOLDEN TEXT.—Through the grace of our Lord Jesus Christ we shall be saved, even as they. Acts xv, 11.

CHRISTIANITY was born in the household of Judaism. It was fitting that it should pay a certain deference to the rules of the household. A pronounced and ostentatious opposition to Judaism on its part would have agreed ill with obligation to its own religious ancestry, and would have been, besides, greatly lacking in prudence.

On the other hand, Christianity was meant for the race. In the words of the Founder it was unmistakably characterized as a message of glad tidings to all nations. As its mission was world-wide, so also its spirit was too large and catholic to admit of narrow bounds.

To harmonize these two requirements, to pay at once a suitable deference to its connection with Judaism and to assert its character as a universal religion, was the great problem which confronted Christianity at the threshold of its career. No task more delicate or more difficult than this engaged the attention of the apostolic Church.

How was the great problem solved? Not simply by theorizing; not merely by the vote of a conclave. It was solved by the providential method of gradual advance. The logic of fact was a conspicuous element in the solution. One event after another was utilized to work toward a general agreement in thought and feeling. Conservatism was not wounded by an abrupt severance from Judaism. At the same time the vocation of the new religion to transcend Jewish limitations was not denied. Stage by stage the Church advanced to a recognition of its true position as the herald of a new and broader dispensation. The appointment of liberal-minded Hellenists to the office of deacons, the scattering of the Church by persecution, the preaching of Philip in Samaria, the forming of a new Christian center at Antioch, the baptism of Cornelius and his household by Peter, the transforming of the strictest and most persecuting Pharisee into the most liberal apostle to the Gentiles, the fruits which rewarded the first great missionary tour in Cyprus and Asia Minor—these were so many successive steps toward preparing an acknowledgment of the independent and universal character of Christianity. They paved the way for the consummating act, the declaration of a relative freedom from Jewish restrictions which was passed by the Council of Jerusalem at the middle of the century. Without the foregoing development that declaration would have been impossible or nugatory.

A reverent mind will confess here the leading of a divine hand. The end was not planned by human wisdom. The apostles themselves did not see it clearly from the start. They needed the outward demonstration of fact to go with the inward illumination of the Spirit in order to become assured that men could be followers of Christ without being made subjects of Moses.

While the events of the score of years which intervened between Pentecost and the council had done much toward dissipating prejudice and enlarging insight, some who had confessed Christ were still far from abandoning their Jewish exclusiveness. In their view, Paul's boldness in extending gospel privileges to the Gentiles was a dangerous liberalism, a contravention of truth upon which twenty centuries had set their seal. It stirred their animosity to think that an economy which had come down from heaven in the divine manifestations of the patriarchal age and the miracles of the Mosaic era, and which had been so wonderfully sustained through the mutations of national fortune, should at length be set aside. The fervor with which this party insisted upon retaining the ceremonial law disturbed the Christians at Antioch and threatened a disruption of the Church. To meet the exigency the most notable assembly which history mentions between the pentecostal gathering and the Council of Nicæa was convened.

In considering this assembly we may notice its composition, its decision, the grounds or motives of its decision, and the lessons which are taught to later times.

1. The Council of Jerusalem was peculiarly *a representative assembly*. Grant that its members came from only a few congregations and a very limited stretch of

territory, still it was one of the most comprehensive assemblies ever convened.

In the persons of the attending apostles the cardinal types of New Testament teaching were represented. No direct mention is, indeed, made of John; but we gather from Paul's statement in the Epistle to the Galatians (ii, 9) that he was present in Jerusalem so as to share in the private conferences which occurred between the apostles. This makes it next to a certainty that he was a member of the council. As for Peter and James, they were foremost actors in the proceedings of the assembly. Now the line which includes these four men circumscribes the main types of New Testament doctrine. In Paul you have the opponent of legalism and the champion of free grace, whose formula is justification by faith as opposed to a servile dependence upon works; in Peter you have the advocate of faith as a principle of triumphant hope and courageous devotion; in James, the exponent of religion on its practical side as a rule of conduct; in John, the portrayer of religion as an inner union with God through the bond of love. On the special question which engaged the attention of the council the position of John has not been definitely indicated to us. Probably at this stage it was not remote from that of Peter, who may be regarded as occupying an intermediate place between Paul and James, scarcely so ready to leap over Jewish restrictions as the former, and less closely attached to Judaism in feeling and practice than the latter.

18

The council was also peculiarly representative in that it included all ranks of Christians. Whatever prerogatives may have been given to the apostles for their exceptional vocation as organizers of the Church in its formative era, their method of administration was vastly remote from that of a dictatorship. In matters of common concern they took pains to elicit the collective verdict of the Christian communion. Accordingly, the action of the Council of Jerusalem is represented as having been taken with the concurrence of the *elders and the whole Church.*

2. *The decision* of the council may be described as the assertion in principle of the independence of the new religion, together with charitable allowances for those who were closely associated with the old religion. By declaring the Gentiles exempt from the obligation of circumcision it acknowledged that in strictness the ceremonial law did not apply to them at all. The duty to regard any part of it became simply the duty of brotherly kindness, which requires avoidance of needless occasions of offense. It was on this ground that the council deemed it fitting to enjoin abstinence from meats offered to idols, from blood, and from things strangled. As James had argued, the Mosaic writings being read weekly in every city, it would be a prolific source of scandal to many minds if Christians should indulge in practices specially reprobated by those writings. The prohibition was a prudential measure, and therefore carried with itself the tacit admission that under changed conditions its enforcement might be waived.

That it should have been thought necessary to include a positive vice with the three practices which were forbidden as offensive to Jewish feeling is at first thought a surprising fact. It may be presumed, however, that in mentioning this vice the council had reference to the ill-instructed neophyte, or to the person who had not yet escaped from the entanglements of his former associations. The occasion for the specification was the appalling laxity of the declining classic world. In the corrupt Gentile society of that era a deed of impurity that did not violate the marriage bond was reckoned only a trivial offense. The prevalence of slavery had helped, among other causes, greatly to deaden conscience on the subject.

3. If we look for *the grounds* which influenced the council to declare for the essential exemption of the Gentiles from the Mosaic law, we find three specially prominent—namely, the cogent presentation of recent facts, the citation of Old Testament prophecy, and a marked exhibition of magnanimity on the part of the recognized champion of the Jewish interest.

The ringing words of Peter must have produced no small effect upon the assembly. Recalling his ministry to Cornelius and his household, he declared that God had clearly indicated therein his equal favor to the Gentiles, since he had given them his Holy Spirit, had purified their hearts by faith, and had unmistakably saved them through the grace of the Lord Jesus Christ, upon which all alike must depend for salvation. Not less must have been the effect produced by the recitals of

Paul and Barnabas, as they told how their preaching in Gentile communities had been favored with the double attestation of signs from heaven and manifest effects upon the hearts of the people.

While the wide prospect which the testimonies of these distinguished witnesses had opened up was in the minds of the audience, the thought arose that this broader outlook was no illicit thing, that it had, in fact, been anticipated by the old prophets. This thought, too, was far from being fanciful. It was one of the most remarkable phases of prophetic anticipation that it mounted ever and anon above Jewish legality and exclusiveness, apprehended a time when a new and more spiritual covenant should be introduced, and brought the Gentiles into view as sharing with Israel the light and blessing of divine revelation. The anticipation may not have been very definite, and may have been clothed in rather vague language, still it worked as a leaven in the minds of the prophets. Selecting one among several passages that might have been chosen, James reminded the assembly of the words of Amos as indicating the extension of God's gracious purpose to the Gentiles. .

The argument of James was only one part of his contribution to the decision of the council. His example told for no less than his reasoning. As head of the Christian community at Jerusalem, he lived in the very citadel of the Jewish interest. He was himself deeply imbued with that interest. All the glimpses that we have of him, whether in the New Testament or in the writings of Eusebius, assure us that he was a man of legal bias, and that he held in great reverence the historic institutions of Israel. He is believed to have taken the vow of the Nazarite, and to have ordered his conduct after the unsparing rule of ascetic piety. The strict Judaizers looked to him as their standard-bearer. That in the face of all this he gave his voice in behalf of liberality, and declared against troubling the Gentiles, was a notable instance of magnanimity. Its influence in uniting the assembly upon a common policy must have been potent.

4. In describing the characteristics of the council and the elements which entered into its decision, we have already indicated in large part *the lessons* which come to us from this great historic scene.

We are reminded that the proper idea of church government is not that of prelate or vicegerent speaking like an absolute monarch from the throne, but rather that of an assembly representative of the whole religious fraternity, and seeking to elicit and to formulate its collective wisdom and will.

Again, we are taught to value the spiritual as opposed to the ceremonial conception of religion. As Peter argued before the council, the possession of the Spirit and the corresponding fruits is a valid token and seal of God's favor, before which artificial distinctions must pass out of sight. The action of the council reflected this sentiment. Those, therefore, who judge by the ceremonial standard, who disfellowship devout and Christ-like men because they have not received a specific ceremonial mark, or disparage their Christian standing because they are outside of certain ecclesiastical lines, place themselves in glaring contrast with this assembly of primitive Christians. They associate themselves with the most prejudiced of the Pharisaic Judaizers rather than with the apostolic group.

Finally we have a striking lesson as to the precious results of a true-hearted consultation for the interests of peace. With more of the pugilistic and less of the forbearing spirit, the council would have ended in strife and division. By holding to principle, and respecting at the same time the scruples of those who were bound by ancestral customs, the leaders of the assembly were able to unite the contending parties, and to lay down a platform admirably suited to an era of difficult transition. This successful consultation for the peace of the Church doubtless helped to foster the cheerful conviction of the council that it had been blessed with the presence and aid of the Holy Spirit. The expression, "It seemed good to the Holy Ghost, and to us," is more properly understood of the confidence and satisfaction of the council in the result of its deliberations than as a declaration of official infallibility.

H. C. SHELDON.

XIII.*

THE BIRTH OF CHRIST.

Luke ii, 8-20.

GOLDEN TEXT.—Behold, I bring you good tidings of great joy.
Luke ii, 10.

FARRAR, in his *Life of Christ*, has said of Palestine as a war ground: "This land has glittered with the lances of the Amalekites; it has trembled under the chariot wheels of Sesostris; it has echoed with the twanging bow-strings of Sennacherib; it has been trodden by the phalanxes of Macedonia; it has clashed with the broadswords of Rome; it has rung with the battle-cry of the crusaders; it has thundered with the artillery of England and France." The lesson narrates a beautiful contrast to all this. We see, not a battle-field, but a pasture; not soldiers, but shepherds. We hear, not the blast of trumpets and shouts of warriors, but a celestial choir. We are taken, not to a redoubt, but a manger. We find, not a dying soldier or grim general, but a living babe. The scene is not Palestine in war, but Bethlehem, "the house of bread," announcing "Peace on earth!" Bethlehem—to the Christian the holiest spot on earth. It was here that Rachel died and Ruth gleaned after the reapers of Boaz. Here David kept his father's flocks

---
* No homily is given for Lesson XII, which is a review.

and was anointed King of Israel. Here, says Stanley, stood the " Tower of Shepherds," and dwelt the prophet Amos. Here Jeremiah foretold the coming of " the Lord our righteousness. But none, nor all, of these have given us Bethlehem. The angels might have met the shepherds and had some other message, and the place now be forgotten. But this " house of bread " as Christ's birthplace has become immortal.

1. *The Angel to the Shepherds.* There was a great city only six miles away ; there were in it palaces that held the representatives of the Cæsars, a splendid temple, and sumptuous houses. In that city were many distinguished circles—the Roman tribunal, the Jewish Sanhedrin, the Jewish Church, the sect of Pharisee, Sadducee, and Essene, the schools of Hillel and Gamaliel. Why did the angel come to this little village and to the shepherds?

Bethlehem had but a manger for a Messiah, but that was better than a prison or a cross, and Jerusalem was in danger of furnishing the latter. And there was nothing arbitrary in the selection of the shepherds. The choicest divine revealings have never come first to those imbedded in sect or party or society circles. The receptive souls, the children, the devout women, the fishermen, the shepherds, get the clearer vision and the higher message. It is the pure in heart, not the keen in thought, nor the mighty in intellect, nor the maker or upholder of systems, who has the promise of seeing God. So the angel passed by a Cæsar, an Annas—Rome and

Jerusalem—and came to those unprejudiced, meditating men on the plains of Bethlehem. This is a part of the truth we need. Abraham leaving Ur, Moses in Midian, David feeding his flocks, Elijah at Horeb, John the Baptist in the wilderness, Paul in Arabia, John at Patmos, join with these shepherds in their silent watches at Bethlehem in teaching us that heaven's messages to earth need solitude rather than society, receptivity more than controversy.

2. *The Message.* The messenger came to but a few; he brought a message of "good tidings to all people." This had been the Messianic hope. However crude or material their notion of the coming One, the devout Jew believed he was to be a joy, and his blessing to reach to all. But this is an unmeasurably larger message to us than to them. An earthly leader, a palace to shelter him, a court to bow down to him, an army to support him, the Jewish nation supreme, the Jewish Church strengthened— that was the best they could interpret this message. So the shepherds must have been puzzled over the announcement: "You shall find a babe in a manger." Was he not to be called Wonderful, Counselor, Mighty God, Everlasting Father, Prince of Peace? A king, not a pauper, a throne, not a manger, was their ideal. And if they had relied now on their traditions or their selfish ambitions they would have stayed with their flocks; but they were men of faith. "And suddenly there was with the angel a multitude;" "a multitude of the heavenly host praising God, and saying, Glory to God in the high-

est, and on earth peace among men in whom he is well pleased." Heaven's chorus did more for them than earth's logic. Lange calls this the first Gospel, and the shepherds accepted it. That song was an appropriate casket for this gospel jewel, but we are to remember it was only that. Had the shepherds, dazzled with this manifestation, forgotten the message, our Christianity would have lost something of its symmetry and strength. Here is a thought for us. We are glad of this miraculous setting for this Gospel. Well has Phillips Brooks said that the marvel is not that miracles attended the coming and the work of Christ; rather would it be strange if such a One should come without something of this kind; but we are not to let the miracle overshadow the message.

The Gospel the angels brought is more vital to us than themselves; the truth they gave than their method of giving it. The kingdom of God is within, and the final appeal must be not to miracle, nor tradition, not to any form of external authority, but the receptive, rational soul.

3. *The Babe.* " Let us now go even unto Bethlehem." The wise men came later; but the first to greet the Saviour were the shepherds. We are glad the wise men came. Christianity is broader and deeper than all humanity. It came to meet the philosopher as well as peasant, Dives as well as Lazarus; but the first welcome from the shepherds was prophetical of all Christianity. The wise men brought gifts; but they were products of

earth. The shepherds brought a flash of the glory which Christ had with the Father, a strain from the song around the throne, a message that meant infinitely more than gold and frankincense and myrrh. It is not the last time the shepherds have contributed to Christianity more than the wise men. Our faith to-day rests upon what the simple, loyal, loving soul brings to its support far more than some of us as philosophers and theologians are ready to admit. "They found the babe."

Why this lowly birth in the hush of night among strangers; the manger instead of the throne; and after this the carpenter-shop instead of palace halls? Perhaps we need the truth pressed to-day that environment is not all of life. The Christ came in the line of descent, on the human side, from the best blood of the world; but he came with surroundings so humble and life so simple that we still almost wonder if Bethlehem and Nazareth were best. But each Christmas-time adds its testimony to confirm the everlasting wisdom of the manner of Christ's advent. The mystery of the babe is more than compensated for by the ministry of the babe. "They wondered, but Mary pondered." Three classes gathered about that manger, and their tendencies have been perpetuated. Herod would destroy, the shepherds were ready to receive, but Mary went beyond them; she would build out of all this a fabric of faith, a temple of life. Destructive, receptive, constructive—these are the bearings of humanity toward this new religion. To seek the young child's life—that is the great heresy.

But to wonder is not enough. The spectacular, the ceremonial, the ritualistic—these may help in certain stages of human development our approach to Christ, but they may also tend to hide him. Not till we stand by Mary's side, in this great cradle scene, with Mary in her purity, her divine experiences, her spirit of thoughtfulness, not understanding all, but pondering, shall we be best equipped.

4. *The Return.* Angels had come to these men; how could they think of sheep? They had been introduced to the Messiah, how could they go back to their earth-work? They had been honored with a concert from the celestial choir—a Gospel from heaven; must they not repudiate their old life? But "they returned." There was to be the same careful watching of flocks, the same wearying and humble round of duties as before. They returned, but not the same. They came to that manger wondering and doubting; they went away from it "glorifying and praising God for all they had seen and heard."

Perhaps here is the choicest truth in this lesson for us. The life that will meet Christ now as those about that manger met him will have a new vision and will hear a new message. There will be much to wonder about, much to ponder over, for humanity cannot yet compass divinity. But after all this there will still have to be the return to farm and store, shop and school. Earth's toil and trial will press upon us, but we may go back to these praising God. There can come in the field as surely as in the temple, to the shop as truly as at the altar, the divine message and leading. Christ in the manger and Christ in the carpenter-shop has made sacred the things called secular, and has made nothing sacred in work or worship that has not the spirit of " peace on earth, good-will to men " in it.

We have in this lesson, this strangely beautiful story, only the opening scene of a great drama, the first touches of a great picture, the first flashes of a great light. Perhaps it needs the closing act, the last touches, the sunset splendor to fully comprehend the Golden Text; but from that Christmas-time until this there has never been a doubt that the birth of Christ has been "good tidings of great joy."

JOHN FAVILLE.

XIII.*

A LESSON IN SELF-DENIAL.

Rom. xiv, 12-23.

GOLDEN TEXT.—We then that are strong ought to bear the infirmities of the weak.—Rom. xv, 1.

SELF-DENIAL is the first step in Christian discipleship. To be worthy it must have some worthy motive. To throw away the food which one needs, and for which one is hungry, may be called penance; it is not self-denial. To give the food one longs to put to his lips to another soul hungry and in need is true denial of self; it is a brotherly going without that to which one has a right in deference to the weakness or need of another.

Christ was preached by the apostles and accepted by people so widely differing that their religious lives had hitherto had little in common. They came into the new faith cumbered with prejudices and customs which long use made it difficult to throw aside. The Jew held fast to circumcision, and some—perhaps, of the Platonizing Gentiles—holding all evil to be rooted in the flesh, could allow only a vegetable diet. They could not believe in the spirituality of Christian flesh-eaters, and felt that their pernicious example would lead astray the young and the weak.

---

* This temperance lesson is optional with the Christmas lesson for December 25, 1892.

A LESSON IN SELF-DENIAL.

Paul has no sympathy with their view of the harmfulness of meats, yet he sees that it is not wise to argue with them. They have accepted Christ in good faith, but if their prejudices be offended before enlightenment comes, they for whom Christ died may be forever lost to his fold. He at once declares his own purpose of self-denial: "If meat make my brother to offend, I will eat no meat while the world standeth." He also puts the spirit of his own act into a saying which makes clear the duty of Christ's men every-where until now: "It is good neither to eat flesh, nor to drink wine, nor any thing whereby thy brother stumbleth, or is offended, or is made weak."

This noble principle has many possible applications in every one's life. Take the question of amusements. One enjoys games of chance. Some of these are most frequently associated with gambling. It is certain that many have been led astray by their knowledge and love of such games. It is not prejudice that leads the intelligent Christian to forsake these pastimes, but a high regard for the influence of one's example.

The theater has many defenders. Let all that is said for it be granted. Still it is true that many have been corrupted by it. Young girls, attracted by the glare of stage life, have lost their love of home, of quiet, of religion, and of virtue. The most respectable theaters will at times corrupt their constituency by outbreaking sins in the shape of the worst plays. A great actress is eagerly caught up even although her chosen rôle is a realistic representation of crimes of which people should not even think. One may justify the theater nine times out of ten, but because in the tenth instance a brother is made weak, one may wisely deny himself and stay away.

Many positions have been taken by earnest advocates of temperance which are disputed by its sincere friends. They have felt that a good cause is weakened by claiming as true that which is yet in honest and learned dispute. It cannot be positively said that the wine used at the marriage in Cana was unfermented. Is alcohol always a poison, and never a good to the human system? It is not yet safe to pledge our great cause to this affirmation. Is a moderate use of wine or beer always harmful to the person who uses it? In the face of so much honest and intelligent denial we do not commend our reform by blazoning this upon its flag and condemning all who deny.

Strong drink is the source or occasion of three-fourths of the crime and poverty to be found in Christian lands. Here is a fact to which personal observation and careful statistics bear witness. One other position will not be denied by any who have the spirit of Christ. We who are strong ought to deny ourselves because of the weakness of others.

The great influence of social custom may be seen by any who will give it a little thought. It has often the strength of despotism in its compelling or restraining voice. Many customs which have no legal, moral, or reasonable force we would no sooner break than the moral law itself.

The force of example is greater in what one does than in what one merely refrains from doing. A boy who lights a cigar sets an example in a stronger sense than those about him who merely refrain from smoking. So the influence of one who puts wine on her table is the more forceful, since it can be quoted as a positive act. A single doing of that which we do not usually allow may be noted and remembered as if characteristic of our whole lives.

This should make us very careful. There are times when wine is put before us at public or social tables, and one's modest fear of being conspicuous is a strong reason for indulging once. We should then reflect that, so far as influence is concerned, it may not be once, but forever.

A Christly regard for our weak brother will lead us to shield him from the temptations with which others would lead him astray. A mere teetotaller is not a great helper of the temperance cause in these days.

The apathy of the temperate and the appetite of the intemperate are the upper and nether millstones between which is ground out to-day the fine flour of human misery. The whole of self-denial leads one to positive endeavor in the suppression of intemperance.

We are proud that the privilege of choosing our legislators and executives is our own. We celebrate the bravery of our fathers in fighting for it, but really the task of doing it is irksome to us. And of good people who profess to do their political duty the greater number leave the larger part undone.

It is not enough to cast the ballot; somebody must prepare the ballot. It is not enough to vote "Yes" or "No" on questions presented; somebody must present questions. It is not enough to discuss issues that may now be before the public mind; somebody must *make* issues of matters that are vital. There has always been a disposition to keep *moral* questions out of politics. We can frame a good excuse for it. But if moral questions excite no interest outside of politics put them into it by all means.

Why should I shout myself hoarse when the only question is whether Tad or Tim—both good fellows—shall be alderman. But if my torch can help to illuminate some great moral question, and my shouting find the ears of the morally deaf, then I'll cheerfully do my part in any demonstration. Christian citizens should "go into politics." They often have been in, but usually only a little way. Let them now, with higher motives, go in as wholly as other men.

There are three tribunals before which a man's life may be held accountable. He may be brought to trial before his fellow-men representing some civil, social, or religious government; in a very real sense he may examine and judge himself; and in the end of the world there is a judgment before God. Now, the first of these is very limited in its reach. It can question fully a man's acts and words. It can sometimes go a little way into his motives, but the great world of his thought and desire is beyond its reach.

Self-judgment has to do with all these. Conscience is the voice of God in the heart because its eye is spiritual and takes notice of the motive rather than the act.

Paul tells us that if we would be sure of living right before our fellows we are to judge ourselves. We may in the exercise of our natural, civil, or church rights do a harm to our brother. Our conduct is legitimate, so far as men can judge it. It is wrong before God. It is unchristian before the eye of our enlightened conscience, because it is a stumbling-block to our weak brother.

So we are to examine constantly our conduct at the bar of this inner and high tribunal, that we may know its influence as well as its rightfulness. Happy is he who, searching his own motives as God will search them, condemneth not himself in that which he alloweth.

J. WEARE DEARBORN.

www.ingramcontent.com/pod-product-compliance
Lightning Source LLC
Chambersburg PA
CBHW022105290426
44112CB00008B/556